D1714461

Talking Time

SECOND EDITION

WEBSTER DIVISION, McGRAW-HILL BOOK COMPANY

St. Louis, New York, San Francisco, Dallas, Toronto, London, Sydney

SECOND EDITION
TALKING TIME

· ·

LOUISE BINDER SCOTT
and
J. J. THOMPSON

AUTHORS

Louise Binder Scott, Associate Professor of Elementary Speech Education, California State College at Los Angeles, is also senior author of three other widely used books with J. J. Thompson, Chairman of the Department of Speech, California State College at Long Beach: *Phonics, Speech Ways,* and *Rhymes for Fingers and Flannelboards.*

Professor Scott, in addition to co-authoring *Singing Fun* and *More Singing Fun* with Lucille F. Wood, has also co-authored *Book R* of the *Time for Phonics* series with Virginia Sydnor Pavelko, and is author of *Books A, B,* and *C* of the same series.

TALKING TIME

SECOND EDITION

Copyright © 1966 by McGraw-Hill, Inc. All Rights Reserved. Printed in the United States of America. This book, or parts thereof, may not be reproduced in any form without permission of the publishers.

ISBN 07-055818-3

5 6 7 8 9 0 VB VB 7 5 4 3 2

Acknowledgments

The authors express their gratitude to Dr. Mary Huber, Professor of Speech, California State College at Los Angeles, for her invaluable assistance in editing chapters on philosophy; to Frances C. Hunte, Consultant in Speech and Hearing, Garvey Elementary School District, California, for many hours spent in advisement, for use of her corrective techniques, and for "My Tongue"; to Virginia Sydnor Pavelko for "Little Squirrel," "Dragonflies," "The Ladybug Parade," "The Tiny, Shiny Cricket," "Woodpecker," and "The Crow Family"; to Lucille F. Wood for "I Yawn"; to Bowmar Records for permission to use "The Dream Fence," "The Sleepy Farm," and "Choo-Choo Engine" from *The Listening Time Albums;* to *The Instructor* for permission to use "The Yawning Puppy" and "What is Thin?"; and to *The Grade Teacher* for permission to use "Caw-Caw, the Crow," "The Basket," "The Strange Sound in the Garden," "It's Christmas," "What Was It?" and "Little Red Rooster."

58201

Table of Contents

CHAPTER 1

An Introduction

"Every teacher is a teacher of speech, either consciously or unconsciously, for the speech habits and the speech development of a child are affected and influenced by the activities that take place in the classroom."

This statement was made almost fifteen years ago in the first edition of *Talking Time*. Today those words may seem commonplace, but only because the philosophy which underlies the statement has since been widely accepted as a fundamental premise of speech education. There remains, however, a great need for materials which will convert this philosophy into practical, everyday classroom experiences. The first edition was developed because of such a need and this revision is presented with the same purpose in mind. Here is a simple, nontechnical book designed to aid in the correction of articulatory speech difficulties in children and to improve general speech proficiency in all children.

FOR WHOM THE BOOK WAS WRITTEN

Talking Time, first of all, is a book for teachers in the classroom. These materials, suitable for use from kindergarten through fourth grade, guide the teaching of speech sounds and listening and speaking skills. All children can profit from a program which helps them to listen selectively, to enunciate carefully, and to speak with a pleasant voice that displays good vocal variety. This point of view is supported by a special report of the American Speech and Hearing Association, which states that "School personnel and parents are becoming increasingly aware of the need for all children — those with normal speech and those gifted with speech skills, as well as children with speech and hearing problems — to develop the ability to communicate their ideas effectively in acceptable speech, voice, and language patterns." [1]

In many classrooms, there are children who fall into that category referred to as the "culturally deprived." For these children in particular, the selections in *Talking Time* stimulate the senses and provide a rich variety of vicarious experiences. These same selections, with their repetitive refrains and their appeal to rhythm and bodily response, are easily adapted to the needs of the mentally limited, the physically handicapped, and other groups of exceptional children.

It should be pointed out that this book was not intended primarily for use by speech specialists in a clinical setting. Experience has indicated, however, that the speech specialist will find these materials of value. They can provide for the child a reassuring common ground between his classroom and his speech-therapy sessions. The classroom teacher and the speech specialist find it difficult, even with the most concentrated and coordinated efforts, to provide sufficient individual attention to children who have serious speech problems. These children need many opportunities to use their newly mastered speech sounds in an environment of acceptance and warmth. A common and familiar body of materials can help to fill this need. When the materials are used by both teacher and speech

---

[1] American Speech and Hearing Association, "Public School Speech and Hearing Services," *The Journal of Speech and Hearing Disorders,* Monograph Supplement 8, July, 1961.

specialist, they help to unify any program for children with articulation problems.

Talking Time can also be used effectively by parents to extend the child's school experiences. The use of *Talking Time* during relaxing time, with parent and child sharing the fun, humor, and delight of these speech-sound-oriented materials, will provide additional auditory stimulation and reinforcement of correct speech patterns. The stories and poems can become a part of the parent's repertoire for reading-aloud time.

WHAT IS A SPEECH PROBLEM?

Classrooms all over the nation, particularly those at the primary level, include numbers of children who have some type of speech problem. These problems result from a variety of causes.

Impaired hearing may cause a child to perceive speech sounds in a distorted manner or not to hear them at all. A child cannot imitate what he cannot hear, so an articulation problem results.

A cleft palate, even though surgically repaired, may make it difficult for a child to build up sufficient air pressure inside the mouth to make such plosive sounds as "p," "b," "t," "d," "k," and "g." Other speech sounds may also be distorted by deeply ingrained speech patterns the child has acquired as a result of his cleft palate. Often such a child has a very nasal voice quality caused by his inability to direct the breath stream through his mouth instead of his nose when he talks.

Cerebral palsy and other types of injuries to the brain may cause a child to have difficulty in controlling the muscles of the speech mechanism or in retaining memory patterns essential to reproducing speech sounds.

Dental abnormalities may prevent a child from placing his lips or tongue in the position to make certain sounds.

Speech problems caused by the physiological and neurological disorders mentioned above are organic in nature — that is, they are the result of some deficiency or impairment of the speech structures or of the physiological and neurological systems which control the muscles of the speech mechanism. Other speech problems, such as stuttering or dysrhythmic, cluttered speech, can be described as psychological disorders resulting from emotional disturbances.

However, the vast majority (approximately 75 per cent, according to most authorities) of the speech defects which occur within the school-age population are classified as functional articulation problems. These defects occur in children who have the ability to reproduce correctly all of the standard sounds of our language, but who nonetheless misarticulate speech sounds. These children may omit certain speech sounds altogether (*at* for *hat* or *un* for *sun*), substitute one speech sound for another (*witto* for *little* and *wed* for *red*), distort sounds, or even add unnecessary sounds to their speech. It is this group of speech-handicapped children who will benefit most from organized and consistent use of *Talking Time*. Further explanations of speech-sound substitutions and other mispronunciations are listed under each separate speech-sound unit.

THE TEACHER AND SPEECH IMPROVEMENT

Speech is an acquired skill and the kindergarten child brings well-established language concepts to his first school experiences. He communicates, yet his speech sounds may be misarticulated. His learned speech habits are acquired from his parents (his mother in particular) and from other members of his family and neighborhood. The child may bring to school dialectal variations or deviant word pronunciations learned in the home and the community.

He may bring shy or aggressive vocal patterns, and his speech sounds may be precise and accurate or they may be muffled, distorted, substituted, or omitted.

The teacher's role in speech development and correction comes into focus at the very beginning of the child's school life. The Research Committee of the American Speech and Hearing Association describes this role in these words: "It consists of systematic instruction in oral communication which has as its purpose the development of articulation, voice, and language abilities that enable all children to communicate their ideas effectively." [2]

The term *speech improvement* is applied to this type of systematic classroom instruction in oral communication to distinguish it from speech correction. Specifically, *speech correction* refers to the efforts of the speech specialist and other persons working with speech-handicapped children in a speech program apart from the regular classroom curriculum. These children have abnormal or deviant speech patterns which have become problems because they call unwanted attention to their speech and interfere with communication.

There is some obvious overlapping of *speech correction* and *speech improvement*. It was indicated above that all children need help in developing and improving their oral communication skills, but all children do not have defective speech. Neither do children develop speech and language skills at the same rate or in the same way. It is difficult sometimes to determine how effective certain techniques are for the child with a speech problem when he is exposed to those techniques in a group situation rather than on an individual basis. However, it has been reported that "Speech improvement programs that have been initiated and carried on for a number of years

---

[2] *Ibid.*, p. 78.

are proving to be beneficial to the general speech of the total population and have reduced . . . speech problems." [3] It was the opinion of 61 per cent of specialists from all over the nation who were interviewed for the report cited above that speech-improvement programs have decreased the number of children requiring special speech therapy. One of the recommendations of the report was that "Speech improvement should be a part of the curriculum from kindergarten through grade 12." [4]

In this way, the classroom teacher becomes an essential part of the speech-correction team by initiating and maintaining an active program of speech improvement in the classroom and working closely with the speech specialist. Even when they cannot diagnose the problems, most teachers will recognize that one child's speech is different from that of other children. Perhaps this child hesitates, stutters, or blocks when attempting to communicate. In all cases, the teacher should seek the help of the speech specialist or guidance director, if such personnel are available. Rather than attempt to counsel parents about the correction of the speech problem, the teacher should refer them to specially trained people on the school staff. The classroom teacher may help the speech specialist by administering simple screening tests explained in this book and by listing what he determines to be the general difficulties. The rhymes and stories in this book will give the child many successful speech experiences through choric speaking, creative dramatics, and puppetry.

Talking Time can help specifically those children who have functional articulation disorders. The teacher is advised to begin his efforts in helping these children by checking his own knowledge of the speech sounds in our language. The teacher should observe himself in a mirror as he produces each of the sounds, so that he will be able

---

[3] *Ibid.,* p. 79.
[4] *Ibid.,* p. 92.

to explain to the child what should be done to make each sound correctly. In this book, each of the units on a particular speech sound begins with a paragraph which describes how the speech sound is made. These units should be used as a guide in noting tongue movements, discovering what the lips and teeth do, and feeling the voice box to find out whether there is vocal-cord vibration. This knowledge will help the teacher to conduct a speech survey with his class. He will have prepared both his eyes and his ears to pick up deviations.

THE SPEECH SURVEY

The speech survey is a means of determining the sound or sounds which are substituted, omitted, added, or distorted. This check should take place early in the school year in order to discover any speech deviations which may exist. Once the class has been screened and the speech differences classified, the program for introducing speech instruction into the curriculum may be planned.

A very simple survey may be made by asking the child to count to fifteen, name the different colors, say the nursery rhyme "Jack and Jill," and identify pictures whose names contain the "ch" and "sh" speech sounds. Small colored squares or circles, or bits of colored ribbon will stimulate the child to say the colors. Miniature objects and small toys also are excellent for testing speech sounds in a more comprehensive manner. A child delights in reaching into a "surprise" box, taking out an object, and telling the teacher what it is. The box may contain such objects as a ring (initial "r"), a fork (initial "f"), a bar of soap (initial "s"), and so on.

To prepare a more thorough speech survey, collect pictures from magazines and inexpensive coloring books. The word lists in each unit of this book are a good source of suggestions for a picture collection. Mount the pictures on uniform-size pieces of tagboard, so that they can be used for speech games as well as for screening speech sounds.

If a comprehensive speech evaluation is to be made, it will be necessary to include pictures, objects, or words that test each sound in initial, medial, and final position. It should be noted that certain sounds do not appear in all three positions. Our language has no words which begin with the "zh" or "ng" sounds or which end with the sounds of "w," "wh," or "h." A complete test will include all the consonant blends involving "s," "r," and "l." These consonant blends may be difficult for the child to pronounce in whole words, even though he is able to produce them in isolated nonsense syllables (e.g., *sta, ste, sti, sto, stu*). Check the appropriate speech-sound units for lists of words containing these consonant blends.

USING THE SPEECH-SOUND UNITS

After completing the speech survey and identifying those children whose speech is defective, turn to those sections in this book which deal with the sounds causing the difficulty. The materials for speech improvement and development are arranged to fulfill specific needs.

Making the speech sound. Each section begins with a description of the sound and how it is produced. Each sound is given one or more characteristic personalities. For example, "s" is called the "teakettle," "snake," or "flat-tire" sound. "L" is the "singing-wind," the "elevator," or the "telephone-wires" sound. Young children are sometimes confused by alphabet designations such as *s* (ess) or *l* (ell). But if they are told that the snake says "ssss" and the singing wind goes "llllll," they will be able to make the association and listen for the sound in their own speech and in the speech of others.

8

Correcting the deficient speech sound. In each speech-sound unit, common defects of articulation are listed and techniques are suggested for helping the child to produce the speech sound correctly. Correction can be a difficult step, since the child has a deeply reinforced habit pattern to overcome. Activity materials are provided in each section to assist the teacher in helping the child establish correct speaking patterns.

Instructions to the child. Instructions for making the sound are presented in language which the child can easily understand. A teacher who is beginning a speech-improvement program for the first time may want to read these instructions to the class directly from the book. However, a few readings will enable the teacher to improvise and adapt these instructions for his own pupils.

Words for practice. The word lists in each speech-sound unit provide an immediate supply of common words containing the sound in initial, medial, and final position. Words containing consonant blends are included under some sections. A complete articulation test for the speech survey may be compiled from these word lists.

I hear it. The "I Hear It" rhymes are designed to help a child learn to discriminate between the desired speech sound and other sounds he may be substituting for the correct sound. If a child cannot differentiate between two sounds when he hears them, he will have difficulty in reproducing the desired sound when he speaks. Each of us must learn to listen to his own speech if he wishes to improve any aspect of it or to modify ineffectual language patterns. We must become aware, however, of what we should listen for. We may ask a qualified person to be an evaluator. Then we may experiment until we obtain an acoustically acceptable pattern. Finally, we must familiarize ourselves with this correct pattern through repeated practice. An explanation of how to use "I Hear It" is given on pages 80-81 in the "s" unit.

Are we listening? Listening is a basic segment of speech and language development. The optimum effectiveness of the materials in this book depends upon the child's ability to attend. These "Are We Listening?" sections have several purposes:

They make it possible for the child's response to include words containing the speech sound with which he is having difficulty.

They aid in the identification of speech sounds and help the child to discriminate between correct and incorrect speech-sound patterns.

They create an awareness of similarities and differences in rhyming words.

They provide pleasurable vocalized expression through which the child can hear and evaluate his own voice.

They give the child an opportunity to use a rich variety of sentence patterns with which to express himself.

They stimulate him to recall a series of statements (within a narrative poem or story) and to make creative responses to these verbal stimuli.

An explanation of how to use the "Are We Listening?" activities is given on page 81. This device is included for the most frequently misarticulated speech sounds.

Stories and poems. Each speech-sound section includes stories and poems that present the speech sound both in isolation and in initial, medial, and final position in words. Materials stressing consonant blends are included in some sections. For most of the sounds, much practice is devoted to hearing, identifying, and producing the single phoneme before a two- or three-letter blend is introduced to the child. Vowels, though represented in words throughout the book, are not discussed, since it is the consonants which present major speech difficulties in the functional articulation problems of children.

Isolated speech sounds form the basis for repetitive refrains in a number of the rhymes and stories in this book. These refrains enable a child to participate immediately and to hear many correct repetitions of a sound. The use of speech-sound personalities helps children remember how to articulate speech sounds in these refrains and in other speaking activities. As children sharpen their ability to hear and identify sounds and the differences between sounds by listening to themselves and others, they begin to develop an awareness of their speech mechanism as it produces specific speech sounds. The process of speech improvement has begun when this takes place.

There is little value in dwelling upon isolated sound elements after the child has learned to differentiate between one sound and another and to identify and produce those sounds in various positions in words. However, until he has established the habit of producing the sound accurately and spontaneously in his speech, it may be necessary to reinforce the learning process by continued use of rhymes and stories that present the sound in isolation. In addition to effective drill, these materials provide stimulating classroom fun which motivates the child's interest in improving or correcting his speech. A child who has mastered a new sound pattern is proud of his accomplishment. His feat is comparable to that of a musician who finally has learned to play a Bach fugue well or of a mathematician who has arrived at the solution to a difficult equation. The child should be allowed to demonstrate his success to the class and should be given recognition for overcoming his mispronunciation. Encourage the child to show his classmates how to make the newly acquired sound. He needs feelings of acceptance, warmth, and affection from his group. In particular, the speech-handicapped child requires praise, patience, and approval from the teacher. The frustrations a child with a speech problem experiences when trying to speak so that he is understood are comparable to those of an adult learning a new language.

Children with speech problems are not going to overcome those problems with a first presentation of speech-correction materials. They may continue to misarticulate speech sounds. The teacher should not feel that he is neglectful of the child when he is allowed to misarticulate. The child in the reading group who is interrupted in the middle of a sentence and asked to repeat a word correctly may not only be robbed of his enthusiasm for the story, but may also be conditioned to become a halting, hesitant reader with a strong dislike for books. The child who is corrected in front of his peers may experience humiliation and feelings of defeat when he cannot repeat correctly what is demanded of him. It must be decided whether it is more important for the child to communicate in some fashion, even though he may make articulation errors, or whether perfection and precision is to be expected in all speaking efforts. Everyone would no doubt agree that it is essential for the child to speak with adequate volume, to sound pleasant, to use variety in rate and pitch, and to gain control of his speech fright. But we also should understand that the child must be permitted to communicate his ideas. His talents and abilities must be recognized. We must give him many opportunities to talk, read aloud, dramatize, and discuss if he is to develop and improve his communication skills.

Two minutes of concentrated individual help on the part of the teacher can be worth a half hour of uninteresting drill on a speech sound. Ten minutes of participation with a rhyme or story containing refrains can help to modify a child's attitudes about his poor speech. The teacher who is eager to help all children develop and improve their speaking skills can make speech a part of every activity during the day if given effective tools. A good speech program includes far more than teaching the bare essentials of correct articulation through drill activities. The selections in *Talking Time* were not devised solely to provide repetitive practice on specific speech sounds. The rhymes and stories balance good speech-improvement materials with a broad variety of other materials that provide for relaxation or for stimulation of sensory perception; teach concepts of color, shape, size, and number; and introduce fantasy and fable, as well as selections about holidays, transportation, the farm, the community, animals, pets, the circus, and the zoo. An index of the selections by themes is included on page 399.

Each rhyme and story is followed by suggestions for creative use of the selection. The teacher may wish to devise additional techniques for presenting the selection and for stimulating pupil responses. Creative responses can be effectively solicited by questions like these:

1. What special sounds did you hear?
2. What words did you like?
3. What did the story (or rhyme) make you want to do? Dance? Sing? Cry? Clap?
4. How did it make you feel? Sad? Happy? Excited? Relaxed?
5. What pictures did you see in your mind as you listened to the story (or rhyme)?

Children who are culturally disadvantaged or educationally handicapped must be given experiences which develop their abilities, attitudes, and tastes and which lead them to appreciate and accept the better things in our culture. *Talking Time* presents stories that incorporate fundamental truths, e.g., "The Lost Song," "The Threap," and "Little Firefly." Moral values are pointed up in stories such as "Turkey-Urkey." The variety presented in the rhymes and stories may help a child to respond and do constructive things he would not have done had he not listened to the selections. When children are encouraged to join in a refrain, to pantomime, or to discuss, they reveal and put to use many talents We may

13

discover that one child has learned to get along with his peers; another has learned to take turns and not to interrupt; still another has learned to evaluate his own performance and those of others; all, hopefully, have learned how to plan with a group.

As it was pointed out earlier, successful accomplishment is not always immediate, but the consistent and systematic presentation of speech-improvement activities will contribute to it. If a child still continues to say *wed* for *red,* perhaps his need to communicate with others has been fulfilled within the confines of his not-altogether-correct speech patterns. We must continue to study the communication problems and progress of our pupils. We will gain new insights into their personality development and their creative talents as we ask ourselves these questions:

Who expresses the most original ideas?
Who recalls details?
Who is inventive in the use of language?
Who asks questions?
Who responds or fails to respond?
Who thinks of logical ways of solving problems?
Who employs extensive vocabulary?
Who enjoys experimenting with words?

CREATIVE IDEAS FOR THE TEACHER

The young child finds rhythm in everything he does. He may make up songs and nonsense rhymes while playing with his toys. He may find his expression in such physical activities as rhythmic clapping, jumping, or spinning around. Creativity may begin with a single idea through which the child discovers the joy of achievement as he acts out or discusses the idea he has in mind. Whatever the mode of expression, he senses that the idea is his and his alone. From the teacher should come encouragement and appropriate materials with which to work and create.

The teacher will find endless ways to use this book. The selections provide a variety of materials that are useful during each day's poetry-story time. The opportunities for creativity offered in these pages stimulate thinking, feeling, and exploration; stimulate a desire to share and be a group participant; and induce self-criticism as the children learn to evaluate their own listening and speech habits. The values of the stories and poems are abundant. Children can be given a deeper understanding of the rewards which the beauty of words offers. They can be helped to experience the sense and meaning of rhyming and rhythmic patterns. They can be exposed to the pleasures of vicarious sensory perception evoked by the imagery of the stories and rhymes. Children seem to feel the intended movement of a line. They can swing into a rhythm pattern almost at once as they anticipate how a line should be said. Little encouragement is required.

The use of repetitive sounds or words is a source of joy to the child, who may overcome timidity and speech difficulties so easily and so gradually that he never realizes there was a concealed purpose behind the selection. Much satisfaction is gained, however, when the child knows that the activity is a purposeful one offered to help him with a specific need, such as enunciating more clearly, speaking more softly or more loudly, speaking more slowly, or using better voice placement and variety to overcome a monotonous way of speaking. Imaginative activities which teach specific facts or values in this way will help the child to retain them and share them with others. Realizing that over-formalization can stifle creativity, this book offers stories, poems, and jingles which afford children freedom of expression through rhythmic body movement, pantomime, creative dramatics, creative art, and creative writing experiences.

Dramatization with puppets can bring a story or poem to life. Most adults and children, at one time or other, have tried their hand at making and manipulating puppets. This is evidenced by the popularity of books and articles on puppetry and by the number of television programs that utilize this method of dramatization.

A puppet play offers the children an excellent opportunity for improvising. As participants rather than spectators, the children can present their fullest and most conscientious efforts. They can express their emotions freely by projecting them through the puppets. The use of puppets in the classroom offers the child many educational experiences.

Puppets help the child to improve his speech. When the child manipulates and speaks through a puppet, he assumes a different character each time he performs. His wish to be heard and understood supersedes his desire to have fun. As the puppet "talks," the child's words are pronounced more clearly, his voice assumes more variety of expression, and his phrasing improves. Although puppetry must be considered a supplementary treatment for stuttering or other emotional problems, it will help to give the stutterer confidence in speech situations, since the listener's attention is focused upon the puppet rather than upon the child. If the stutterer keeps his attention on the puppet, he usually will find himself able to speak with fewer hesitations, repetitions, or prolongations.

Puppets can help the child to develop listening skills. Since listening is necessary to the improvement and correction of speech, the child's attention must be caught and maintained. He must discriminate between speech sounds he hears, and he must be able to associate and identify them with something in his own experience. A puppet sometimes can perform an instructional task much more effectively than the teacher alone. One speech specialist uses a clown puppet to tell the children in the classroom it is time to have special help with their speech sounds. One first-grade teacher has a small puppet that "whispers information to her" which she then relays to the children. The puppet's admonitions do not go unheeded. Puppets encourage a child to listen more attentively.

Puppetry helps the child to improve social relationships. Puppetry is a sharing activity and, when a group decides to dramatize a story or poem, cooperative effort is called for. Each puppet must do its share. Each puppet must observe good listening behavior. Human relationships are improved as the children plan and work together and adapt their activities and behavior to those of their companions. Puppetry provides a way of learning behavior that is acceptable and expected in our society. Courtesy and self-control are achieved and the child becomes a better-adjusted individual. His ideas have been considered worthwhile. He has acquired esteem in the eyes of his associates. He has gained self-respect and respect for others, and he has learned to discipline himself.

Among the many stories and poems which can be presented with puppets are "Funny Old Pig" (page 303), "Rooster Red" (page 120), and "Peepers, the Hungry Chick" (page 318).

THE FLANNELBOARD AND THE MAGNETIC BOARD

Flannelboard or magnetic board presentations motivate the child to listen more attentively and to recall a sequence of ideas and events more precisely. Instruction can be made vital and enjoyable. It is suggested that the children be encouraged to draw, color, and cut out figures for stories and rhymes which they wish to dramatize with the help of this medium. The following suggestions may help the teacher to make full use of the flannelboard and the magnetic board.

Have a junk box. Fill it with scraps of cloth, beads, buttons, sequins, blocks of wood, bamboo sticks, tongue depressors, old venetian blind slats, wallpaper, paper bags of various sizes, pipe cleaners, yarn, cotton, fur, and bits of felt, flannel, and other fabrics. The children may feel free to create their own puppets or flannelboard figures.

Materials for figures. Use materials like felt, pellon, or outing flannel to make figures for the flannelboard. Figures made from these materials need no special backing to make them adhere to the board.

Use magnets. Buy small magnets at a hardware store. Glue them to small toys, objects, or pictures for use on your magnetic board.

Use pictures. The children may use pictures that they have drawn and colored or have cut from magazines and discarded books. These pictures will need backing to make them adhere to the board. Cover the back of the picture with plastic glue, press it on a piece of outing flannel, allow it to dry beneath a heavy book, then cut it out. Strips of flocking, bits of blotting paper, or sandpaper of a fine-grained quality may also be used for backing.

Use a minimum of figures or characters. Ask the class to choose the most important characters which will appear frequently in the story or poem. The board should not appear too cluttered. Make a container for each selection to be used with the board by taping a manila folder at the sides to form an envelope. File each story or poem with its figures in a box on the browsing table so that the children may make their own choice when they wish to retell a selection.

Making backgrounds. Backgrounds may be cut from large pieces of colored outing flannel and used for grass, sky, and hills.

The language in which the story is told is as important as the content of the story itself. Therefore, it is advisable to read the story to the children rather than attempting to tell it, since much of the flavor and effectiveness are lost with the omission of the particular words used by the author. Carefully chosen words in a story have the same compelling power that effectively sequenced tones of pitch have in a musical composition. The right words can help gain and maintain interest and attention. Without concentrated attention there can be no effective hearing, seeing, feeling, tasting, and smelling. Words can form distinct impressions and well-defined images. But even the right words require clear articulation and vocal variety on the part of the reader if they are to "paint pictures" in the child's mind.

The teacher should become aware of a few important considerations which will help to improve the presentation. See that the class is ready to listen before beginning a story. Speak with animation and conviction, yet do not overdo the interpretation with gestures or a quality of expression that calls attention to itself. Be interested and look alert so that the class will sense your attitudes. Use a well-modulated voice. Enunciate clearly, being careful not to be overly pedantic and remembering that *the* and *a* should usually be pronounced as *thuh* and *uh* when used in unaccented positions in speech. Pause or phrase carefully to help the children listen more easily and enjoyably.

Telling a flannelboard story. In telling a flannelboard story, it is well to keep a few basic rules in mind. Refrain from cluttering the board with figures. Remove pictures when they no longer function as part of the story. Place the pictures in left-to-right order whenever possible for good left-to-right eye movements. Arrange the pictures to be used in proper sequence behind the board so that they can be found easily. Check each picture before story time to make sure it will stick. Just in case, keep a cushion of corsage pins handy to secure the figure on the board. Place each figure on the board as it is mentioned in the story, and not before.

CHORIC SPEAKING

Choric speaking is a most satisfying group experience for children. Many of the selections in this book can be used for choric speaking which will help the child to control his speed, pitch, and loudness and to acquire a more desirable vocal quality.

Some children with harsh or strident voices may be helped through regular exposure to the beauty of words in poems and other narrative materials. Such exposure gives children the desire to make their speech pleasant to listen to. Shy children who appear to have weak voices show more strength of tone as they gain the confidence that results from participating in choric speaking. It is recommended that the teacher make optimum use of his own vocal mechanism in order to demonstrate effective pitch patterns and variety in rate, volume, and quality.

One main value of choric speaking is that all children in a class may participate. Although certain arrangements have been suggested, the teacher should feel free to try other ways and to solicit ideas from the children about which lines or words should be said softly or loudly, said by boys or girls, said by the group or used as solos, expressed slowly or rapidly or with emphasis, or given special vocal expression.

Aside from benefits of group participation, there are many values which can accrue from the use of choric speaking.

It can improve articulation.

It can help the child to lose self-consciousness.

It can help the aggressive child to take turns, to share, and to recognize achievement in others. Such a child discovers new satisfaction in being a part of the group.

It can improve rhythm in speech.

It can create an awareness of rhyming words.

It can improve vocabulary usage.

It can help the child with a speech defect as he hears the speech sound frequently repeated in a selection and gains practice in pronouncing the sound in words.

It can provide a cooperative effort for programs and can be used as a highly effective termination activity for a unit of study. This speech activity can be taken easily from the school into other parts of the community, since scenery, costuming, properties, and special lighting are not required and there is a minimum of rehearsal preparation.

CHAPTER **2**

Sensory Perception

The best instructional materials and activities for young children are those which sharpen their sensitivity to sights, sounds, tastes, smells, and textures and which make them receptive to learning new things through their senses.

As we study the primary child's interests and his spontaneous expressions, we discover how large a part the senses play in his learning. When little Tommy asks a question, our response is usually stated in terms of physical action and sense perception, for the very young child examines the world about him with his muscles and senses rather than with the logic of cause and effect. The inquiries children make are those, then, which lead them to expand their experiences through ever-widening circles of hearing, seeing, touching, smelling, and tasting. The seemingly helpless baby is born with all the potential equipment necessary to explore and learn through his five senses — the chief means for developing his communication skills.

The sense of hearing is essential to the child as he begins to listen for and identify all the sounds in his environment, including the speech sounds which he must imitate before he can learn to talk.

moke from a chimney and soap on my hands and a
clean, starched dress."

Alexa's mother added, "And your nose is a sound box
for three speech sounds — *m* as in *mother, n* as in *nose,* and
ng as in *sing.*"

Alexa drew a picture of her wonderful nose.

She asked, "Why do I have a tongue?"

Mother said, "You have a tongue that helps you taste.
It helps push food into the back of your mouth so that
you may swallow it. It has little taste buds to help you
know whether something is sweet, sour, salty, or bitter."

Alexa thought about this a bit and then said, "My
tongue and my nose are good friends."

"That they are," agreed Alexa's mother. "The little
nerves inside your nose tell your brain if something is
good to eat. Scientists call them olfactory nerves."

"If something smells bad, I would never eat it, of
course," said Alexa. "But I know something else about
my tongue. It moves inside of my mouth to help me talk.
I can feel my tongue go up and down in back when I talk.
I can feel the tip go up. Oh, my tongue really is
WONDERFUL!"

Alexa drew a picture of her wonderful tongue.

"Why do I have two hands and ten fingers, Mother?"
asked Alexa.

The sense of sight is one of the first senses to come
into play. When the infant's nervous system has matured
enough to control the movements of the six small muscles
of each eye, he begins to discriminate visually. At eight
weeks he is attracted by motion. By two and a half or
three months, he is interested in color and often will stop
crying at the sight of a bright-colored toy.

The sense of touch is the sense that enables the baby to
reach out and feel the warmth of his mother. Through
cuddling and pleasant words, he receives assurance that
he is loved. An awareness of touch during those first
months is necessary to his emotional development.

The senses of taste and smell complement the other
three senses. The mouth provides an area of exploration
for the young child. His sensitive lips and tongue tell him
if he is tasting old leather or a sweet cookie. Taste and
smell feature strongly in his development.

The child, then, learns and develops through all
sensory avenues. As Dr. Linderman has pointed out,
"Whenever a child's aesthetic needs are met, there is in-
tegration of his ability to think, feel, and perceive the
world he experiences." [1] In this way, the child's personality
is enriched, his sensibilities are increased, and the human
relationships which exist in his environment are enhanced.

A variety of motivational material which emphasizes
further development of sense perception is welcomed by
the primary teacher. One way in which he may help children to experience sensory stimulation is to teach them
to be more observant of the world about them, beginning
with the classroom itself. Vocabulary for expressing the
nature of dimension and capacity and textural consistency
can come from the children themselves as exemplified by
a group of kindergartners who described boxes as *square,*

1 Linderman, Dr. Earl, "A Thing of Beauty," *The Grade Teacher,* April,
1963.

short, long, tall, round, and *big.* One box was *full* of crayons, while another was *empty.* "Play-doh" was "squizzy" and "gooey," and some children noted that it could make any shape at all. In expressing themselves, the children used every part of speech and more than seven different sentence patterns.

Another kindergarten group listened to "rattlers" made from small cereal boxes and baby-food cans. Such objects as tacks, short crayons, rice, bits of glass, beads, beans, dried peas, tiny bells, and pencil stubs were placed in these containers. The children identified the sounds which the rattlers made as *sharp, dull, rattly, soft, jingly, high, low,* and *nice.* Auditory perception was intensified and refined as the children listened in order to group the sounds as *soft, loud, medium, louder,* and *softer.* To create an increased awareness of the emotional feelings aroused by sensory perception, some children were asked these questions:

What is the loveliest thing you have ever seen?

If you had a special pair of eyes, what might you be able to see?

If you could have just one thing to eat, what would it be?

Imagine the rain has stopped. The earth has a good smell now. How does it smell?

How does pudding taste in your mouth?

How does jelly feel in your hand?

How does popcorn sound when you eat it?

Name something in the room that you would like to feel. Point to it. Get it and show it to us. Tell why you like to feel it.

In addition to teaching opposites and rhyming words and providing practice with repeated speech sounds, the conceptual rhymes in this book, such as "What Is Thin?" (page 172), will be of considerable help in developing sensory perception.

"Mother, why do I have two ears?" asked ⸢

Alexa's mother answered, "You have two ca⸥ you hear and to keep your balance."

Alexa said, "Yes, my ears help me hear. I ca⸥ bird sing and a dog bark. I can hear a bee make⸥ buzz, 'zzzz.' I can hear rain on the roof, drip, dri⸥ and I can hear a tiny whisper. But how do my t⸥ help me keep my balance?"

"There is a tiny balance mechanism insid⸥ head," replied Alexa's mother. "It is filled with flu⸥ it is in the inner part of your ear deep inside your⸥ Sometimes it makes you feel dizzy when you turn s⸥ saults too fast, or spin like a top. But it helps you⸥ your balance when you jump rope, climb trees, play⸥ scotch, follow tracks on the sidewalk, and do many, n⸥ things where you must move in different directions⸥ your ear has two jobs to do, you see."

Alexa said, "Yes, it has two jobs to do. The ear⸥ me hear and it helps me keep my balance."

Alexa drew a picture of her two wonderful ears.

"Why do I have a nose?" Alexa asked her moth⸥

Her mother replied, "You have just one nos⸥ little hairs inside that serve as nose-sweepers to b⸥ dust and germs from the air you breathe and to ⸥ passageway that leads into your lungs nice an⸥

Alexa smiled. "My nose helps me to smell. It⸥ smell cookies and oranges and fresh-cut grass. I ⸥

Her mother answered, "You have two hands and ten fingers to tell you how things feel."

Alexa looked at her hands and fingers. "Sometimes things feel squishy like mud or rough like sandpaper," she said. "Some things feel AWFULLY good to me. I like to feel the smooth fur on my kitty's back. Even if Daddy's whiskers are rough, I like to feel them. I like to feel the soft pillow under my head when it is sleepy time. I like to taste and feel cold ice cream and warm chocolate on my tongue."

Mother said, "Yes, you would not want to feel cold ice cream or warm pancakes with your hands, would you?"

Alexa laughed at that. She said, "I can tell what shapes are by feeling them with my eyes closed. Some shapes are square. Some are round, triangular, or rectangular. I learned that in kindergarten."

Alexa drew a picture of her two hands and ten fingers.

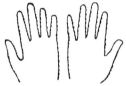

Then Alexa asked, "Why do I have two eyes?"

Her mother replied, "You have two eyes to help you see. Your two eyes can look big and round to show surprise. They can look right and left, because six little muscles control the movements of each eye. Your eyes are blue, but some eyes are brown, gray, or green."

Alexa said, "With my two eyes, I can see lovely pictures. I can watch for red, yellow, and green traffic lights. I can see the first snow in winter and the first robin in spring. I can see a spider working on his web. I can see leaves that have turned red and brown in the fall. And I can READ! I hear the words I read. The words make sentences. Words help me learn. I can sit up tall and hold my book straight when I read,"

Alexa drew a picture of her two wonderful eyes.

She said, "I hear, I smell, I taste, I touch, and I see. That is how I learn."

—L.B.S.

THE SENSES AND YOUR SPEECH HELPERS

The following lesson plan will help the teacher to explain the five senses further.

There are five pathways to your brain, boys and girls. They are hearing, sight, touch, taste, and smell. Your brain is the engine of your speech train, and it guides all the movements of your body. The senses send messages to your brain to tell it that you have heard a sound, seen a color, felt a shape, smelled an odor, or tasted food.

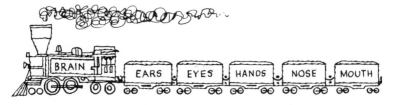

Your ears helped you learn to walk, because of the tiny canals in the shape of three loops inside each ear. They helped you keep your balance so that you would not take too many tumbles. Your ears helped you hold yourself upright and take steps to explore your new and exciting world.

And of course your ears helped you learn to talk. You heard your mother and daddy make sounds and those sounds joined hands and made words. The words helped to recall pictures recorded in your brain so that you would know what things were. You were like a little mockingbird because you imitated words you heard and you used those words to remember and to tell what you needed and wanted. You used words to help express your feelings, too.

You said "Da-da" and "Ma-ma" and suddenly you found that your talking helpers could do all sorts of amazing things! You could press your lips together and open them and then round them into a small circle when you said, "*Me, ah, oo.*" You could make an acrobat out of your tongue and you could make your voice motor hum. "La, la, la! Hummmmmmmm." When your teeth came through, they helped you to say, "Fine," when someone asked how you were feeling. Your nose tingled when you said, "Mmmmmmmmmy!" You experimented with your speech helpers and it was such fun!

Your fingers made you want to talk about things. They knew if something was cuddly and soft like your favorite teddy bear, or square and hard like a block, or round and rubbery like a ball. You felt with your sensitive finger tips and they helped you learn and remember the names of things.

You tasted oatmeal and applesauce and vegetables, and you learned the names of things you liked and disliked. When you put that dirty old rag in your mouth, it did not taste good at all. But when your daddy gave you a spoonful of ice cream, oh, that was different!

You smelled the things you tasted and those two senses, smell and taste, worked together so that you would not make a mistake and eat something which was not meant to travel to your stomach.

—L.B.S.

Ask members of the class what each of their senses do. Ask them what each of their speech helpers do.

TOMMY'S FIVE SENSES

Tommy's ears help him hear
And keep his balance, too.
Tommy's eyes help him see
If something's red or blue.
Tommy's hands help him touch
And know just how things feel.
Tommy's tongue helps him taste
A sour lemon peel.
Tommy's nose helps him smell
The food he likes to chew.
Tommy's senses help him think,
Decide, and learn to do.
Tommy has five senses as
This picture of him shows.
Tommy's helpers: ears and eyes
And hands and tongue and nose!

—L.B.S.

Cut a large face shape from pink outing flannel, and add yellow yarn for hair. Place it on the flannelboard, and let individual children add features cut from felt as the poem is said by the class. Features: eyes, nose, two ears, and red tongue. The hands are placed six inches below the face. Suggested additional parts are a red cap and a blue bow tie.

WHAT DO YOU LIKE TO HEAR BEST?

CHILDREN: What do you like to hear best?
           Oh, what do you like to hear best?

TEACHER: The crickets at night,
An owl in its flight,
A foghorn at sea,
Someone calling to me.

CHILDREN: Those things I like to hear best.
What do you like to see best?
Oh, what do you like to see best?

TEACHER: A favorite book,
A sparkling brook,
A cloud drifting by,
A bright butterfly.

CHILDREN: Those things I like to see best.
What do you like to taste best?
Oh, what do you like to taste best?

TEACHER: A chocolate éclair,
A delicious ripe pear,
A bowl of oatmeal,
A nippy orange peel.

CHILDREN: Those things I like to taste best.
What do you like to smell best?
Oh, what do you like to smell best?

TEACHER: The earth after rain,
Yellow ripening grain,
Clean sheets on a line,
Purple grapes on a vine.

CHILDREN: Those things I like to smell best.
What do you like to feel best?
Oh, what do you like to feel best?

31

TEACHER: A baby's smooth face,
A small bit of lace,
The warmth of dry sand,
My mother's soft hand.

CHILDREN: Those things I like to feel best.
—L.B.S.

This rhyme stimulates the children to tell spontaneously and individually the things which appeal to their senses. Write down some of their favorite sense impressions and make a class book of them or use them for a wall chart.

THE STRANGE SOUND IN THE GARDEN [2]

ALL: Did you hear a strange sound in the garden today?
What WAS that strange sound?
SOLO 1: Who can tell?
SOLO 2: Who can say?
TEACHER: Was it Little Green Gartersnake swishing around
Making a slippery, slithery sound?
CHILDREN: It was not Little Green Gartersnake swishing around
Making a slippery, slithery sound.
TEACHER: Was it Chirrupy Cricket hop-hopping along
Fiddling his crickily, crackily song?
CHILDREN: (Let the group repeat the question as a negative statement, or encourage various children to give individual responses.)
TEACHER: Was it Bella the Bumblebee humming a tune
While making sweet honey this fine afternoon?
CHILDREN: (Respond.)

---

[2] By special permission of *The Grade Teacher*. Poem by Louise Binder Scott.

TEACHER:	Was it Little Gray Fieldmouse away down inside
	His cozy dark burrow, where he likes to hide?
CHILDREN:	(Respond.)
TEACHER:	Was it Little Brown Toad trying hard to get chummy
	With a pudgy old fly to fill up his fat tummy?
CHILDREN:	(Respond.)
TEACHER:	Did YOU hear something strange in the garden today?
ALL:	What WAS that strange sound?
SOLO 3:	Who can tell?
SOLO 4:	Who can say?
SOLO 5:	It was Sally May using her shiny new hoe
	And chopping the weeds so her flowers would grow.
CHILDREN:	(Repeat.)
ALL:	Scritch-scratching, scritch-scratching, scritch-scratching away.
	That's the sound that I heard when I went out to play.
	That's the sound that I heard in the garden today.

This poem creates an awareness of sounds in the environment. Ask the children to tell about some strange sounds they may have heard. Ask what kind of flowers Sally May raised in her garden. Words in the poem which could be used for practice on initial "s" are *strange, swishing, song, slippery, slithery, something, Sally, say, scritch-scratching, spring,* and *sound.* Words for medial "s" are *inside* and *gartersnake.* Words for final "s" are *makes, this, fieldmouse, likes.*

IMPRESSIONS IN RHYME

Sounds: Crickets at night that sing with delight,

Swishing cold rain on a large windowpane,

Laughter in June on a hot afternoon,
Crackling dry leaves, water dripping from
    eaves,
These sounds we like to hear!

Sights: Silver sun rays on cloudy, dark days,
A lamb new and sweet with tiny black feet,
Dewdrops on the grass like small chips of
    glass,
A forest of pine in the crisp wintertime,
Just you and ME and the dolls having tea,
Those sights we like to see.

Smells   Earth dampened by rain, and freshly cut
and   grain,
Tastes: Spicy cake on a tray on Thanksgiving Day,
Perfume in the room like a garden in
    bloom,
A tangy gold cheese, a fresh ocean breeze,
Iced strawberry pop, and an orange lolli-
    pop,
Those things we smell and taste.

The teachers in an extension class at California State College,
Los Angeles, were asked to elicit sensory responses from the children
in their classes and compile them in a poem. The assignment re-
sulted in the poem above. Note how internal rhyme has been used.
Ask the children to listen for the two rhyming words in each line.

MY SENSES

When I close my eyes,
What do I see?
I see a flower,
And maybe a tree!

When I close my eyes,
What do I hear?
Soft sounds, loud sounds,
Far and near.

When I close my eyes,
What do I taste?
Striped stick candy,
And white toothpaste.

When I close my eyes,
What do I smell?
Strawberry ice cream,
Or brown caramel.

When I close my eyes,
What do I touch?
My kitty's soft fur
That I like so much!

—L.B.S.

Divide the class into five or six sections. Ask each section to decide what they can see, hear, taste, feel, and smell when they close their eyes, and let them share their imagined sensory experiences with the class.

Though presenting speech sounds is secondary to the main purpose of this poem, there is emphasis upon the "s" speech sound in *see, soft, taste, striped, stick, toothpaste, smell, strawberry,* and *ice.*

Have you heard soft tinkling bells
When everything is still?
Have you smelled the scent of pine
High upon a hill?
Have you felt cold, crispy air
Upon your fingertips?
Have you tasted flakes of snow
Wet upon your lips?
Have you seen the packages
Wrapped in ribbon gay?
These are signs to let you know
That this is Christmas Day!

Ask the children to tell what Christmas sounds, sights, smells, tastes, and feelings they have experienced.

FIVE LITTLE RABBITS

ALL: Five little rabbits on the big, big farm
           Turned their floppy ears to catch the sounds,

SOLO 1:   Heard a cow moo,
SOLO 2:   Heard a horse neigh,
SOLO 3:   Heard a dove coo,
SOLO 4:   Heard a mule bray.

ALL: Five little rabbits on the big, big farm
           Looked all around with their little pink eyes,

SOLO 5:   Saw a chickadee,
SOLO 6:   Saw a black crow,
SOLO 7:   Saw a bumblebee,
SOLO 8:   Saw a scarecrow.

[3] By special permission of *The Grade Teacher*. Poem by Louise Binder Scott.

ALL:	Five little rabbits on the big, big farm
	Wiggled their whiskers and sniffed the air,

SOLO 9:	Smelled a cabbage green,
SOLO 10:	Smelled the growing wheat,
SOLO 11:	Smelled the earth so clean,
SOLO 12:	Smelled a carrot sweet.

ALL:	Five little rabbits on the big, big farm
	Were hungry for lunch, so they started to munch.

CHILDREN:	(*Tell what the rabbits ate.*)

—L.B.S.

The children may draw and color pictures for the twelve scenes depicted in the poem, and show them as they say the solo lines. Additional pictures may be created for foods the rabbits ate.

ON HALLOWEEN

Hear the brownies
    pattering,
        chattering.

Hear the goblins
    moaning,
        groaning.

Hear the night wind
    sighing,
        crying.

See the witches
    gliding,
        riding.

See the pumpkins
staring,
glaring.

See the black cats
biting,
fighting.

Feel the dry leaves
whirling,
swirling.

Feel the cold air
nipping,
snipping.

Feel the bat wings
rushing,
brushing.

ON HALLOWEEN!

—L.B.S.

This rhyme builds word pictures that appeal to the senses. The verb forms ending in *ing* can be used for practice on the *ng* speech sound.

QUIET, QUIET, QUIET

TEACHER: Quiet, quiet, quiet! What can I hear?
The bells in the chapel ringing slowly, long, and clear.
I can hear an orchestra of crickets in the night.
I can hear a hummingbird whirring in its flight.

CHILDREN: Quiet, quiet, quiet,
                 quiet, quiet, quiet! (*Voices grow softer.*)

TEACHER: Quiet, quiet, quiet! I can hear the bees
                 Flying from the clover to their beehives in
                     the trees.
                 I can hear the crackling and snapping of a fire.
                 I can hear the singing of a little children's
                     choir.

CHILDREN: Quiet, quiet, quiet,
                 quiet, quiet, quiet!

TEACHER: Quiet, quiet, quiet! I can hear the rain
                 Swishing off the sidewalks and washing down
                     the drain.
                 I can hear the ocean with its lapping lullaby.
                 I can hear a bell buoy and a lonely sea gull's
                     cry.

CHILDREN: Quiet, quiet, quiet,
                 quiet, quiet, quiet!

—L.B.S.

Ask individual children to tell things they can hear when they are quiet. This selection encourages relaxation and readiness for other activities. It provides practice with the sound of the *qu* ("kw") blend in the word *quiet*.

OF SMELLS I LIKE

I like the smell that fills the air
    when gardens are in bloom.
I like the smell that always comes
    from Mother's new perfume.
At school, I even like to smell
    our open jars of paste;

39

And cookies baking smell so good
    I cannot wait to taste!
A farmyard has a special smell;
    a candy store does, too.
The smell of busy traffic makes
    you want to hurry through.
There are fresh washed sheets and popcorn, too,
    and burning leaves as well;
A forest wet with summer rain;
    all these I like to smell.
So why not come along with me!
    We'll take a little hike.
We'll sniff and sniff along the way
    and find some smells you like.

—J.J.T.

Ask the children to write their own poems about smells they like. The poem offers useful drill with the *sm, sp, sn,* and *sk* consonant blends.

WHAT WAS IT? [4]

CHILDREN: Tommy could smell something!
                 Oh!
                 What was it? Tommy really didn't
                 know.

SOLO 1:   Was it a ripe tomato growing in a
                 patch?

SOLO 2:   Or a baby chicken trying hard to
                 hatch?

ALL: It was not a ripe tomato growing in a
                 patch,
                 Or a baby chicken trying hard to hatch.

SOLO 3:   Was it a humming top turning
                 round and round?

[4] By special permission of *The Grade Teacher.* Poem by Louise Binder Scott.

ALL: No! A top has no smell. It just has
a sound.
SOLO 4: Was it a rose?
SOLO 5: Or a pancake?
SOLO 6: Or a piece of apple pie?
SOLO 7: Or a puppy in the rain that was
shaking himself dry?
ALL: It was none of those,
Sniffed Tommy's little nose.
SOLO 8: Was it a peach?
SOLO 9: Or asparagus?
SOLO 10: They both smell so good.
ALL: It was nothing like that.
It was no kind of food.
Tommy could smell something—
Mmmmmm, so fresh and fine!
SOLO 11: Could it be white sheets that had
hung on the line?
SOLO 12: Could it be brown bread?
Mmmmmm! How nice!
ALL: No, it was not *food*. We have said
that twice.
Think of gardens,
Think of meadows,
Think of things YOU like to smell.
Think of words that will describe
them.
Are you ready now to tell?
CHILDREN: (*Give individual responses.*)
SOLO 13: Tommy smelled a scent of perfume
That was coming from the South.
CHILDREN: OH! IMAGINE!
ALL: It was a black-and-white skunk
With a flower in his mouth!

The suggested arrangement is helpful if the selection is to be
used for programs or with a flannelboard.

CHAPTER **3**

Listening and Relaxing

Listening is the basic communication skill by means of which a child builds his speaking, reading, and writing skills. There are many different kinds of listening. A child may listen for pure enjoyment, appreciatively and passively. He may listen actively and creatively as he offers his experiences to the materials being presented. Or he may listen for a functional purpose as he sorts out facts, gains information, and makes decisions. Whatever form of listening he is using, he must be ready to give his attention to the subject at hand. Attention will be more easily maintained when his interest is aroused by materials that stimulate the senses.

The child's ability to listen and concentrate depends to a great extent upon the kinds of listening he has experienced in the home. Children who have had a rich background of varied listening experiences, whose speech and language patterns have developed so that they can express desires, needs, and emotions, will no doubt find it easier to pay attention than will children who have been deprived of worthwhile listening experiences.

An atmosphere, then, of good conversation, music, and literature in the home helps inculcate acceptable listening patterns and encourages both self-control and self-realization. The old saying that "the child attends if he has been listened to, talked to, and read to" cannot be emphasized too vehemently. The child who is nagged and who must daydream in his own more pleasant world, the child who is given no turns to talk, the child whose opinions are not considered, and the child who tunes out significant sounds around him because of a bombardment of noises in the household can be helped immeasurably by a teacher who understands his background and who knows why he is inattentive and restless.

The child's inner turmoils subside and he becomes more amicable and relaxed as his mind and body respond to the controlled, well-modulated voice and the rich, colorful, selective vocabulary of the classroom teacher.

The movements of the teacher, as well as his manner of speaking, play an important role in establishing effective listening and an atmosphere of tranquility in the classroom. The teacher should realize that he need not move constantly and look "busy" to prove that he is a good teacher. He can sit quietly as he reads or tells a story. He can conserve some of his energy and still set a climate of firmness, friendliness, stability, poise, and inner strength which will help his pupils build feelings of well-being and calmness.

The classroom teacher, then, can create an atmosphere of security and provide experiences which will help to counteract listening deficiencies and physical and emotional tensions during the time the child is in the classroom and can hope that as the child feels "still inside," he will become more receptive to learning. The stories and poems contained in this section are designed to motivate relaxation. They can be used to follow either a concentrated learning activity in which movement has been restricted or an intense physical activity in which the children have been overstimulated by much movement.

THE SLEEPY FARM [1]

Once there was a pleasant little farm. Its neat white house spread out like a clean white sheet on a grassy meadow. It had a friendly barn. It had fields of sweet-smelling clover where, over and over, bees buzzed a drowsy tune on almost any warm afternoon:

> It was a grazy day,
> A hazy day,
> A sleepy, slumbery, lazy day,
> A fine day for just buzzing around —
> A day peaceful with sound.

The farm made you feel all quiet inside, because — because it was — *Shhhhhhhhh!* — a sleepy farm!

On that sleepy farm lived a little white chicken.

"Cheep, cheep, cheep!" peeped the little white chicken. "I think it must be *time*."

> So he snuggled down
> In his mother's nest,
> And under her feathers
> He had a good rest.

On that sleepy farm lived a fuzzy baby duckling.

"Quack, quack, quack!" quacked the fuzzy baby duckling. "I guess it's *time*. Quack!"

> So he found some leaves
> Which he used for a bed,
> And under his wing
> He tucked his head.

---

[1] By special permission of Bowmar Records, 1015 Burbank Avenue, North Hollywood, Calif. Story by Louise Binder Scott from the *Listening Time* albums.

On the sleepy farm lived a playful brown puppy with long ears.

"Ruff, ruff, ruff!" barked the playful brown puppy with long ears. "I've played very hard, and now I can rest for awhile."

> So he stretched—— and he stretched——
> In the pleasant sun.
> He was much too lazy
> To jump and run.

On the sleepy farm lived a little black pig with a curly tail.

"Oink, oink, oink!" grunted the little black pig with a curly tail. "This is the part of the day I like best. Ho-hum! I must be going."

> So he found a mud puddle
> All oozy and warm,
> And he wallowed and slept
> On that sleepy farm.

On the sleepy farm lived a little red rooster who was just learning to crow.

"Er, er, er, er, errrrr!" crowed the little red rooster. He was very, *very* tired.

> So he flew to his favorite
> Branch in the tree,
> Behind some green leaves
> Where no one could see.

On the sleepy farm lived a plump kitten.

"Mew, mew, mew!" mewed the plump kitten. "I am — mew — so little — and so sleepy. I simply must have my catnap."

So she found a cool place
By the garden wall,
And she curled herself up
In a wee round ball.

On the sleepy farm there lived a little boy. It was the warmest time of the afternoon. The little boy yawned, "Ho-hummmmm," and again he yawned, "Ho-hummm-mmmmm." He tried to keep back the yawns, but he just couldn't. They came out one after the other.

So he lay on some grass
In the nice, cool shade,
And he watched the shapes
That the fluffy clouds made.

And before you could even count to three,
He was sleeping as quietly as could be.

By now, I am sure
You will all agree
That the farm was the sleepiest
Place to be.

If you'd like to visit
That farm some day,
Just come with me;
I'll show you the way!

On a grazy day,
A hazy day,
A sleepy, slumbery
Lazy day!

This story should be read slowly, and the voice should be soft in order to induce feelings of relaxation and quiet. After a few readings, the class may be encouraged to say refrains.

THE DREAM FENCE [2]

I am sure that you know about Wee Willie Winkie who lives in Mother Goose Land.

Well, Wee Willie Winkie built a dream fence to separate Wide-awake Land from Sleepy Land. He asked Miss Muffet's spider to spin a shimmering silver web between each fence post, all of which lean lazily over to one side.

Now, to see this sleepy dream fence, you will need to close your eyes, for that is how you can see it best. Close your eyes and think about it with me as I tell the story.

Wee Willie Winkie's dream fence is covered with moonbeams — as soft as cotton — as soft as down on a baby duckling — as soft as *velvet,* even.

Little shadow pictures fall along the side of the fence. These shadow pictures never seem the same, no matter how often you look at them.

Sometimes they are white, sometimes they are gray, and sometimes they are a deep blue, depending on how big the moon is and how brightly it is shining.

If there is only a thin slice of moon, the shadows make tiny silver dots all over the fence. If the moon is round like a cookie, the shadows make big splashes on the fence. You never know what to expect, and that is why the dream fence always holds such lovely surprises.

When you close your eyes, the nicest things happen! You can see soft, fuzzy baby chicks, or cuddly puppies — and sometimes you can see shadows that remind you of flowers, or leaves, or dancing butterflies. It is so much fun imagining those shadow pictures, and the more you think about them, the sleepier you become — until you cannot hold up your head anymore at all. *Ahhhhhhh!* (*Sigh.*) Your eyelids feel *sooooo* heavy and your whole body feels *sooooo* limp that about the only thing you *can*

---

[2] By special permission of Bowmar Records. *Listening Time, Album 2.*

do is to go to sleep. It makes me sleepy just telling about it, so I know exactly how you must be feeling right now as you listen — all cozy and dreamy and comfortable. I am so sleepy myself that I'm afraid I can't tell anymore just now. Ho-hummmmmm. (*Children yawn.*)

—L.B.S.

This relaxation story is designed to quiet the children and instill feelings of repose. Read the story in a very soft voice and slowly enough for the children to form vivid mental pictures of the dream fence.

IN THE NIGHT

Benny puts on his pajamas and gets into bed. He snuggles down under the warm and friendly covers.

In the lovely night, Benny hears wind sounds. The wind makes a tree branch go swish, swish, swish against the windowpane, but Benny is not afraid.

The wind sings an "oo——" mournful song up and down the scale, but Benny is not afraid. He says, "The wind is singing a lullaby to put me to sleep."

Sometimes, the rough wind roars and soars and rolls and rattles the doors. It bangs the shutters. But Benny is not afraid. He knows that the blustery-flustery wind is blowing up a rain which will water the little seeds and help them grow.

Sometimes the thunder goes "Rrrrrroom, rrrrrroom" like a big bass drum, and the lightning makes a zigzag streak across the sky. But Benny is not afraid because thunder and lightning are part of the rainstorm that will water the little seeds and help them grow.

The rain comes down — drip, drip, drip, drop, drop, drop. And the raindrops come faster and faster — pit, pit, pit, pit, pit, pit, pit!

How soothing the rain sounds. Benny's eyes droop and he feels *sooooo* sleepy. Benny knows that the earth likes the cool rain. Benny is sure that the little seeds are turning in the softened earth and soon will begin to push their way upward.

Then the rain stops and big yellow moonbeams shine through Benny's window, casting a light along the floor. And Benny gets up to open the window to let in the delicious, fresh night air.

Sometimes in the lovely night, Benny hears scramble, scramble, scramble, across the floor. But it is only a tiny, sleek mouse looking for a morsel of food.

Sometimes Benny hears a train whistle in the distance and it makes him think of faraway places he hopes to see someday.

In the lovely night, Benny hears little crickets playing their fiddles. And sometimes, he hears a humming sound, "Mmmmmmmmmmmmmmmm." But it is only a little mosquito hoping that it might get into Benny's room. But of course it can't, because there is a screen on the window.

And sometimes Benny hears, "Hoo— hoo— hoo!" He knows that sound is made by a barn owl.

Benny hears footsteps. Then he hears a *squeak-squeak,* and he knows that Daddy is coming upstairs and stepping on that squeaky step that needs fixing.

Benny is glad to hear footsteps coming, for he likes to have Daddy and Mother come to see if he is covered up.

Benny hears the tick-tock of a little clock on the night stand and it seems to say, "Tick-tock, tick-tock. Night sounds are good sounds. Tick-tock, tick-tock."

Benny feels safe, for he knows that the sounds he hears are part of the lovely night. Night is an important time, just before you go to sleep, to think of the marvelous things you have done during the day.

Night is soft and gentle like tiptoeing feet. Night brings shadow pictures on the furniture. Night means a fuzzy blanket that keeps Benny snug and comfortable. And Benny sleeps, sleeps, sleeps through the lovely night.

—L.B.S.

When read slowly, this story induces quietness and a deep sense of repose. It is also very effective when used therapeutically to alleviate fears of the dark.

THE YAWNING PUPPY [3]

Once there was a puppy who did nothing but sleep and yawn. Oh, dear! When he wasn't sleeping, he was yawning, and when he wasn't yawning, he was sleeping. Without a doubt, he was the LAZIEST puppy in the world!

In the morning, as soon as the sun was up, he would find a tree with spreading branches. Then he would yawn, "Ow-oop!" After that, he would lie down with his hind legs stretched out behind and his front legs stretched out in front and snooze the morning away.

At noon, he would wake up just long enough to eat some lunch. Then back he would go to his shady tree — stretch — yawn, "Ow-oop!" and close his eyes for another nap.

In the evening, he always chose his favorite rug in front of the fireplace, for in winter it was warm and in summer it was cool. He would stretch his legs wide apart behind him and with a BIG yawn, "Ow-oop!" he would place his nose between his two front paws and go to sleep.

Now a yawn is one of the most catching things ever. It is even more catching than measles. But, of course, it is far pleasanter to yawn than to have measles. Everyone who saw the puppy yawning would catch his yawn, and

---

[3] By special permission of the F. A. Owen Publishing Company: *Stories That Stick,* by Louise Binder Scott.

he would have everybody yawning long before the sun had gone down behind the old red barn.

One evening, Father was reading his newspaper. All at once, the puppy opened his mouth — oh, so big — showed his white teeth, curled up his long pink tongue, and yawned, "Ow-oop!"

Mother was knitting a sweater for the baby who was coming soon to live with the family. She opened her mouth and yawned, "Ho-hum!" It was a very ladylike yawn. Then Father opened his mouth and yawned, "Awk — oh — ahhhhhh!" It was a rather noisy yawn.

Grandfather caught that yawn. He put down his knife and whittling stick. His face wrinkled up into what everyone thought would be a laugh, but the laugh did not come. No, siree! Out came the biggest, loudest yawn you ever heard: "Ay — yuh — rrrrrrk, hummmmm, rup!"

Grandmother caught Grandfather's yawn. Her eyes closed for a minute. She laid down her mending and raised her hand to shut off the yawn. Too late! Out it came! "Awk — ohhhhh — ummmmm."

Of course they all went to bed at once!

The same thing happened evening after evening. Everyone was in bed by sundown and all because of the yawning puppy.

The unmended socks piled up in a great heap in the mending basket. The baby's sweater did not get knitted. The newspaper was never read. And the whistle that Grandfather was whittling did not get whittled.

Finally, one evening just as everyone was beginning to catch the puppy's yawn again, Father decided to do something once and for all. He took a hammer and went out to the old red barn. There he measured and sawed and hammered until he had built a fine doghouse.

"There you are, puppy," he said. "I am putting you off by yourself. Now you may yawn as much as you please. We cannot keep our eyes open while you are in the house."

The puppy did not seem to care a bit. The doghouse had a woolly blanket on the floor and a snug, warm covering for the door. The puppy was more comfortable than a bug in a rug or a bear in a lair or a chickadee in a cherry tree. He yawned and slept as much as he liked.

Then one day, Baby Robert came to live at the house. He was wee and pink, and when he opened his mouth, the biggest sound came out! "Wah! Wah! Wah! Wah!"

Father patted Baby Robert.

Mother sang lullabies to Baby Robert.

Grandfather said, "Nice baby," and tried to make Baby Robert laugh.

Grandmother jiggled Baby Robert on her knee.

But Baby Robert kept on making that loud sound. "Wah! Wah! Wah! Wah!"

"Dear me," complained everyone. "We are getting no sleep at all." But they could not be angry with Baby Robert for crying, because they loved him so.

Father had no time to do the chores.

Mother had no time to cook dinner.

Grandfather had no time to wind the clock.

Grandmother had no time to piece a quilt.

There was no time for anything but Baby Robert, who kept on crying, "Wah! Wah! Wah! Wah!"

Now the yawning puppy grew lonely for his favorite spot in front of the fireplace. So he went to the house, scratched at the door, and Father let him in.

The puppy walked over to Grandfather's knee. Grandfather was holding Baby Robert. Then the yawning puppy opened his mouth and yawned, "Ow-oop!"

Baby Robert stopped crying and looked at the yawning puppy.

The puppy yawned again, "Ow-oop!"

Baby Robert's eyelids began to droop. Before you could say *three,* he went sound asleep and Mother laid him in his crib.

"Good puppy," said Grandmother. "Now I can begin to piece my quilt."

"Good puppy," said Mother. "I'll begin to get dinner right away."

"Good puppy," said Grandfather. "Now I can finish my whittling."

"Good puppy," said Father. "Now I can get my chores done."

"Good puppy," they said all together. "You will not need to live in the doghouse all the time. You may come into the house as often as you wish. We need you to help Baby Robert go to sleep when he cries."

Now I suppose you are wondering whether

the newspaper was read,
the sweater was knitted,
the socks were mended,
the chores were done,
the dinner was cooked,
the clock was wound,
and the quilt was pieced!

YES! All of those things were done — well, most of the time. For you see, Baby Robert grew out of his crying, and the yawning puppy became a bouncing, bounding, barking dog who was so busy helping around the farm that he didn't have time to yawn.

The children may participate in the story by repeating the yawns whenever they occur. Suggest that the children draw a yawning picture of their favorite animal or pet.

A HO-HUM STORY

TEACHER: Once there was a sleepy little kitten.
She said, "Ho-hum! I need a catnap. I need it now.
So I will curl right up. Mee-ow!"

CHILDREN: And she did. Ho-hum!
When kittens are sleepy as they can be,
They yawn — and yawn — like you and me.
Ho-hum!

TEACHER: Once there was a dear baby lamb. He said,
"Ho-hum! I will find my mother sheep,
And then I will fall fast asleep."

CHILDREN: And he did. Ho-hum!
When lambs are sleepy as they can be,
They yawn — and yawn — like you and me.
Ho-hum!

TEACHER: Once there was a panting puppy.
He said, "Ho-hum! I chased a cat.
I ran a mile, and now I'll have to rest awhile."

CHILDREN: And he did. Ho-hum!

TEACHER: Once there was a long-eared rabbit. He said,
"Ho-hum! Rabbits play and rabbits hop,
But sometimes rabbits have to stop."

CHILDREN: And he did. Ho-hum!
When rabbits are sleepy as can be,
They yawn — and yawn — like you and me.
Ho-hum!

TEACHER: Once there was a brown calf. His legs were
wobbly
Because he was so very young and new;
And he could not make a very loud moo.
He said, "Ho-hum! Because I was just born
today,
I think I'll lie down in this hay."

RAGGEDY ANN

ggedy Ann is my best friend.
is so relaxed; just see her bend,
st at the waist, and then at the knee.
r arms are swinging, oh, so free!
r head rolls around like a rubber ball.
e hasn't any bones at all.
ggedy Ann is stuffed with rags.
hat's why her body wigs and wags.

—L.B.S.

ren enjoy Raggedy Ann and Andy dolls. Ask the chil-
tomime the actions of the poem. Change Ann to Andy
time you say the poem with the children.

YAWNS ON THE LAWN

I saw a tiny puppy yawn—
Yawn— yawn— out on our lawn.
I caught the yawn,
And I yawned, too!
Now just what would YOU do?

N: Why, yawn— yawn— yawn!

I saw a tiny kitten yawn—
Yawn— yawn— out on our lawn.
I caught the yawn,
And I yawned, too!
Now just what would YOU do?

EN: Why, yawn— yawn— yawn!

—L.B.S.

the children to yawn each time they say the word *yawn*.
m to discuss other animals which they have seen yawning.

CHILDREN: And he did. Ho-hum!
When calves are sleepy as they can be,
They yawn — and yawn — like you and me.
Ho-hum!

TEACHER: Once there was a little boy (girl). He closed
his eyes,
And his mouth opened wide, with a yawn
inside!
He said, "I — want — to — go — to — sleep!"

CHILDREN: And he did. Ho-hum! Goodnight, all!
Ho-hum!

—L.B.S.

This story is a relaxing activity, but it may also be used for
practice with the "h" speech sound.

SLEEPY THINGS WITH WINGS

Once there were some sleepy things,
And every one of them had wings.

There was a bat, all velvet brown,
And he slept as bats do, upside down.

A butterfly, blue, green, and red,
Poised with her wings above her head.

An oriole forgot to sing,
And tucked his head beneath his wing.

A whippoorwill, all speckled gray,
Sat upon his log all day.

A white hen rested on her nest;
This was the place that she liked best.

55

An owl sat still and nothing said;
His glowing eyes stared straight ahead.

Yes, once there were some sleepy things,
And every one of them had wings.

—L.B.S.

Ask the children to name other birds and insects and tell how they sleep. They may draw sleepy pictures of their favorite animals and create stories about them.

HUSH!

Hush— hush! Oh, please!
There can't be *any* noise,
Because my cat is sleeping,
And so are all my toys.

Hush— hush! Oh, please!
We cannot make a peep,
For everything needs quiet now
To sleep — to sleep — to sleep!

—L.B.S.

The following couplets may be substituted for the last two lines above: "I'm covering up my dolly, And now she's fast asleep." "My puppy's in his basket, And now he's gone to sleep." The poem may be read to the children with an autoharp providing soft background music. The "sh" sound in *hush* should be prolonged.

SOFT THINGS

TEACHER: Tiny, fuzzy kitten has soft, soft fur.
              Touch her gently, and she'll say,

CHILDREN: "Purr, purr, purr!"

TEACHER: Downy, yellow chicken is cuddled there
               asleep.
              Touch him gently, and he'll say,

CHILDREN: "Peep, pe

TEACHER: Little brig
              Touch him

CHILDREN: "Quack, qu

TEACHER: Little hamst
               cheeks.
              Touch him g

CHILDREN: "Squeak, squ

The appeal in this poem to
helps some children feel comfor
trate relaxed animals and people
has emotional problems.

STILL

I do not feel like
I'm tired as I can
     (*Palms together*
I'll sit right down,
And fold my hand
     (*Children fold*
And close my eyes
     (*Children close e*
My body now is qui
I can keep so very s
You ask me how I k
Because I say, "I wil

This kind of poem, with its pantom
when the children come in from reces
actions yourself, the children will imita

Ra
Sh
Fi
H
H
Sh
R
T

All child
dren to par
the second

CHILDRE

CHILDR

Ask
Ask the

CAN'T YOU GUESS?

TEACHER: Boys and girls, what are you doing?
CHILDREN: Can't you guess?
TEACHER: Are you sitting quietly?
CHILDREN: Yes, yes, yes.
TEACHER: Boys and girls, what are you doing?
CHILDREN: Can't you guess?
TEACHER: Are you listening? Are you listening?
CHILDREN: Yes, yes, yes.
TEACHER: Boys and girls, what are you doing?
CHILDREN: Can't you guess?
TEACHER: Are you watching? Are you watching?
CHILDREN: Yes, yes, yes.
TEACHER: Boys and girls, what are you doing?
CHILDREN: Can't you guess?
TEACHER: Are you thinking? Are you thinking?
CHILDREN: Yes, Yes, Yes.

—J.J.T.

This rhyme encourages attention and concentration and can be used at various times during the day when children appear restless.

SNOWFLAKES

TEACHER: Pretend snowflakes are falling
CLASS: Down . . . down . . . down.
(Begin with hands above head and lower them gently with fingers fluttering.)
TEACHER: There must be snow for Santa's sleigh,
Or he will never find his way.
CLASS: Down . . . down . . . down.
(Repeat movements.)
TEACHER: Hush now. It is so very still.
I see upon the windowsill
Soft fluffy snowflakes as they play
All through the night, all through the day.

59

CLASS: Down . . . down . . . down.
           (*Repeat movements.*)
TEACHER: On every rooftop in the town.
CLASS: Down . . . down . . . down.
           (*Repeat movements.*)
           Down . . . down . . . down.
                                        —L.B.S.

This poem is most effective when it is said very slowly. Pause each time after the word *down*.

READINESS

Now shall we sit up tall in rows,
With listening ears and quiet toes?
So — close your eyes; your head drops down.
Your face is smooth without a frown.
Now roll your head just like a ball,
Then nod at me and sit up tall.
Lift up your chin and look at me.
Take one deep breath and count to three.
Then smile a smile; fold hands in lap,
And make believe you've had a nap.
So — you have rested from your play!
I hope you'll have a happy day!

                                        —L.B.S.

Ask the children to act out this poem as you read it slowly. Record it on tape which a substitute teacher may use to relax the children when they come in from play or grow restless on a rainy day.

FUNNY OLD SCARECROW DAN

I am funny old Scarecrow Dan.
I flip and I flop as a scarecrow can!
I move my arms, (*Move arms to and fro.*)
I move my wrists, (*Shake wrists.*)

I move my legs,
   (*Hold out one leg at a time.*)
And I shake my fists. (*Shake fists.*)
I bend way down; (*Bend from waist.*)
I bend way back. (*Bend backward.*)
I jump up and down
Like a jumping jack! (*Jump.*)
I stop right here, (*Point to floor.*)
And I don't make a sound.
   (*Forefinger to lips.*)
Then I sit right down
Upon the ground! (*Sit on floor.*)

—L.B.S.

The children may act out this relaxation poem after a seatwork activity.

GRUMPETY GROANS

There once was a man named Grumpety Groans,
And would you believe it — he had no bones!
   (*Children flop arms.*)

From top to toe, there were no bones at all,
And his head rolled around like a rubber ball!
   (*Children roll heads.*)

He wibbled and wobbled when he walked,
   (*Children act out.*)
And he spoke very slowly when he talked.
   (*Read line slowly.*)

And when he yawned, his mouth was so wide
That twenty gumdrops could hide inside.
   (*Children yawn.*)

And when his shoulders started to sag,
He looked like a great big burlap bag.
   (*Children imitate.*)

His arms would dangle, his chin would drop,
And his jelly-like legs would flippity-flop.
    (*Children act out.*)

Grumpety Groans went strolling one day,
And the sun was so hot he just melted away!
    (*Children sink to floor.*)

                                        —L.B.S.

This nonsense rhyme creates a feeling of emotional tranquility
and of muscular relaxation in various parts of the body.

MY SHADOW

When the sun shines, I can see
My shadow right in front of me.
When I walk, my shadow walks!
When I hop, my shadow hops!
When I jump, my shadow jumps,
And when I stop, my shadow stops!

Oh, it is such fun to see
A shadow that belongs to me!
When I skip, my shadow skips!
When I slide, my shadow slides!
When I creep, my shadow creeps,
And when I hide, my shadow hides!

                                    —L.B.S.

Ask the children to act out this poem as you read it slowly.
Pause briefly at the end of each line to be pantomimed. Since there
is repetition, the class will be able to learn the poem by rote. It
may be used for drill on the "sh" speech sound in *shadow*.

WIGGLE GAME

Wiggle, wiggle here, and a wiggle, wiggle there;
Wiggle your fingers all around in the air!

62

Wiggle your shoulders up and down;
Wiggle your nose and smile like a clown!
Wiggle your legs, both left and right;
Wiggle your thumb with all its might!
Wiggle, wiggle here, and a wiggle, wiggle there.
Now sit right down upon your chair!

—L.B.S.

As an additional activity, sing "I Wiggle" from *Singing Fun*, Lucille F. Wood and Louise Binder Scott, Webster Division, McGraw-Hill Book Company, 1955.

LITTLE LEAF [4]

Little leaf, little leaf,
Fly, fly, fly. (*Move hands.*)
The cold wind will take you
Up to the sky! (*Raise arms over head.*)
The cold wind will take you
Around and around.
      (*Turn body around.*)
Then slowly — so slowly —
You'll fall to the ground. (*Sink to floor.*)

—L.B.S.

SCARY SCARECROW

Scary Scarecrow stood in the middle of a cornfield that belonged to Farmer Boggs. Scary looked, indeed, like a scary scarecrow, because he was made to scare crows away from the ripe corn. A scarecrow HAS to be scary to do that!

Farmer Boggs made Scary because he was angry and DISGUSTED by the way his corn was disappearing. Of course, Farmer Boggs knew the reason why. So he said in a most furious voice:

[4] From the Teacher's Edition for *Book B, Time for Phonics,* Louise Binder Scott, Webster Division, McGraw-Hill Book Company, 1962.

"It is Inky Crow! I know, I know!
As sure as I'm born, he is eating my corn!"
(*Children join in.*)

So Farmer Boggs made up his mind to do something about what was happening. He took a worn-out pair of trousers with patches at the knees, a bright-red shirt, and an old felt hat with a hole in the top, and he made Scary. And that was how Scary Scarecrow came to be.

Oh, what a lazy scarecrow! Oh, what a flippy-floppy scarecrow! His arms hung down, and his neck bent over to one side so that his stuffed head looked as if it were going to drop right off his straw body. His whole body drooped. (*Children imitate different postures.*) Tufts of straw stuck out of his trouser legs and even out of the hole in the top of his old felt hat.

Scary Scarecrow stood quietly in the middle of the cornfield — and nothing happened. Absolutely nothing! It was stiller than still in the cornfield, so something was BOUND to happen.

Inky Crow sat in a tree at the edge of the cornfield and kept watch. He saw Farmer Boggs put Scary Scarecrow in the cornfield. He watched Scary Scarecrow with his sly and beady bright eyes. He cawed in a loud cawing voice:

"OH, ho, ho! OH, no, no!
I'm not afraid of THAT scarecrow!"

Inky Crow flew straight to a stalk of corn. He found a choice ear and *purrrrrrt!* He gobbled up the corn as sure as you're born. He winked one beady eye to nobody in particular and cawed:

"OH, ho, ho! OH, no, no!
I'm not afraid of THAT scarecrow!"

Poor Farmer Boggs watched his corn disappearing day by day, and he said sadly,

"It is Inky Crow. I know, I know!
As sure as I'm born, he is eating my corn."

It was early autumn. The leaves were turning red and gold, and birds were winging their way to a warmer climate. The corn was waiting to be picked — what there was left of it. But if something were not done about Inky Crow, there would be no corn to pick at all.

Now Scary Scarecrow knew this and he tried hard to move. But please tell me how a scarecrow CAN move when there is no wind. Scarecrows need wind, for how else can they flip and flap and flop? Farmer Boggs said, oh SO sadly:

"It is Inky Crow. I know, I know!
As sure as I'm born, he is eating my corn."

Farmer Boggs looked angrily at Scary Scarecrow. He shook his fist at Scary Scarecrow. He stamped his foot at Scary Scarecrow, and he said loudly, "A FINE scarecrow YOU are! You are not worth the straw you are stuffed with. It is plain to see that YOU cannot protect my corn. I'll make another scarecrow, I will!"

So Farmer Boggs stomped out of the cornfield and went to the shed, and he made a second scarecrow and named him Stuffy.

Now Stuffy was stuffed with so much straw that he was round as a balloon and stiff as a broom handle, though, of course, not so thin. My! How important Stuffy looked. Farmer Boggs, pleased with himself and his new scarecrow, took Stuffy to the cornfield. Then he said to Scary Scarecrow, "Bosh! You couldn't scare a doodlebug. But don't worry. I won't take you out of the cornfield. You may stay and see for yourself what makes a good scarecrow."

So Farmer Boggs set Scary to one side of the cornfield. And he went to the house to have lunch with Mrs. Boggs.

Now Inky Crow saw the new scarecrow and he laughed:

"OH, ho, ho! OH, no, no!
I'm not afraid of that other scarecrow,
And I'm certainly not afraid of this new scarecrow, either."

All afternoon — well, until about three o'clock — Inky Crow had a fine feast. *Purrrrrrt!* Nothing happened. *Purrrrrrt!* Still nothing happened. Then — oh, then — a small breeze came up, and the little breeze began to blow — slowly and softly at first — then harder and harder. WHOOOOOOOO! WHOOOOOOSH! Scary Scarecrow began to move. But Stuffy stood stiff as a broom handle, because he was just too full of straw to move. Scary's head flipped and flapped and flopped, first to the left and then to the right. But Stuffy stood stiff as a broom handle. Scary's arms moved to the left, to the right. Whoosh! Swoosh! Scary had to hang onto his old felt hat with the hole on top! He almost lost his balance! He swayed back and forth — back and forth — back and forth. By that time Inky Crow was so frightened he flew out of that cornfield with a loud CAW, and he never did come back again — well, not to that *particular* cornfield.

"Say!" cried Farmer Boggs. "That Scary Scarecrow is a helpful scarecrow after all. From now on, I will let him stand guard and I'll take Stuffy away.

So Scary Scarecrow now once again stood in the middle of the cornfield; and the wind helped Scary as it moved his arms, his head, and his body to the left, to the right, and every which way. And Inky Crow never ventured within a mile of the cornfield again.

Farmer Boggs had a VERY good crop of corn that fall, and all because Scary Scarecrow had been such a fine helper.

—L.B.S.

The child experiences the differences between physical tension and relaxation by imitating the movements of the two scarecrows.

Ask the children to participate in saying the refrains each time they occur. Suggest that children draw pictures of the two scarecrows, color them, cut them out, and back them with bits of flannel or blotting paper, so that the story may be told with the flannel-board. The children may want to portray the characters and act out the story.

CHAPTER 4

Our Speech Helpers

Lips, lips, lips!
They are active, don't you see,
When I say "pretty butterfly"
And "popsickle" and "bee."

Teeth, teeth, teeth!
Of course, they help me make
The first sound in "fisherman"
And "valentine" and "snake."

Tongue, tongue, tongue!
The tip goes up so high
To help me say "tall ladder"
And "duck" and "nest" and "tie."

Jaw, jaw, jaw!
It's useful, I've no doubt.
Its hinges move it up and down
To let my speech sounds out!

Nose, nose, nose!
It helps three sounds to hum
When I say "my nice mother"
And "sing a song" and "drum."

Roof, roof, roof!
Now what do you suppose?
The hard palate separates
My mouth from my nose.

Soft palate, soft palate!
It rises up so high
To keep the sounds out of my nose,
Or they'd go sliding by.

Larynx and voice box —
They are one and the same.
The larynx buzzes when you say
The voiced sounds in your name.

Ear, ear, ear!
It should not seem strange to you,
Since both your ears help you to hear,
That they are speech helpers, too!

—L.B.S.

THE TONGUE AS A SPEECH HELPER

Control and flexibility of the tongue is essential to distinct articulation. If there is any physical abnormality, if the web of tissue underneath the tongue "ties" it to the floor of the mouth so that movement is restricted, or if the tongue is sluggish, the selections in this section will help the teacher to detect these deficiencies so they can be reported to the speech specialist and the school nurse for further analysis, diagnosis, and therapy.

Frequently, control of the tongue tip is faulty. When the child substitutes "w" for "r," as *wed* for *red,* it is the lips which are called to the child's attention at first and not the tongue tip. First, the lips must be spread in a smile. We get rid of those rounded lips. Say to the child: "Let's use the 'magic' mirror (a small hand mirror) which is a wonderful teacher. If you cannot make a speech sound, it will help you by showing you pictures of your mouth, teeth, and tongue. To make a plain 'rrr' sound, we must make a happy smile. 'Rrrr' is a pleasant, happy sound so we spread the lips in a pleasant look."

"Elevator" sounds, or sounds in which the tongue tip rises and touches the alveolar ridge behind the upper teeth, are "t," "d," "n," and "l." Of these speech sounds, "l" presents the most difficulty. Again the lips come into play, for the child rounds his lips in an "oo" position as he substitutes "w" for "l," as *wamp* for *lamp*. Once again, we use the "magic" mirror, and this time we can see the tongue tip go up like an elevator and stop on the top floor. Sometimes the child can produce "r" by first making the "l" sound and then allowing the tongue tip to move and curl back.

In a lateral lisp, air is emitted over the sides of the tongue in a slushy manner. This lisp is alleviated by exercises that can help the child to achieve central emission of air. Speech sounds affected by this faulty emission of air are "s," "z," "sh," "zh," "ch," and "j."

If the child is malnourished, the tongue, as well as other muscles of the body, may become flaccid. Proper nutrition under medical supervision should then be considered if there appears to be a serious lack of good muscle tone.

Retraining and exercising of the tongue should be made interesting through the use of dramatization. As with the speech sound, the tongue may assume a personality and become a real friend who helps the child to "talk more plainly." The child will take pride in his new-found friend, his tongue, and in directing all of its movements.

MY TONGUE

My tongue can do so many things.
Just watch and you will see!

It can sweep,
   (*Tongue tip sweeps inside cheeks between
   lips and teeth as lips are closed.*)
Go up and down,
   (*Tongue tip touches ridge behind upper
   teeth and sweeps downward rapidly.*)
And make the sound for *t.*
"T, t, t!" (*Make sound three times.*)
Now it sweeps around, around;
   (*Repeat first movement.*)
Now way inside it sweeps.
   (*Sweep roof of mouth from front to back.*)
Now it jumps gaily up and down;
   (*Tongue tip protrudes and moves toward
   chin and then nose several times.*)
Now out it slyly peeps!
   (*Tongue tip protrudes between slightly
   parted lips.*)

My tongue can do so many things.
It is very useful, you can see.
It can sweep,
Go up and down,
And make the sound for *t.*
"T, t, t!" (*Repeat first three actions.*)
                              —FRANCES C. HUNTE

MR. TICKY TONGUE

Mr. Ticky Tongue is a curious little man.
He jumps out the window,
   (*Open mouth and protrude tongue tip.*)

And he jumps back again!
  (*Retract tongue tip and close mouth.*)
He jumps to the north, (*Lift tip toward nose.*)
He jumps toward the south.
  (*Protrude tip toward chin.*)
Then he jumps right back
Inside of my mouth. (*Close mouth.*)

—L.B.S.

PINKY TONGUE

Pinky Tongue thought he would have some fun.
He peeked out slowly to see the sun. (*Protrude tip.*)
He peeked to the left, (*Move tip to left.*)
He peeked to the right, (*Move tip to right.*)
And he peeked around at everything in sight.
  (*Move tip outside the mouth in a circle.*)

Then Pinky Tongue, without any excuse,
Made the sound of Old Mrs. Goose!
"Th— th— th!" (*Protrude tip and make voiceless "th."*)
But he stayed behind my teeth to make
The hissing sound of Mrs. Green Snake.
"Sss— sss— sss!" (*Teeth together. Make "s" sound.*)
Pinky Tongue lifted himself up higher
To make the sound of the telephone wire.
"Lll— lll— lll!" (*Rest tip on ridge behind upper teeth
  and make voiced "l."*)
Pinky Tongue raised himself at the back
To make the cough sound in click-clack.
"K, k, k! K, k, k!"
  (*Raise back of tongue and press against soft palate.*)

Oh, he is clever as clever can be!
Mr. Pinky Tongue is MINE! He belongs to ME!

—L.B.S.

THE LIPS AS SPEECH HELPERS

The lip sounds "m," "p," and "b" usually are acquired very early in the child's speech development. He rarely has a problem producing them unless there is a cleft palate and lip which make it difficult for him to build the air pressure inside the mouth necessary to release the explosives "p" and "b." Sometimes, because of overbite or misalignment of the teeth, the lips may not close firmly enough in connected speech to articulate "p" and "b" precisely.

The rounded lip sounds "w" and "wh" can be troublesome, too. Most children substitute the voiced "w" sound for the voiceless "wh" in such words as *why* and *when*. Exercises involving these two sounds will help the child with his auditory discrimination as well as his lip mobility. See the sections on "p," "b," "m," "w," and "wh" for selections which will help the child to use his lips more effectively.

NONSENSE EXERCISE

May, pay, bay, may, pay, bay;
My two lips press together this way.
Wee and whee! Wee and whee!
My lips are round as they can be!

—L.B.S.

THE JAW AS A SPEECH HELPER

The lower jaw is used continually in the articulatory process and therefore should move with facility. If the child is tense or concerned about his speech, or if he is experiencing speech fright, his jaw muscles may be less easily controlled because of muscle tension. Careless speech or mumbling may cause the jaw to become lax. Jaw exercises have a place in speech improvement, for they create an awareness of the speech mechanism with all parts working together.

Selections such as "The Crow Family" (page 289), in which the "aw" vowel sound in *caw* is repeated, will provide help for the child who is not articulating plainly. The following rhyme may be used to motivate jaw mobility:

THE CROW AND THE DONKEY

The crow and the donkey decided to sing,
And oh, it was funny as anything!
    Ee-aw, ee-aw, caw, caw, caw!
    Ee-aw, ee-aw, caw, caw, caw!

The crow opened his beak, and the donkey his jaw,
It was as funny a sight as I ever saw!
    Ee-aw, ee-aw, caw, caw, caw!
    Ee-aw, ee-aw, caw, caw, caw!

—L.B.S.

THE PALATE AS A SPEECH HELPER

The speech sounds "k," "g," and "ng" are produced through action of the back of the tongue being pressed against the soft palate. Sections in this book which emphasize those speech sounds may be found on pages 285-307 and 367-374.

NONSENSE EXERCISE

Lunka, lunka, lunga, lung.
Listen to the sounds I make with my tongue.
Lugga, lugga, lugga, lack.
My tongue goes up at the front and the back!

—L.B.S.

THE NOSE AS A SPEECH HELPER

The velum, an extension of the hard palate, rises to coordinate with the musculature of the back wall of the throat to prevent speech sounds from passing through the nasal cavity. When its action is weak, nasal speech results.

Denasality, or lack of nasality, may be caused by enlarged tonsils and adenoids which block the nasal passages and cause *m, n,* and *ng* to be pronounced as "b," "d," and "g," e.g., *sig a sog for be* (sing a song for me). Temporary inflammation of the naso-pharynx, such as caused by the common cold, may also block nasal passages.

The following exercise can help the child to feel vibration as he places his fingers beside his nose, on his cheeks, or on the lower part of the throat or Adam's apple.

SING A SONG

Sing a long song,
Sing a new song,
Sing a wrong song,
Sing a true song.
Sing a night song,
Sing a moon song,
Sing a right song,
Sing a June song.

—L.B.S.

THE TEETH AS SPEECH HELPERS

Good teeth are necessary not only for proper chewing; they are important to proper speech as well. A number of consonant speech sounds are dependent upon good dental adjustment. Among them are "f," "v," "th" (*voiced and voiceless*), "s," "z," "ch," "j," "sh," and "zh." If poor spacing, missing teeth, or misalignment occurs, the child may have difficulty in articulating clearly. Referral to the school nurse or the speech specialist is recommended. Selections from the appropriate speech-sound sections will be useful in correlating classroom activities with those of the speech therapy sessions.

THE LARYNX AS A SPEECH HELPER

Within the larynx are the vocal folds (cords) which are set into vibration by the pressure of air from the lungs as it ascends upward through the trachea (windpipe).

Some consonant speech sounds are voiced, while others are breathed, or voiceless. The voiced consonant sounds have vocal-cord vibration and include "b," "d," "g," "j," "l," "m," "n," "ng," "th" (voiced), "zh," "r," "v," "w," "y," and "z." All vowels are voiced.

Customary voice disorders which may be found among groups of primary children are nasality, denasality, monotony (lack of variety), pitch that is too high or too low, and excessive loudness or weakness. In the case of chronic hoarseness, the child should be referred to the school nurse.

CHAPTER 5

The "S" and "Z" Speech Sounds

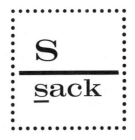

MAKING THE SPEECH SOUND

This sound is made with the lips in a slight smiling position and the teeth nearly closed. The tongue tip is hidden behind the lower front teeth. It varies as to position. There is no vocal-cord vibration and the soft palate is raised.

Research has shown that the high frequency "s" is the most frequently misarticulated speech sound in the English language.

You may call "s" the "snake" sound, the "teakettle" sound, or the "flat-tire" sound.

CORRECTING THE DEFICIENT SPEECH SOUND

The most common defect is the substitution of the voiceless "th" sound for "s," e.g., *Tham* for *Sam* or *thum* for *some*. This is called the *central, frontal,* or *protrusion lisp,* because the tongue tip touches the teeth or protrudes between them. Asking the child to try to keep the tongue tip from showing and encouraging him to watch his endeavors in a mirror can help him to acquire the proper position. At all times he should be reminded to *listen* to the teacher as the sound is produced and to himself as he practices for correct tongue position. Self-hearing is extremely important, since the child himself must be able to differentiate the correct from the incorrect articulatory pattern.

A second "s" deviation is the *lateral lisp* in which air escapes laterally around the sides of the tongue as it is held in a flat position. This type of lisp may be caused by imitation of poor models, misalignment of the teeth, defective hearing, sluggish tongue, improper auditory perception, or the wish of the child to continue to "talk like a baby," which gives him comfort and security.

Self-hearing and imitation of the correct sound are essential. The child should be encouraged to experiment with tongue positions as he holds his cheeks with the palms of his hands and attempts to make the "steamy" sound by directing the air stream away from the sides and down the center groove of the tongue to the tip. Holding a plastic straw between the teeth and directing the stream of air through it sometimes helps the child to achieve correct tongue placement.

If the deviation is a *whistling* "s," again the child must learn to hear what he is producing and try to soften the sound by using less force. Other substitutions for "s" are "t" (*tee* for *see*), "sh" (*shee* for *see*), and "f" (*fee* for *see*). The sound also may be omitted completely (*ee* for *see*).

Should the problem be one of dentition or tongue thrust resulting from incorrect swallowing habits, orthodontic or speech therapy services should be recommended.

The teacher should motivate the child by bringing into play as many of the senses as possible. In this way, the child will *hear* the sound, *feel* the movement of the speech organs as he produces the sound, and *see* both the teacher and himself (in a mirror) as he attempts to establish a correct pattern.

INSTRUCTIONS TO THE CHILD

"Close your white gate (teeth). Hide your tongue tip. While it is hiding, make the 'teakettle' sound with me: 'Sssssssss.' Now listen as I do it: 'Sssssssss.' Let me hear your 'teakettle' sound. (Reponse.) Did yours sound like mine? Let's try to put that 'steamy' sound into some words: *ssssee, sssssay, ssssso.* Did you hear the steam? Look into the mirror to see what your teeth are doing. Are they closed? When you hear the 'steamy' sound, clap your hands: *saddle, soap,* ball, *Santa,* fan. Sammy Snake makes the 'sss' sound, too. Join in saying the 'snake' sound as we do this rhyme:

> I can make a 'snake' sound,
> And you can, too.
> When I make a 'snake' sound,
> This is what I do: 'Sss— sss— sss.'
> You can make a 'snake' sound;
> Try it now and see.
> You can make a 'snake' sound;
> Do it with me: 'Sss— sss— sss.'

Now we can walk and make the 'snake' sound at the same time:

> Walk in a circle, a circle, a circle;
> (*Prolong the 's' sound at the
> beginning of* circle.)
> Walk in a circle around and around."
>
> —L.B.S.

Note: Use other movements such as running, jumping, hopping, and skipping. The word *circle* begins with the "s" sound.

WORDS FOR PRACTICE

Initial	*Medial*	*Final*
seven	Alaska	gas
Santa	basket	horse
soap	sister	grass
seal	biscuit	plus
safe	lesson	goose
sand	Thanksgiving	bus

Initial and Final Consonant Blends:

*sk*in	*sm*ile	*sn*ow	*scr*een	*sl*ed	*sp*ace
*sk*y	*sm*oke	*sn*ake	*scr*ap	*sl*ip	*sp*in
*spr*ing	*st*op	*str*aw	*sw*im	*squ*eal	
*spr*ead	*st*ick	*str*eet	*sw*eet	*squ*are	

ro*ck*s	lam*p*s	ca*p*s	car*t*s	ca*t*s	bea*k*s
boo*k*s	stum*p*s	to*p*s	hur*t*s	ea*t*s	chee*k*s
ne*ck*s	bel*t*s	nes*t*s	bea*t*s	cho*p*s	
wor*k*s	hal*t*s	ves*t*s	ne*t*s	li*p*s	

X has the "ks" sound: bo*x*, fo*x*, mi*x*, si*x*.
Sometimes *c* has the "s" sound: fa*c*e, voi*c*e, pea*c*e, poli*c*e,
Gra*c*e.

USING THE "I HEAR IT" DEVICE

The following "I Hear It" rhyme contains not only the
speech sound which the child should be producing but
also the speech sound which he may be substituting. Distinguishing separate speech sounds from one another and
identifying them in words are initial steps toward the correction of any articulatory defect.

Read the "I Hear It" selection slowly, pronouncing
the speech sounds precisely. Ask the class or an individual
child to make the single speech sound when it occurs. The

second time the selection is read, ask the children to repeat each line after it has been said. Always prolong the speech sound whenever possible so that it may be identified more easily.

I HEAR IT

I hear it in *sigh,* but not in *tie.*
I hear it in *so,* but not in *toe.*
I hear it in *sell,* but not in *tell.*
    I hear it in *bass,* but not in *bath.*
    I hear it in *pass,* but not in *path.*
    I closed my white gate and I let the air through.
    I kept my tongue hidden. Did you? Did you?
    "Sssssss— sssssss!" *See, sigh, so, soo.*
I hear it in *saw,* but not in *thaw.*
I hear it in *sing,* but not in *thing.*
I hear it in *sank,* but not in *thank.*
    I hear it in *Sue,* but not in *shoe.*
    I hear it in *said,* but not in *shed.*
    I closed my white gate and I let the air through.
    I kept my tongue hidden. Did you? Did you?
    "Ssssssss— ssssssss!" *See, sigh, so, soo.*

—L.B.S.

ARE WE LISTENING?

Increasing attentiveness, memory span, concentration, and attention to specific detail is essential in helping children to form new speech patterns. Read each story slowly. Ask questions to elicit responses which contain the "s" speech sound. Encourage complete-sentence answers.

1. Are we listening? One *Christmas* morning, *Sally* found a pair of *skates* under the tree. Bill found a red *sled.* Mother found a *silk scarf.* Daddy found a *striped* tie. Are we listening? Let's see! Who found a pair of *skates?*

What did Mother find? What kind of tie did Daddy find? What did Bill find?

2. The family went on a picnic. They took peanut-butter *sandwiches, soft* drinks, chocolate *ice* cream, and potato *salad.* They forgot the *strawberries* and left them at home. Are we listening? Let's see! What was made from potatoes? What did the family leave at home? What kind of drinks did they take? What was made from peanut butter? What kind of cream did they have for dessert?

3. In the kitchen, we *see* a *sink.* We *sleep* in a *soft* bed in the bedroom. In the dining room, we eat pudding with a *spoon.* In the evening, we eat *supper.* What do we see in the kitchen? What kind of bed is in the bedroom? How do we eat pudding? What meal do we eat in the evening? Were we listening? How many answers did you get right?

—L.B.S.

SEE-SAW

See-saw, see-saw,
Watch me go!
See-saw, see-saw,
High and low.
See-saw, see-saw,
Ride with me!
See-saw, see-saw,
See-saw-see!
See-saw, see-saw,
See-saw-see!

—L.B.S.

Ask the children to stand and move the arms up and down at the sides to imitate a see-saw. Suggest that the child look into a mirror to see whether he is making the "s" sound correctly.

82

MY DADDY'S TIRE

The tire on my daddy's car
Is big and round and fat;
But when the air comes out of it,
That tire goes down flat!

Sssssssssssssssssssss! (*Loud to soft.*)

I listen to the flat-tire sound,
And it is very clear;
When I say *Sally, Sam,* or *Sue,*
This flat-tire sound I hear:

Ssssssssssssssssssssss! (*Loud to soft.*)

Ssssssally! Ssssssam! Sssssssue!
I heard it! Say! Did YOU?

—L.B.S.

Self-hearing is extremely important if the child is to improve articulation or correct a speech-sound mispronunciation. Ask the child to place a hand behind each ear as he makes the "sss" speech sound. This procedure will magnify the sound, so that the child can hear it more accurately. Ask the children to name some words which begin with the "flat-tire" sound.

STOP FOR ME!

Big brown dump truck
With round, round wheels,
The faster you go, oh!
The nicer it feels!

Dump truck, stop for me!
(*Children clap rhythm.*)
I want to take a ride.
Dump truck, stop for me
And let me climb inside!

83

Blue, blue automobile
With round, round wheels,
The faster you go, oh!
The nicer it feels!

Automobile, stop for me!
I want to take a ride.
Automobile, stop for me
And let me climb inside.

—L.B.S.

Add other vehicles: green jeep; white-and-black police car; red, red fire truck; silver, silver airplane; black, black engine; orange, orange garbage truck; yellow, yellow bus; red, red street car; orange, orange wheelbarrow; and blue, blue helicopter. Ask the children to make pictures of the vehicles for the flannelboard and use them as the rhyme is said. They may make up their own rhymes about modes of transportation. Tell the children you will listen for the "snake" sound in *stop,* or the "rooster" sound in *round.*

STEP, STEP, STEP

Step, step, step, step
To the tip-top!
Step, step, step, step,
And now we will stop!

Step, step, step, step,
Down to the ground.
Step, step, step, step,
And turn right around.

—L.B.S.

The *st* consonant blend is emphasized in this selection. Draw eight double stairsteps on the chalkboard and ask the children to say the rhyme as you point to each step going up and coming down. Then let the children take turns doing this.

FIVE ROUND PUMPKINS

TEACHER:	Five round pumpkins were sitting in a row.
CHILDREN:	See, so, so, See, so, so!
TEACHER:	The first one said, "It is Halloween, you know!"
CHILDREN:	See, so, so, See, so, so!
TEACHER:	The second one said, "There are witches in the sky!"
CHILDREN:	See, sigh, sigh, See, sigh, sigh!
TEACHER:	The third one said, "My! Something just flew by!"
CHILDREN:	See, sigh, sigh, See, sigh, sigh!
TEACHER:	The fourth one said, "Ghosties dance and goblins play."
CHILDREN:	See, say, say, See, say, say!
TEACHER:	The fifth one said, "I am going to roll away!"
CHILDREN:	See, say, say, See, say, say!
TEACHER:	But the five round pumpkins sat all in a row,
CHILDREN:	See, so, so, See, so, so!
TEACHER:	While the moon in the sky laughed, "Ho, ho, ho!"
CHILDREN:	See, so, so, See, so, so!

TEACHER:	Then the five round pumpkins — well, what did they DO?
CHILDREN:	See, soo, soo, See, soo, soo!

TEACHER:	They became jack-o'-lanterns for me and you and YOU!
CHILDREN:	See, soo, soo, See, soo, soo!

—L.B.S.

One technique in helping children with the lips is to use the isolated speech sound with syllables containing different vowel sounds. In this nonsense rhyme, practice is afforded not only on initial "s," but also on five vowel sounds. Suggest that the children draw and color pumpkins for use on the flannelboard as the selection is used. Clapping emphasizes the primitive rhythm of the refrains and adds to the children's enjoyment.

STOP, SLOW, AND GO

Go to the store and buy some purple thread;
Stop, stop, stop, if the light turns red!

Go anywhere, but be very careful, fellow!
Slow, slow, slow, if the light turns yellow!

Go to the station for a tank of gasoline;
Go, go, go, if the light turns green!

—L.B.S.

This safety rhyme presents the *st* and *sl* consonant blends in *stop* and *slow*. Make a large rectangular-shaped traffic light out of black tagboard; cut three appropriately spaced circular holes in the tagboard and cover with red, yellow, and green crepe paper. Let one child hold a flashlight behind the appropriate circle as the rhyme is said by the class.

86

SMALL

Small is the snowflake I taste on my lips;
Small are the baby's sweet fingertips.

Small is the ant that works, oh, so hard;
Small is the leaf I pick up in my yard.

Small is the seed that grows under the ground;
Small is the bead all shiny and round.

Small is the goldfish that swims in a bowl;
Small is the earthworm that burrows a hole.

Small is the ladybug dressed in bright red;
Small is the crumb from a slice of fresh bread.

Small is the guppy and small is his fin;
Small is the speck of dirt there on your chin.

—L.B.S.

Ask the children to name other things which are small. Tell them that you will listen for the *sm* consonant blend when they say *small*. After a second reading, many children will be able to supply the last word in each couplet.

SUPPOSING

Supposing the clock forgot to tick,
And supposing the paste forgot to stick.

Supposing a puppy forgot to bark,
And supposing the night was never dark.

Supposing the wind forgot to blow,
And supposing the snow forgot to snow.

Supposing an engine had no wheels,
And supposing potatoes had no peels.

We know that things do not happen this way,
But *supposing*'s a very fine game to play!

—L.B.S.

Ask the children to make up their own fanciful happenings using the word *supposing*. This word contains the initial "s" and the medial "z" speech sounds.

SI, SI, SI!

Piñata, piñata, piñata,
With candy for you and for me.
Will you break the piñata?

CHILDREN: Sí, sí, sí!

Sally will hit the piñata,
One and two and three.
Sally will break the piñata.

CHILDREN: Sí, sí, sí!

—L.B.S.

Substitute the names of children in the class. Practice is gained on the "s" sound in *sí*.

LITTLE SQUIRREL

Little squirrel, little squirrel, in your hollow tree,
Little squirrel, little squirrel, come out and visit me.

I will give you acorns and pretty berries red;
I will find some maple leaves to line your little bed.

Little squirrel, little squirrel, in your hollow tree,
Little squirrel, little squirrel, come and live with me.

88

I will give you sweet seeds and nuts of gold and brown;
Little squirrel, little squirrel, won't you please come
    down?

Little boy, little girl, I cannot visit you.
Little boy, little girl, that I cannot do.

I must not leave my babies up in this hollow tree.
I cannot come to live with you, for squirrels must be free.

—VIRGINIA SYDNOR PAVELKO

This poem, which emphasizes the *squ* consonant blend in the word *squirrel,* can be easily learned by rote because of its repetition. Suggest that half of the class ask the questions and the other half give the answers. Suggest that the children tell what they know about squirrels.

DEER IN THE SNOW

TEACHER: A deer came out of the forest
As cautiously as could be;
And right in the clearing near our house,
He steadily looked at me!

CHILDREN: Stay, please stay, deer in the snow!
Stay, please stay! Do not go!

TEACHER: His eyes were so large and lovely;
His two antlers, like a dead limb,
Would soon drop off and there would grow
A brand-new pair for him.

CHILDREN: Stay, please stay, deer in the snow!
Stay, please stay! Do not go!

TEACHER: His sensitive nostrils quivered.
Oh, I stood very still that day,

For one footstep would send him leaping,
And my deer would be frightened away.

CHILDREN: Stay, please stay, deer in the snow!
Stay, please stay! Do not go!

—L.B.S.

The refrain should be said quietly and with feeling. Consonant blends *sn* and *st* are emphasized in the words *snow* and *stay*. A discussion on deer and their habits should follow the reading of this poem.

LITTLE ECHO MAN

I know a little echo man
Who lives across the way.
I always like to call to him
When I go out to play.
My funny little echo man
Is courteous as can be.
No matter what I say to him,
He always answers me.

Can you stand? (*Echo answers.*)
Can you swing?
Can you sneeze?
Can you sing?
Can you skate?
Can you squeak?
Can you slide?
Can you speak?

—L.B.S.

The children echo each question containing the *st, sw, sn, sk, sq, sl,* and *sp* consonant blends. Any speech sound or groups of sounds may be substituted, however. This rhyme provides an effective listening experience. Let the children take turns using a variety of sentence patterns for the class to imitate. Statement of fact: "I am six years old." Command: "Show me your thumb." Strong feeling: "Wow! Look at that rain come down!"

THE SPARROW'S SECRET

The sparrow had a secret;
He whispered it to me —
A most important secret
About something in the tree.

Refrain: Whisper, whisper, whiss— whiss— whiss!
                Whisper, whisper, whiss— whiss— whiss!

The robin saw the secret,
And he stopped along the way
To tell his friend, the oriole,
Who told the old blue jay.

Refrain: Whisper, whisper, whiss— whiss— whiss!
                Whisper, whisper, whiss— whiss— whiss!

He told his friend, the redbird,
Who told the gray fieldmouse
That Mr. and Mrs. Sparrow
Had some birdies at their house.

Refrain: Whisper, whisper, whiss— whiss— whiss!
                Whisper, whisper, whiss— whiss— whiss!
—L.B.S.

The refrain should be said softly. The word *whisper* contains medial "s" and *whiss* contains "s" used in final position. Ask a child to whisper a "secret" to his neighbor, who whispers the same secret to the next child, and so on. The last child repeats the secret aloud. This is an excellent listening activity.

TIMMY TEAKETTLE

Timmy Teakettle was very sad. He sat on the toy shelf with last year's Christmas toys and waited for Penny to play with him.

Penny owned Timmy Teakettle. She loved him dearly, but not meaning to do so, she had put Timmy on the shelf and had forgotten all about him.

Timmy wanted to make a steamy sound, "Sssssss." But how could he make steam if nobody filled him with water and put him on the stove?

To make a good teakettle sound, Timmy had to have water inside him and the water had to boil.

One day Timmy decided to take matters into his own hands, or rather into his own spout, since Timmy Teakettle didn't have any hands.

He took a big breath, puffed out his teakettle cheeks, and out came a sound. Was it *sssss*? No, it was not *sssss*. The sound Timmy Teakettle made was "Th— th— th— th." (Voiceless *th*.)

"Oh," said Timmy Teakettle, "that is the sound Mrs. Goose makes when she puts out her tongue. I cannot put out a tongue for I haven't one. The steam should come out my spout. Oh, dear me!"

But Timmy Teakettle decided to try again.

He took a big breath, puffed out his teakettle cheeks, and out came a sound. Was it *sssss*? No, it was not *sssss*.

The sound Timmy Teakettle made was "Sh— sh— sh!"

"Oh, oh," cried Timmy Teakettle, "that is the wrong sound again. It is the sound the seashell makes and not a good sound for a teakettle at all."

But Timmy Teakettle tried not to be discouraged. He took a big breath, puffed out his teakettle cheeks, and out came a sound.

Was it *ssss*? No, it was not *ssss*.

It was an angry sound that went, "F, f,f,f,f,f,f!"

"Why," said Timmy Teakettle, "that is the sound the angry pussycat makes. I want to make a happy sound, not an angry one."

Timmy Teakettle sat on the toy shelf growing sadder and sadder.

Day after day passed. And nobody paid any attention to Timmy Teakettle.

One day Penny came into the playroom. She said, "I am tired of my toys. What shall I play with?"

She looked all around her playroom.

Suddenly she said, "Oh, I know! I will have a party for my dolls. And I will use Timmy Teakettle!" You can imagine how happy Timmy Teakettle was to hear that!

Penny set the table with her little blue dishes and tiny knives, forks, and spoons. Then she went to the toy shelf and took down Timmy Teakettle. She took him to the sink and filled him with water from the faucet. Then she put Timmy Teakettle on the stove!

Timmy was so pleased because he knew he was going to be able to say something. What was it? *Ssss?* Yes, indeed, and very *ssssoon!*

Timmy Teakettle sat on the flame and the water inside him began to bubble — bubble — bubble and boil — boil — boil!

This time Timmy did not have to take a big breath and puff out his teakettle cheeks. The steam came out his spout *sooooo* easily, just like this: "Sssssssssss!"

He made the best steamy sound you ever heard. "Sssss." He made a loud one: "SSSSS." Then he made a very tiny *"sssss."*

Timmy Teakettle sat on the stove and he sang and he sang and he sang, because he was so happy that he could make his very own teakettle sound: "Sssssssssss!"

—L.B.S.

Each time the "teakettle" sound occurs, the children imitate it. Suggest that they retell the story in relays.

SUNNY SNAKE LEARNS TO MAKE A "SNAKE" SOUND

A snake family lived under an old musty tree stump at the edge of the meadow. There was Mrs. Snake, who was the mother, and there was Mr. Snake, who was, of course, the father.

Now the snake family made a funny hissing sound which you can make, too, if you will remember to keep your pink tongue tip from showing. Make it like this: *sssssssss*. (*Children make the sound.*) Mrs. Snake could say, "Sssssssss," and she also could say her name, which was Mrs. Ssssssssnake. (*Children imitate.*) Mr. Snake could say, "Sssssssss," and he could say his name, too: Mr. Sssssssssssnake. (*Children imitate.*)

Mr. and Mrs. Snake were not the only members in the family. They had two girl children and two boy children.

Saucy and Silky were the girl children. Sometimes Saucy was a bit naughty. She curled up on some leaves that were exactly her colors. When Mother Snake tried to find her, Saucy could not be seen, although she was right there. Most of the time Saucy minded her manners quite well and Mother Snake did not care if she played a joke now and then. Saucy made quick little hisses like this: "S— s— s— s."

Silky was tiny and dainty. Her scales shone like sparkling silver and she made a soft ladylike hiss like this: "Sssssss— ssssssssss." (*Children imitate.*)

Stripey and Speckles were the boy children. Stripey had streaks on his sleek body, just like his father. Stripey was a brave snake. When Scorpy Scorpion came in sight, Stripey would hiss loudly, and Scorpy would swish his long, narrow tail back and forth and scurry away. Stripey could make a very good snake sound: "Sssssssssss." (*Children imitate.*)

Speckles had speckled skin just like his mother. He was a helpful little snake. He found delicious bugs for the family supper, and he kept the beds neat with fresh, damp moss from the woods. He could make a snake sound, too: "Sssssssssss." (*Children imitate.*)

Every member of the snake family could say his own name, which we know had the "snake" sound in it, and each one could say everyone else's name that had the same sound: Mrs. Snake, Mr. Snake, Saucy Snake, Silky Snake, Stripey Snake, and Speckles Snake. (*Children imitate names.*)

But there was somebody else in the snake family. His name was Sunny. Sunny looked mostly like his father and mother except that he was much, much smaller. He was a dear little snake, but he could not say his own name, *Sunny.* (*Children imitate.*) And he could not say the "snake" sound, *Sssssssss.* (*Children imitate.*) Sunny tried and tried to say his name, but he just could not do it. His kind mother wanted to help him.

"Your name is Sunny," she would say. "Try to say your name. Please!"

And all Sunny could say was *Thunny,* which you know is not right because it does not begin with a good, plain "snake" sound.

"Let us practice," said Sunny's mother. "I will help you."

But when Sunny tried to say *sink,* it came out *think.* When he tried to say *some,* it came out *thumb.* And when he tried to say *saw* and *sank,* they came out *thaw* and *thank.*

And what did his mother do? *Nothing!* Because she was a kind and understanding mother and she knew Sunny could not help it because he was still just a baby snake and had to grow up in his talking.

"Never mind, Sunny," said Mother Snake, "I love you just the same. One of these days you will be able to make the best "snake" sound in the whole family." Then she curled up her long snaky body around Sunny and made him feel safe and comfortable. She sang a special song to him that only snakes can understand. It went this way, "Sssss— sssss— sssss— sssssssssss," which does not sound like a pretty song to us, but to Sunny it was a lovely lullaby.

That fall, Sunny started to snake school. He was so excited. But on the very first day, the snake teacher, whose name was Mrs. Serpent, asked each of the snake children to tell his name. When she came to Sunny, he stretched out importantly and said, "Thunny Thnake."

Some of the children laughed, but Mrs. Serpent looked quite cross, and they knew this was not the polite thing to do. Sunny Snake guessed he had found a good friend in Mrs. Serpent when she tried to help him make a "snake" sound during recess. Sunny liked Mrs. Serpent a lot, and he tried doubly hard to make the sound for her sake.

Sometimes when the snake children went to the playground for games like "Slither-slither, Which Way to Go," Sunny would be teased about his funny "snake" sound. Sweetie Snake was a little girl snake who was cute as a button, but she did a *very* thoughtless thing. She said to Sunny:

> "You talk like a baby.
> If I were you,
> I would try to talk
> Like other snakes do."

If Mrs. Serpent had heard this, she would have asked Sweetie to apologize for her rude manners, but she could not be around every minute, so sometimes the teasing went on and the only thing Sunny could do was to try not to hear it or let it bother him.

Sunny's brothers and sisters tried to help him. His sister Saucy said, "I will polish your scales so that they will sparkle like diamonds if you will say 'sssss.' "

His sister Silky said, "I will find seven bugs for you to eat if you make the sound, 'ssssssssss.' " (*Children imitate.*)

His brother Stripey said, "I will bring some special damp moss for your bed if you will say 'sssssss.' " (*Children imitate.*)

Now Sunny knew that "sss" was a very important sound, because you cannot say *six* or *seven* without it. You cannot say *sock* for your foot, or *soap* for clean hands, or *sing* a pretty *song* without making a "snake" sound. Try it and see: *sock . . . soap . . . sing . . . song*. You could not ask *Santa* for things like *skates . . .* or *sleds . . .* or *snowsuits . . .* or a pet cocker *spaniel*. (*Children repeat.*)

You could not ask for certain foods when you are hungry, like *spaghetti . . .* ice-cream *sundae . . .* apple *sauce . . . spinach . . .* or *sweet* red *strawberries*. (*Children say the italicized words.*)

And what if we had no word for *smile . . .* or *speak . . .* or *sing!* Imagine! What would we do if we wanted to write a *story* about a *spaceman* or the *solar system?* Or the United *States* of America — if we had no "snake" sound? We could not even *study science*, could we? (*Children imitate each italicized word.*) So now you know how important it was for Sunny to make a good "snake" sound.

One day when Sunny was feeling especially sad, he said, "I am going to crawl away." And he DID. He slithered away, his little snaky body making humps as he moved himself along the ground.

Soon he came to a farm. He knew that it was a farm, because he could hear farm noises like "oink, oink" and "baa-baa" and "moo, moo."

Then he heard a *dreadful* sound. It went, "Th— th— th— th!"

Sunny saw what was making that sound. It was a goose! She put out her tongue and came right at Sunny, who was so frightened that he crawled away from there fast. When the goose's "th-th" sound could no longer be heard, Sunny stopped to rest. All tired out, he curled up on a rock beside a clear, sparkling pool. He could see his reflection in the pool, but to get a better look, he uncoiled himself and crawled closer . . . and what he saw gave him a start.

Instead of a little baby snake in the looking-glass water picture, he saw an almost grown snake — as big as his sisters and brothers, but not quite so big as his father and mother.

"I MUST make a good 'snake' sound," said Sunny when he saw how big he had grown, and then he realized that he had never really practiced before. It took practice to make a good "snake" sound and nobody else could do it for him.

Sunny thought about the dreadful "goose" sound: "Th— th— th— th!"

"Why," said Sunny, "I have been making a *goose* sound and not a *snake* sound at all. I just *thought* I was making a "snake" sound, but now I know different."

And Sunny practiced and he practiced and he practiced until he could make a "snake" sound without even thinking about it: "Sssssssss." (*Children imitate.*) And he practiced saying his own name, *Sunny.* And he practiced saying the names of his brothers and sisters, *Stripey, Speckles, Saucy,* and *Silky.* (*Children say each name.*)

Then when *Starry,* the new baby snake came to join the snake family, Sunny helped her make a "snake" sound: "Sssssssssss." (*Children imitate.*)

—L.B.S.

HIDE-AND-SEEK

Some fieldmice were playing hide-and-seek in the grassy meadow.

It was Little Fieldmouse's turn to hide. So he called:

"Squeak, squeak, hide-and-seek;
Squeak, squeak, do not peek!
Squeak, squeak, I won't speak;
And you won't find me in a week!"

Little Fieldmouse felt very frisky as he darted everywhere and nowhere in particular. It was very important that he find a place where he would not be found, *squeak, squeak,* in a week.

The woods smelled of dogtooth violets and fern, and Little Fieldmouse's whiskers moved as he sniffed the air and enjoyed the woodsy fragrance.

Up in a high tree, Little Red Squirrel went, "Chatter-chatter." His bright eyes looked at Little Fieldmouse's sleek body and tiny paws. Little Red Squirrel would NEVER hurt Little Fieldmouse.

Little Fieldmouse went right on trying to find the best place to hide and, as he ran, he sang his hide-and-seek song:

"Squeak, squeak, hide-and-seek;
Squeak, squeak, do not peek!
Squeak, squeak, I won't speak;
And you won't find me in a week!"

99

Behind a rock sat Mr. Hop-Frog. Little Fieldmouse heard Mr. Hop-Frog say "Glub!" as he puffed up his chest and pointed his toes toward each other. He would NEVER hurt Little Fieldmouse.

Little Fieldmouse took a drink from the brook and got his whiskers all wet, but they soon dried in the sun. He went right on trying to find a good place to hide, and as he ran, he sang his hide-and-seek song:

> "Squeak, squeak, hide-and-seek;
> Squeak, squeak, do not peek!
> Squeak, squeak, I won't speak;
> And you won't find me in a week!"

Little Fieldmouse felt SO frisky as he darted here and there and everywhere and nowhere in particular.

Then — oh, then — right there in front of Little Fieldmouse sat a fat cat. The fat cat sat. She sat looking at Little Fieldmouse and she did not move.

And you can bet that Little Fieldmouse was too scared to move.

The fat cat sat and sat and sat. Then she opened her wide, hungry mouth, curled up her long red tongue, and made a TERRIBLE yawn, so that Little Fieldmouse could see way down the fat cat's throat.

Little Fieldmouse was off in a streak and he let himself be found by the other fieldmice right away.

After that, when the mice played hide-and-seek, Little Fieldmouse hid close by. But he still sang his hide-and-seek song:

> "Squeak, squeak, hide-and-seek;
> Squeak, squeak, do not peek!
> Squeak, squeak, I won't speak!"

But Little Fieldmouse left out the part that went:

> "You won't find me in a week!"

—L.B.S.

100

THE SPACEMAN

Do you like stories that begin "once upon a time"? When you hear those words, you know that usually the story will not be true and stories which are not true are called *fairy tales*. Fairy tales are make-believe, and they are a great deal of fun to tell and hear.

Sooooo— once upon a time, there was a spaceman who decided to descend from his space station in faraway outer space and make a trip to a new planet. The spaceman decided which planet he was going to visit, and no doubt you can guess which one it was. Yes, it was the earth, the big, round earth with its mountains and oceans and rivers and cities and plains.

Swifter than sound, came the spaceship. "Ssssssssss-ssssssss!" Zip, zoom, zip on its long trip came the spaceship. "Ssssssssssssssssssssss!"

Suddenly, the earth came into view, the big, round earth with its mountains and oceans and rivers and cities and plains.

The spaceman had studied planets for years. He knew that he saw the earth, and he was pleased to see that it was all that he imagined and more.

The spaceship had traveled fast — oh, so fast. "Ssssssss-ssssssss!" It had traveled through the solar system, past the stars, past Saturn, and the planet Mars. The ship sped downward, downward, downward. "Ssssssssssssssssss!"

The spaceship passed through high clouds and now the spaceman was very close to the earth, the big, round earth with its mountains and oceans and rivers and cities and plains.

With a swirl and a swish, the spaceship landed on the surface of the earth.

All was quiet.

The spaceman opened the window of his spaceship and he looked out. He peered through his green goggles and he saw things he had never seen. He heard things he had never heard. He felt things he had never felt.

Two larks were singing and the spaceman thought:

> It was the sweetest music he had ever heard,
> But for the music he had no word.

Since he had landed on a long, wide beach beside an ocean, he could hear waves rushing as the tide came in. And the spaceman thought:

> It was the sweetest music he had ever heard,
> But for the music he had no word.

The spaceman walked away from the beach and his ship, and soon he came to a cool, green wood. He smelled the blossoming earth and wild flowers.

> For him such beauty these things held;
> They were the sweetest he had ever smelled.

He smelled pine cones and fresh grass after a spring rain.

> For him, such beauty these things held;
> They were the sweetest he had ever smelled.

And then he YELLED! "Gubba, gubba, gulla!" he yelled. What do you think that meant? (*Individual response.*)

A bushy-tailed squirrel looked at the spaceman, its black beady eyes taking in the strange helmet and green goggles. It darted to the top of the tree when the spaceman held out his hand, and the spaceman felt sorry that the little squirrel was afraid of him.

He picked up a nut and felt it. He put it into his mouth, but the shell was hard and it hurt his teeth, so he threw it away. However, he saw some nut shells on the ground and this gave him an idea. He cracked the nut with his shoe, picked up the seed, and ate it. It tasted good.

Suddenly, the spaceman saw an odd-looking creature. It had a head with eyes, nose, mouth, chin, ears, and hair. The head belonged to a body with neck, shoulders, arms, hands, legs, and feet. The spaceman could see ten little bare toes.

"Hello," said the creature whose name was Andy.

The spaceman thought, "This must be an earth creature who wants to be friendly." So the spaceman smiled and said, "Ubba, gubba." What do you think that meant?

"My name is Andy. What is yours?" asked the boy.

"Goona, watta, luta," replied the spaceman, not understanding a word, because *we* know that the boy spoke the English language.

"I know that you do not understand me," said Andy. "But I am sure you must be a spaceman. You came from outer space in your spaceship. 'Ssssssssssssssssssssss!' "

The spaceman knew this was the sound of his spaceship. He said happily, "Ssssssssssssssssssssss!" Then he pointed to the beach where his spaceship lay. Andy and the spaceman walked to the beach.

"So this is a spaceship," said Andy. "I thought so. It looks just like the picture of one that I drew for our science project at school."

The spaceman pointed toward the heavens. He said, "Ssssssssssssssssssssss!"

"Yes," said Andy. "You came from outer space. Will you stay on earth with its mountains and oceans and rivers and cities and plains?" The spaceman smiled at Andy. It was all strange, this earth creature and this language he talked. "Please stay," begged Andy. Andy held out his hand.

The spaceman took it in his own for a second, and then he walked toward his ship. He again pointed toward the heavens. He said softly, "Ssssssssssssssssssss!"

103

"I understand," said Andy. "You must return to your home, wherever that is."

The spaceman opened the door of his spaceship and climbed inside and, with another smile, started the motor. With a wave of his hand, he was off: "Sssssssssssssssss!"

Up, up, up through the clouds, past Mars, past Jupiter, past many stars. "Sssssssssssssssssss!" And out of sight!

Andy said, "What fun it would have been had the spaceman decided to stay on earth, and what fun I would have had teaching him about this wonderful earth with its mountains and oceans and rivers and cities and plains."

—L.B.S.

Suggest that individual children dramatize this story. It also may be used with sack puppets. Ask the children to add other episodes to the story. Ask: "What words beginning with the "spaceship" sound would Andy have taught the spaceman? The spaceman's name, perhaps? Can you remember any words in the story that began with the 's' speech sound?"

THE LITTLE SEEDS

Some little seeds lay under the dark earth. It was winter and the little seeds were warm, for the dark earth made a comfortable quilt that protected them. The little seeds heard nothing, because they were sleeping soundly.

> But there were sounds to be heard.
> There were sounds of icicles creaking
>   on the roofs,
> Sounds of clopping horses' hoofs,
> Sounds of winds that whir and blow,
> Sounds of galoshes in the snow,
> Sounds of skating on the lake,
> And sounds that children's voices make.

But the little seeds heard none of this, for they were fast asleep in the dark winter earth.

Upon the hill a snowman sat,
And on his head there was a hat.
Oh, my! He looked especially grand
With a wooden broomstick in his hand.

The snowman heard wonderful sounds,
Sounds of laughter, sounds of talk,
Sounds of footsteps on the walk,
Sounds of songs and happy cheer,
Sounds of church bells ringing near.

The snowman loved all of these sounds and he liked the cold and he said, "I want to stay forever and ever and ever."

But one day — ah, one day — the air grew warmer, for spring had come. The snowman began to melt slowly — and he melted — and melted — and melted — and while the snowman was melting, a bunny rabbit came by with his basket of dyes. The bunny rabbit was so glad that it was time to color eggs for the boys and girls. He was so excited that he did not see a stone, and KERFLOP! He stubbed his toe and spilled all of his colors. And the colors ran everywhere, because they were thinner even than finger paint.

But this didn't bother the bunny rabbit at all. He just went back to his burrow to get more colors.

The big sun smiled down upon the snowman and the snowman melted — and melted — and melted — and the water from the snowman ran down the side of the hill. The water ran right over the place where the little seeds were sleeping in the dark earth. The water gave the little seeds a cool drink and, as it seeped down through the dark earth, it tasted mighty, mighty good to those little seeds.

All of the little seeds woke up and drank and drank and drank of the cool water, for they were very thirsty after their long winter's sleep under the dark earth. They began to sprout and push their way upward and, as they did this, each little sprout chose a color from the dyes the bunny rabbit had spilled — red, blue, green, orange, yellow, and purple.

In the time it takes for flowers to grow, there were so many flowers in a beautiful patch at the bottom of the hill that it dazzled everyone's eyes just to look at them.

Children passing by said, "It is spring at last! Look at those lovely flowers!"

The flowers stayed right there at the bottom of the hill for a long time.

Spring came and went.
Summer came and went.
Fall came and went.
Winter came — and behold!

Upon the hill a snowman sat,
And on his head there was a hat.
Oh, my! He looked especially grand
With a wooden broomstick in his hand.

And more little seeds slept in the dark earth, waiting for spring and the time to grow beautiful at the bottom of the snowman's hill.

—L.B.S.

The second time this story is told, the children will be able to participate in the refrains. Ask questions to elicit responses which will give practice on the "s" speech sound: "What sounds do you hear in winter? Fall? Spring? Summer? How would you make a snowman? Is this a good story? Why?"

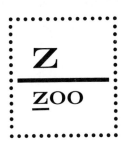

MAKING THE SPEECH SOUND

The "z" speech sound is produced like "s," except that it has vocal-cord vibration. It is a speech sound frequently misarticulated by adults as well as by children. Common mispronunciations among children are *thoo* (voiced "th") for *zoo*, or *doo* for *zoo*. Or a child may allow air to spill over the sides of the tongue and pronunce the *z* with a lateral lisp. Children who learn English as a second language may substitute *s* for *z*, e.g., *boyssss* and *girlssss*.

You may call "z" the "bee" sound.

CORRECTING THE DEFICIENT SPEECH SOUND

See the section on correcting the "s" speech sound for techniques in helping the child to overcome mispronunciations of "z," but keep in mind that the "z" speech sound is voiced and "s" is voiceless.

INSTRUCTIONS TO THE CHILD

"Watch me closely as I close my teeth, keep my tongue out of sight, and buzz like a bee: 'zzzzzz.' Did you hear it? I will name some words which begin with the 'bee' sound: *zoo, zipper, zebra.* Did you hear the 'bee' sound at the beginning of each word? Try it with me, now. Hold up this mirror to see if your teeth are together and your pinky tongue is out of sight: 'zzzzzz.' Good for you! Let's put that 'bee' sound into some words: *zip, zero, zoo.* We have a poem to say, too. Join me when I make the 'bee' sound."

> Little bee, little bee,
> Make some honey for me.
> "Zzz— zzz— zzz!"
>
> Hum a soft drowsy tune
> On this warm afternoon.
> "Zzz— zzz— zzz!"
>
> —L.B.S.

WORDS FOR PRACTICE

Initial	*Medial*	*Final*
zoo	buzzard	fuzz
zipper	razor	buzz
zoom	lazy	Oz
zebra	wizard	blaze
zigzag	freezer	breeze
zero	dizzy	froze

BUSY HONEYBEE

Busy little honeybee
Buzzes near the honey tree.
> "Zzzzzzzz— zzzzzzzzz— zzzzzzzzz!"

You can hear her drowsy tune
On a summer afternoon.
> "Zzzzzzzz— zzzzzzzzz— zzzzzzzzz!"

Busy bee likes clover sweet
Where she can find a pollen treat.
> "Zzzzzzzzz— zzzzzzzzz— zzzzzzzzz!"

Then she flies back to the tree
To tell each little honeybee.
"Zzzzzzzzz— zzzzzzzzz— zzzzzzzzz!"

The children make the "bee" sound when it occurs. Remind them to keep the tongue tip out of sight.

LITTLE BEES

One little bee flies round and round;
One little bee can make this sound:
"Zzzzzzzzzzzzzzz!"
Two little bees fly round and round;
Two little bees can make this sound:
"Zzzzzzzzzzzzzzz!"
Three little bees fly round and round;
Three little bees can make this sound:
"Zzzzzzzzzzzzzzz!"
Four little bees fly round and round;
Four little bees can make this sound:
"Zzzzzzzzzzzzzzz!"
Five little bees fly round and round;
Five little bees can make this sound:
"Zzzzzzzzzzzzzzz!"
Five little bees fly far away,
But they will come again some day.
"ZZZZZZzzzzzzzzzzzz!"
*(Softer and softer until voices
cannot be heard.)*

—J.J.T.

This exercise is a drill which can be used as a creative dramatics activity, with the class making the "bee" sound while five children act out the parts. It can be adapted easily to flannelboard use by preparing pictures of the five little bees, or by attaching tagboard bees to tongue depressors and using them as puppets. The selection may also be used to review the "r" sound in *round*.

I'M ZIPPY THE ZEBRA

ALL: I'm Zippy the zebra,
The zebra, the zebra.
I'm Zippy the zebra
Who lives in a zoo.

TEACHER: And tell us, do you like the zoo?
CHILDREN: Oh, yes! Oh, yes, of course I do.
ALL: I'm Zippy the zebra,
The zebra, the zebra.
I'm Zippy the zebra
Who lives in a zoo.

TEACHER: And did you travel very far?
CHILDREN: Oh, yes! I came from Zanzibar.
ALL: I'm Zippy the zebra,
The zebra, the zebra.
I'm Zippy the zebra
Who lives in a zoo.

TEACHER: Oh, you are such a curious sight.
CHILDREN: It's 'cause my hide is black and white.
ALL: I'm Zippy the zebra,
The zebra, the zebra.
I'm Zippy the zebra
Who lives in a zoo.

—L.B.S.

The refrain affords practice on the "z" sound in *Zippy, zebra,* and *zoo.* The rhythm of the refrain makes it easy to set to music.

THE TOUCH GAME

I make my fingers touch my nose,
touch my nose,
touch my nose.
(*Prolong "z" sound in nose.*)

I make my fingers touch my toes,
        touch my toes,
        touch my toes.
        (*Prolong "z" sound in toes.*)
I make my fingers touch my knees,
        touch my knees,
        touch my knees.
        (*Prolong "z" sound in knees.*)
We make our voices sound like bees,
        sound like bees,
        sound like bees.
        (*Prolong "z" sound in bees.*)
"Zzz— zzz," touch my nose.
"Zzz— zzz," touch my toes.
"Zzz— zzz," touch my knees.
"Zzz— zzz," sound like bees.
        (*Voices grow softer and softer.*)
                    —J.J.T.

Use this rhyme as a readiness activity or to help the group release restlessness through a controlled activity.

Other touch games may be found in *Rhymes for Fingers and Flannelboards*, Scott and Thompson, and in *More Singing Fun*, Wood and Scott, Webster Division, McGraw-Hill Book Company.

WINTER AT THE ZOO

I have a pair of zipper boots,
And zipper jacket, too.
I zip them up and go to see
The zebra at the zoo!

        At the zoo, zoo, zoo!
        The zebra at the zoo!
        His stripes that zigzag up and down
        Are wound and wound
        Around, around
        The zebra at the zoo!

The zebra does not seem to mind
The zero air outside,
Because he's dressed for winter cold
With warm and furry hide.

At the zoo, zoo, zoo!
The zebra at the zoo!
His stripes that zigzag up and down
Are wound and wound
Around, around
The zebra at the zoo!

—L.B.S.

Words that begin with the "z" speech sound are *zebra, zoo, zipper, zigzag,* and *zero.* Children who have difficulty with the "z" sound should concentrate upon one "z" word at a time. Tell them that you are going to listen for the "bee" sound in *zoo.* Ask them to discuss each word that has the "z" sound and to use it in a sentence. Cite the two meanings of the word *zero.*

The words *wound* and *round* are confused aurally. Review the two words in sentences like this: "The zebra's stripes are *w*ound *r*ound and *r*ound." Ask the children to listen for the difference in pronunciation.

THE LITTLE BEE

One day Little Bee found her first pink clover blossom. "Zzzzzzzzzzz! Zzzzzzzzzzz! Zz, zz, zz, zz, zz!" buzzed Little Bee excitedly. Then she flew back to the hive to tell all of the other bees about the lovely pink clover blossom she had discovered. On the way she met Chirpy Cricket.

"Why are you so happy, Little Bee?" he asked.

"I have found my first pink clover blossom," replied Little Bee. "Zzzzzzzzzzz! Zzzzzzzzzzz! Zz, zz, zz, zz, zz! That's why I'm so happy."

So Chirpy Cricket went back to his thicket and began to play his fiddle.

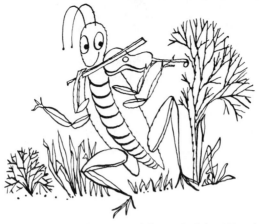

"Why are you so happy, Chirpy Cricket?" asked Vee-Vee the Fly who just happened to be flying by.

"I am happy because Little Bee has found her first pink clover blossom and she is full of happy buzzes, 'zzzzzzzzzzzz.' So that is why I play my fiddle," said Chirpy Cricket.

Hearing this, Vee-Vee the Fly began to make his special kind of hum: "Vvvvvvvvvvvvv."

"Why are you so happy?" asked Flutterby the Butterfly who just happened to be fluttering by.

"Vvvvvvvvvvvvv," hummed Vee-Vee the Fly. "I am happy because Chirpy Cricket is playing his fiddle because Little Bee has found her first pink clover blossom and is full of happy buzzes: 'zzzzzzzzzzzz.' "

Then Flutterby the Butterfly spread her beautiful orange and black wings and began to flutter them very rapidly.

A tiny ant saw this lovely sight and he asked, "Why are you so happy, you magnificent butterfly?"

Flutterby rested on a vine with her wings closed and she said, "I am fluttering because Vee-Vee the Fly is making his special hum because Chirpy Cricket is playing his fiddle because Little Bee has found her first pink clover and she is full of happy buzzes: 'Zzzzzzzzzzzzzzzz.' "

Some little children heard these exciting insect noises and they asked, "Why does that butterfly flutter her wings in the sunlight? Why does the cricket play his fiddle in the thicket? Why does the fly have a special kind of hum? And why does the bee buzz?"

A wise teacher replied, "Perhaps these things are done so that little children will ask questions, for asking questions is the beginning of wisdom and understanding."

—ADAPTED BY L.B.S. FROM AN ANONYMOUS TALE

This story emphasizes the "z" sound in *zoo* and *zebra*. The children are also given many opportunities to produce this sound in isolation as they imitate Little Bee. You may wish to remind the children to keep the tongue tip out of sight when they make the "z" sound.

Ask the class: "What might you wish to know about the bee? The fly? The cricket? The butterfly? The ant? Can you think of any words that begin with Little Bee's sound?"

Suggest that the children add other characters to the story as they retell it. Ask them to make up original stories using these suggested titles which will help stimulate creativity: "The Bee that Lost His Buzz," "The Butterfly that Wanted to Be an Ant," "The Cricket that Forgot to Play His Fiddle," and "The Ant that Won First Prize." Listen for the basic truths which are expressed frequently by children.

CHAPTER 6

The "R" and "L" Speech Sounds

MAKING THE SPEECH SOUND

The "r" speech sound may be produced by saying "ah" with a wide open mouth and letting the tongue tip curl up gradually toward the roof of the mouth. Prolong the "ah" sound and, as it is continued, raise the tongue tip. If the tongue tip curls and moves backward, the change in pronunciation should be a semblance of "r" or a correct pronunciation of "r" as in *red*. The child may make "l" and gradually move the tongue tip backward away from the alveolar ridge. One teacher uses a trilled "rrrrrr" to help achieve tongue mobility. The trilled "rrrrrr" should be followed by a vowel as "rrrrrr-ee" or "rrrrrr-ay." Another teacher reminds the children that the lips are in a lazy position, emphasizing that there must not be "rounded lips as if you were going to kiss your mother good-by."

In normal speech, the tongue tip is elevated and the sides may contact the upper teeth, though not necessarily.

The soft palate is raised and the teeth and lips are parted slightly. Since the "r" speech sound is a voiced consonant, there is vocal-cord vibration when it is produced.

The "r" speech sound is one of the most frequently misarticulated sounds. It is difficult to hear and to produce. Since "r" is a semi-vowel, it may be difficult for some children to hear the difference between "r" and short "oo" as in *book*. The sound is made inside the mouth, so that the child must depend largely upon auditory acuity rather than upon the position of the lips or teeth in order to imitate it.

You may call "r" the "rooster" or the "growling" sound.

CORRECTING THE DEFICIENT SPEECH SOUND

Medial and final "r" are not stressed in certain areas of the United States. Regional differences in the pronunciation of the "r" speech sound are significant in identifying some of the dialects within the United States. One may recognize the locale of an individual if he "growls" or overaccents the "r" in *carrrr* or gives the *ar* a short *o* sound in *apartment*.

The selections in this chapter stress the initial rather than the medial or final "r" sound.

The most common substitution for "r" is "w," e.g., *wed* for *red*.

It is difficult to direct children as to how to move the tongue tip in order to get results. Therefore, it is important to encourage the child to experiment with his tongue and to give him many auditory experiences. One teacher holds out the palm of the hand and lets the finger tips curl back to help the child understand how his tongue tip moves. Another molds a tongue shape from clay and shows the child how his own tongue might look as he produces "ah" and "r."

INSTRUCTIONS TO THE CHILD

"I am pretending that my tongue is fast asleep in bed with its 'toes' touching the 'foot of the bed,' or my lower front teeth. (*Demonstrate.*) Now I will lift the 'toes' or the tip of my tongue very slowly and let it curl back: 'ah— . . . rrrrr.' Did you see what my tongue did? Listen as I name some words that begin with the 'rrr' sound: *red, rag, read.* Did you hear the sound? We call that the 'rooster' sound. Now, some roosters crow, 'Cock-a-doodle-doo,' and for some stories that is fine. But when we are learning to make an 'r' sound, our roosters crow, 'Er, er, er, er, errrrrr!' Try to make the 'rooster' sound with me as we say this rhyme:

> Every morning I can hear
> A rooster crowing loud and clear.
> 'Er, er, er, er, errrr!'
> He says, 'Get up, you lazy one!
> Another day has just begun!
> Er, er, er, er, errrr!'
>
> —L.B.S.

Repeat these words after me and listen to your 'rooster' sound as you say each word: *rrrrabbit, rrrrradio, rrrrocket.* If you could not do this, then your tongue will have to be helped, won't it? At first, we may have to keep the lips back in a smile as we make the 'rooster' sound. We do not want to round our lips in an 'oo' sound."

Note: Beginning practice on the "r" sound should not involve words that contain the sounds of long *o* (rope), long *oo* (room), or *oy* (Roy), because the lips must be rounded to produce those words. If the tongue tip curls back too far, the sound may assume a guttural quality. At first, ask the child to keep his lips in a smile position until the new pattern is formed.

117

WORDS FOR PRACTICE

Initial	Medial	Final
ring	berry	car
robe	market	stair
rabbit	perfume	fire
run	parrot	ear
red	orchard	four
rain	church	bear

Consonant Blends:

cross	trick	broom	dress	frame	grass	press
crown	train	brass	drink	friend	ground	prune

barge	hurt	learn	farm	harp	park	cars
large	part	burn	warm	sharp	work	fairs

curl	word
girl	card

I HEAR IT

Follow the directions under the *s* speech-sound section for suggestions on using the "I Hear It" activity.

I hear it in *read* but not in *weed*.
I hear it in *run* but not in *one*.
I hear it in *rest* but not in *west*.
> I hear it in *rocket* but not in *locket*.
> I hear it in *rain* but not in *lane*.
> I curl my tongue tip and smile just a bit.
> My lips are not round. Can you do it?
> "Rrrr— rrrr— rrrr."

I hear it in *rag* but not in *lag*.
I hear it in *rail* but not in *wail*.
I hear it in *rake* but not in *wake*.
I hear it in *ram* but not in *lamb*.
I hear it in *rap* but not in *lap*.
I curl my tongue tip and smile just a bit.
My lips are not round. Can you do it?
"Rrrr— rrrr— rrrr."

—L.B.S.

ARE WE LISTENING?

1. *Rags* is a dog. He lives on a *ranch*. *Rags* is *Robert's* pet. *Rags* follows *Robert* everywhere, even to school. *Robert* said, "*Rags* is a real pal! I can *run* with him. I can even *read* to *Rags* and he listens. He likes to hear me *read*." Are we listening? Let's see! Who is *Rag's* master? Where does *Rags* live? Why is *Rags* a good pal? Can you think of a good name for a dog? Try to describe *Rags*.

2. *Randy* has three pets — a *rat,* a *rooster,* and a *rabbit*. The *rooster* is *red*. The *rat* is white. The *rabbit* is brown. The *rat* and the *rabbit* are *rodents*. The pets live in *Randy's* back yard. Are we listening? Let's see! Name *Randy's* three pets. What color is the *rooster?* Which of the animals is white? What are the *rat* and the *rabbit* called? Would you rather have a *rat,* a *rooster,* or a *rabbit?* Why?

3. Here are some birthday presents people like. Babies like *rattles*. Daddy likes a *bathrobe*. Mother likes a dozen *roses*. Bill likes a jump *rope*. Susan likes a *raincoat*. Are we listening? Let's see! What does Baby like? Daddy? Bill? Susan? Mother? Which of these things would you like for your birthday?

—L.B.S.

119

ROOSTER RED

Rooster Red,
Rooster Red,
What a pretty comb
Upon your head!
     "Er, er, er, er, errrrrr!"
I'll teach you how to say *hello*
If you will teach me how to crow.
     "Er, er, er, er, errrrrr!"

Rooster Red,
Rooster Red,
Every day you get me
Out of bed.
     "Er, er, er, er, errrrrr!"
I like to learn sounds that are new,
So teach me how to crow like you!
     "Er, er, er, er, errrrrr!"

—L.B.S.

Ask the entire class to join in with the crows, then suggest that individual children be roosters. Teachers often have good success in helping the child with a speech-sound misarticulation by encouraging him to imitate a puppet. When the puppet does the "teaching," the child usually responds with enthusiasm. A rooster puppet is included in the *Time for Phonics Paper-Bag Puppet Patterns,* Webster Division, McGraw-Hill Book Company.

THE GROWLY SOUND

Monday, I visited the dogs at the pound,
And I heard one big dog make this sound:
     "Rrrrrrrr-uff, rrrrrrrrr-uff!" (*Loudly*.)
Tuesday, I visited the dogs at the pound,
And I heard two big dogs make this sound:
     "Rrrrrrr-uff, rrrrrrrrrr-uff!" (*Fiercely*.)

Wednesday, I visited the dogs at the pound,
And I heard three little dogs make this sound:
    "Rrrrrrr-uff, rrrrrrrrr-uff!" (*High voices.*)
Thursday, I visited the dogs at the pound,
And I heard four puppies make this sound:
    "Rrrrrrrrr-uff, rrrrrrrrr-uff!" (*Softly.*)
Friday, I visited the dogs at the pound,
And I chose a special one that made this sound:
    "Rrrrrrrrr-uff, rrrrrrrrr-uff!" (*Happily.*)

—L.B.S.

Ask children who appear to need individual help with the "r" speech sound to be the dogs. The first time the rhyme is presented, ask the children as a group to join in with the growls. The children may discuss their own dogs and the different sounds they make.

ANIMAL GROWLS

The polar bear out at the zoo
Growls softly when he talks to you.
    "Gurrrrrrrr— gurrrrrrrr— gurrrrrrr!"

The tiger's stripes go up and down,
And when he growls, he makes a frown.
    "Gurrrrrrr— gurrrrrrr— gurrrrrrrr!"

When Mr. Wolf walks round and round,
He makes this angry growling sound.
    "Gurrrrrrr— gurrrrrrr— gurrrrrrr!"

My dog is brave as he can be.
He thinks he's taking care of me.
    "Gurrrrrrrr— gurrrrrrrrr— gurrrrrrrr!"

—J.J.T.

Ask the class to join in on the growls, or let various children take turns making the "growly" sound of the different animals.

THE WOODPECKER

The woodpecker has a remarkable bill
Which serves as a chisel and also a drill.
To drum on a billboard, he's pleased and content;
It's really a wonder his bill is not bent!
    "Rrrrrrrrrr— rrrrrrrrrr— rrrrrrrrrr!"
    (*Trill the "r."*)

Have you seen how he climbs? How he jumps with both
    feet?
How his tail makes a prop when he hunts things to eat?
He pecks at the soft-growing bark of the tree,
And he actually hears where the fat bugs will be!
    "Rrrrrrrrrr— rrrrrrrrrr— rrrrrrrrrrr!"

Mister Woodpecker spears them and eats them, and maybe
He carries them home to his woodpecker baby.
He may waken you early, but pardon it please ——
He's just eating the pests that are killing your trees!
    "Rrrrrrrrrr— rrrrrrrrrr— rrrrrrrrrrr!"
       —VIRGINIA SYDNOR PAVELKO AND LOUISE BINDER SCOTT

Children who have difficulty in producing the "r" sound sometimes are helped through practice on a trilled "r."

RIDDLE-RIDDLE-REE

CHILDREN: Riddle-riddle-ree,
              What color do I see?
TEACHER: It starts with the "rooster" sound
              And ends with a *d.* (*red*)`
CHILDREN: Riddle-riddle-ree,
              What color do I see?
TEACHER: In the middle is the "rooster" sound;
              It starts with a *p.* (*purple*)
CHILDREN: Riddle-riddle-ree,
              What color do I see?

TEACHER:	The "rooster" sound is second,
	And it starts with a g. (*green*)
CHILDREN:	Riddle-riddle-ree,
	What color do I see?
TEACHER:	The "rooster" sound is second,
	And it starts with a b. (*brown*)
CHILDREN:	Riddle-riddle-ree,
	What number do I see?
TEACHER:	In the middle is the "rooster" sound;
	It ends with double e. (*three*)
CHILDREN:	Riddle-riddle-ree,
	What number do I see?
TEACHER:	It ends with the "rooster" sound
	And follows number three. (*four*)

—J.J.T.

Ask the children to make up their own riddles for colors and numbers. You may wish to ask older children to make up sentences that use words beginning with "r" as the subject.

FIVE RED ROSES

Five red roses are drooping in the sun,
Five red roses dropping petals one by one.
   (*Children sink slowly to the floor.*)
But the cooling raindrops chase the sun away,
Pitter-pattering they fall on a summer day.
Now the pretty roses raise their heads again
   (*Children rise slowly.*)
And whisper very softly, "Thank you, lovely rain."

—L.B.S

The children may act out this poem by using red scarves to represent the roses, gray scarves for raindrops, and a yellow scarf for the sun. Words which contain initial "r" are *red, roses, raise, raindrops,* and *rain.* The *dr* consonant blend is represented in the word *raindrops.*

RED, RED THINGS

A red, red apple, juicy sweet,
A red, red radish, fresh to eat,
A red, red stripe around my ball,
A red, red flower growing tall,
A red, red mitten with a thumb,
A red, red drumstick for my drum,
A red, red horn that makes big toots,
A red, red pair of rubber boots,
A red, red raspberry ice-cream cone,
A red, red plastic telephone,
A red, red shirt, a red, red dress,
A red, red lots of things, I guess!
A red, red blanket on my bed —
Oh, how I love the color red!

—L.B.S

Suggest that the children draw and color pictures of all the "red things" for use with the flannelboard as this rhyme is said. Ask them to name other things which are red.

DRAGONFLIES

ALL: Dragonflies, dragonflies,
       Periwinkle blue —
       Fiery red ones
       And green ones, too!

TEACHER: All darting to and fro
             With wings of spun glass,
             Sweeping up mosquitos that are
             Crawling in the grass.

ALL: Dragonflies, dragonflies,
       Periwinkle blue —
       Fiery red ones
       And green ones, too!

TEACHER:	Fluttering, hovering, Each a precious gem, Resting as they cling to A pussy willow stem.

ALL:	Dragonflies, dragonflies, Periwinkle blue — Fiery red ones And green ones, too!

—VIRGINIA SYDNOR PAVELKO

Note the words in the refrain which contain the "r" speech sound: *dragonflies, periwinkle, fiery, red,* and *green.* This poem may be used for a lesson on natural science.

IF I HAD ——

If I had a ribbon, a red satin ribbon,
I would tie up a present and give it to you!
But I don't have a ribbon, a red satin ribbon,
So some other present will just have to do.

If I had a rooster, a perky red rooster,
I would feed him some corn and I'd give him to you!
But I don't have a rooster, a perky red rooster,
So some other present will just have to do.

If I had a jump rope, a red-and-white jump rope,
I would jump a few times, and I'd give it to you!
But I don't have a jump rope, a red-and-white jump rope,
So some other present will just have to do.

If I had three roses, three lovely red roses,
I would put them in water and give them to you!
But I don't have three roses, three lovely red roses,
So some other present will just have to do.

125

If I had an apple, a round mellow apple,
I would polish and shine it and give it to you!
But I don't have an apple, a round mellow apple,
So some other present will just have to do.

Oh, I DO have a rhyme! It's an excellent rhyme!
It's about a rhinoceros that lives in a zoo.
It's a very good rhyme, and maybe sometime
I will say it and play it and share it with you!

—L.B.S.

Words that begin with the "r" sound are *roses, round, ribbon, red, rooster, rope, rhyme,* and *rhinoceros.* Because of the simple repetition in each stanza but the last, the children can participate immediately. Suggest they make up rhymes and share them with their friends. Motivate this activity by first asking them to rhyme some words: *zoo, you, too, boo, do; red, bed, head, said, fed; cat, rat, bat, hat, sat, mat, pat.*

RED APPLE

Red Apple was on a tree. One day, Red Apple fell to the ground and began to roll and roll and roll. He rolled and he rolled and he rolled. (*Whirl hands around each other in circular motion.*) Round and round and round Red Apple rolled. (*Children repeat.*)
Rover Dog saw Red Apple rolling. He said,

"Stop, Red Apple.
Stop! Please do!
Stop, Red Apple,
I want YOU!"
(*Children participate.*)

Red Apple called to Rover Dog,

"No, I cannot stop for you.
You will eat me if I do!"
(*Children participate.*)

126

Red Apple rolled on. He rolled and he rolled and he rolled, round and round and round. (*Whirl hands.*)

Ready Rooster saw Red Apple. He called,

"Stop, Red Apple.
Stop! Please do!
Stop, Red Apple,
I want YOU!"

But Red Apple said,

"No, I cannot stop for you.
You will eat me if I do.

I have rolled away from Rover Dog and I can roll away from YOU."

Red Apple rolled and he rolled and he rolled, round and round and round.

Brown Rat saw Red Apple. He called,

"Stop, Red Apple.
Stop! Please do!
Stop, Red Apple,
I want YOU!"

But Red Apple said,

"No, I cannot stop for you.
You will eat me if I do!

I have rolled away from Rover Dog and Ready Rooster, and I can roll away from you, too!"

Red Apple rolled and he rolled and he rolled, round and round and round.

A little boy saw Red Apple. He called,

"Stop, Red Apple.
Stop! Please do!
Stop, Red Apple,
I want YOU!"

Red Apple said, "I will stop for you."
Red Apple stopped rolling.

"Thank you," said the little boy. He picked up Red Apple. He put Red Apple into his pocket. Then he took Red Apple to school to give to his teacher.

—L.B.S.

This story contains repetitive words (*round, rolled,* and *red*) which provide practice on the "r" speech sound. The story may be dramatized with children playing the parts of Red Apple, Rover Dog, Ready Rooster, Brown Rat, and the little boy.

LITTLE RED ROOSTER [1]

Once there was a cute little red rooster. He was a very young rooster, for he had hatched out of a brown egg not too many weeks before. But it did not take Little Red Rooster long to begin growing up. Little Red Rooster was proud of his feathers. He was SO proud of his comb, and he was TERRIFICALLY proud of his crow!

"Er, er, er, er, errrrr!" crowed Little Red Rooster one day, long before the sun was up. "Er, er, er, er, errrrr!" (*Children imitate.*)

"Wuff, wuff!" growled Wolfie the watchdog. "What is the idea of waking me up?"

"I am so sorry," apologized Little Red Rooster.

"See that it does not happen again," growled Wolfie, going back to sleep.

Little Red Rooster flew to the top of a fence post and crowed again, "Er, er, er, er, errrrr!"

---

[1] By special permission of *The Grade Teacher.* Story by Louise Binder Scott.

"Why do you crow before the sun has come up?" asked Mooley Cow, rising from her bed in the hay.

"I really do not know," replied Little Red Rooster.

"Don't know! How silly!" scoffed Mooley Cow. "One must have a reason for everything he does. Of course, you are extremely young and inexperienced. You DO have a lot to learn, so perhaps you can be excused for your thoughtlessness."

Mooley Cow ambled toward the barn. "I suppose I may as well wait for the milking machine now," she grumbled. "There is no sense trying to get back to sleep again."

Little Red Rooster was truly sorry, but before he could control it, another crow came, "Er, er, er, er, errrrrr!"

"Botheration!" cried Nanny Goat. "The sun is not even beginning to appear over the horizon, and that rooster has crowed three times." Nanny Goat butted her head at Little Red Rooster.

"Pardon me," said Little Red Rooster.

"Certainly," returned Nanny Goat, "but do you HAVE to make all that noise?"

"I don't know," replied Little Red Rooster meekly.

"Well, please try to show better manners," advised Nanny Goat sharply.

Little Red Rooster was ever so sorry. He flew up into a tree and for a long time just sat there quietly. But the morning air was so sweet and the day promised to be so pleasant that before he knew it, well, you guessed it — out came another crow, "Er, er, er, er, errrrrr!"

129

"Dear me," said the farmer, opening one sleepy eye, turning on the light, and looking at the clock. "It is not time to get up. Little Red Rooster will have to learn that there is a time and place for everything." The farmer turned out the light and tried to get back to sleep.

"WHAT is wrong with Little Red Rooster?" asked Wolfie the watchdog.

"Yes, what IS wrong with Little Red Rooster?" asked Mooley Cow.

"I wonder what COULD be wrong with Little Red Rooster?" asked Nanny Goat.

But do YOU know? There was absolutely NOTHING wrong with Little Red Rooster. No, indeed! He was just like any other little red rooster who had to grow up, and his crow was a big part of growing up.

You see, if the truth must be known, roosters crow *just to hear themselves crow*. And Little Red Rooster was no different from all other little red roosters when he crowed, "Er, er, er, er, errrrrr!"

This story may be used for practice on the "r" speech sound. The children may draw, color, cut out, and back pictures to illustrate the story so it can also be used with the flannelboard.

TURKEY-URKEY

Turkey-Urkey was a handsome gobbler. His wattles were bright red and his feathers were a shiny black that glistened with rainbow colors when the sun shone on them. When he strutted, his tail feathers spread wide in a magnificent white-edged fan. His wings swept along the ground and made a rustling sound like dry leaves at autumn time.

One bright spring day, Turkey-Urkey decided to go for a walk. The sunshine was warm and pleasant. Turkey-Urkey felt so good that he began to strut. His tail feathers fanned out. His wing feathers spread wide. As he strutted, Turkey-Urkey gobbled to himself,

"What a gorgeous creature am I, am I,
What a gorgeous creature am I."

Red-Head the woodpecker sat high in a tall oak tree, drilling a hole. When he saw Turkey-Urkey strutting down the path gobbling to himself, he stopped drilling and began to laugh,

"Ha, ha, ha, and he, he, he!
You're the funniest turkey
I ever did see!"

Turkey-Urkey stopped strutting, looked curiously at Red-Head the woodpecker, and asked,

"Oh, dear, oh, dear! Oh, me, oh, me!
Why am I the funniest turkey
You ever did see?"

Red-Head the woodpecker answered,

"You should be red like my lovely head,
Red, red, red like my lovely head.
Red, red, red is what I said.
Go home, Turkey-Urkey, and dye yourself red."

Turkey-Urkey was so impressed with what Red-Head the woodpecker had said that he hurried back home and dyed himself red — as red as the woodpecker's head. Proudly he continued his walk, with his red feathers spread wide to catch the sunlight.

Mrs. Green Snake was crawling along the path when she saw Turkey-Urkey strutting toward her. She stopped,

coiled up into a ring, held her head high, and began to
laugh,

> "Ha, ha, ha, and he, he, he!
> You're the funniest turkey
> I ever did see!"

Turkey-Urkey looked down at Mrs. Green Snake and
asked,

> "Oh, dear, oh, dear! Oh, me, oh, me!
> Why am I the funniest turkey
> You ever did see?"

Mrs. Green Snake answered,

> "A turkey red is a sight to see!
> Green, green, green is the color to be,
> Green as the grass or the leaves on a tree.
> Go dye yourself green! Be green like me."

Turkey-Urkey was so impressed with what Mrs. Green
Snake had said that he hurried home and dyed himself
green — as green as the greenest snake. Proudly he continued his walk, with his green feathers spread wide to
catch the sunlight.

Quacky Duck was out hunting bugs for her lunch when
she saw Turkey-Urkey strutting toward her. She was so
astonished at seeing a green turkey, that she stopped stock-
still and began to laugh,

> "Ha, ha, ha, and he, he, he!
> You're the funniest turkey
> I ever did see!"

Turkey-Urkey stopped strutting and listened carefully
to Quacky Duck. Then he asked,

132

"Oh, dear, oh, dear! Oh, me, oh, me!
Why am I the funniest turkey
You ever did see?"

And Quacky Duck answered,

"Oh, your green feathers are strange to see.
Orange like my bill is the color to be,
Orange, bright orange; please be like me!
Go dye yourself orange, bright orange," said she.

Turkey-Urkey was so impressed with what Quacky
Duck had said that he hurried back home and dyed himself orange — as orange as the duck's long bill. Proudly
he resumed his walk, with his orange feathers spread wide
to catch the sunlight.

Grumpy Gopher had just popped up out of his hole
to get a breath of fresh air when he spied Turkey-Urkey
strutting down the path. He was so astonished at seeing an
orange turkey that he stopped sniffing the fresh air and
began to laugh,

"Ha, ha, ha, and he, he, he!
You're the funniest turkey
I ever did see."

Turkey-Urkey looked sadly at Grumpy Gopher and,
with a forlorn look in his eye, he asked,

"Oh, dear, oh, dear! Oh, me, oh, me!
Why am I the funniest turkey
You ever did see?"

Grumpy Gopher stopped laughing and replied,

"Orange is for pumpkins and not for you;
Brown is your color, I tell you true.
Be brown, plain brown like me; please do.
Go dye yourself brown, the color for you."

Turkey-Urkey was so impressed with what Grumpy Gopher said that he hurried back home and dyed himself brown — as brown as the gopher who lived in the brown earth. Proudly he continued his walk, with his brown feathers spread to catch the sunlight.

Mrs. Cow was chewing the sweet grass that grew among the wild purple violets. When she saw Turkey-Urkey strutting down the path, she was so astonished, that she stopped chewing grass and began to laugh,

"Ha, ha, ha, and he, he, he!
You're the funniest turkey
I ever did see!"

Turkey-Urkey stopped strutting and listened to Mrs. Cow, then asked,

"Oh, dear, oh, dear! Oh, me, oh, me!
Why am I the funniest turkey
You ever did see?"

Mrs. Cow replied,

"Brown is not your color, I fear
Purple is for you; be purple, my dear,
Purple like the violets growing here.
Go dye yourself purple! Be purple, my dear!"

Turkey-Urkey was so impressed with what Mrs. Cow had said that he hurried back home and dyed himself purple — as purple as the wild violets that grew among

134

the sweet blades of grass. Proudly he continued his walk, with his purple feathers spread wide to catch the sunlight.

Hoppy the frog was hopping along the path when he saw Turkey-Urkey strutting toward him. The sight of the purple turkey set him to laughing,

> "Ha, ha, ha, and he, he, he!
> You're the funniest turkey
> I ever did see!"

Turkey-Urkey looked down at Hoppy the frog and asked,

> "Oh, dear, oh, dear! Oh, me, oh, me!
> Why am I the funniest turkey
> You ever did see?
>
> I've dyed myself brown, orange, green, purple,
>   and red,
> As red as the redheaded woodpecker's head.
> I've tried to make each friend I met glad,
> But making them glad has been making me sad."

Hoppy the frog replied,

> "Perhaps, friend, you've learned what I know to
>   be true.
> What is fine for another, may not do for you.
> One cannot please all; sometimes, only a few.
> Now go home and change yourself back into you."

Now, Turkey-Urkey was very impressed by what Hoppy the frog had said. He did not hurry back home, but walked slowly, very slowly, thinking about what Hoppy the frog had said. By the time he reached his home, he knew why he had been a funny-looking turkey. He washed off the purple color so that his shiny black

feathers once more glistened with the colors of the rainbow when the sun shone on them. Proudly he continued
his walk, with his feathers spread wide to catch the sunlight. As he walked, he gobbled to himself,

> "Ha, ha, ha, and he, he, he!
> I'm happy Turkey-Urkey,
> Who likes being me."

—J.J.T.

This story presents the "r" sound initially in *red;* medially in
Turkey, orange, and *purple;* and as part of a consonant blend in
brown and *green.* The repetitive refrains can be learned quickly
by the children. The story lends itself well to the flannelboard.

THE ROUND, ROUND PUMPKIN

The round, round pumpkin wanted to do something.
He was tired of lying in the pumpkin patch when it was
so near Thanksgiving, so he decided to roll away.

> He rolley, rolley, rolley, rolled,
> And rolley, rolley, rolley, rolled,
> And rolley, rolley, rolley, rolled.

The round, round pumpkin bumped into a chicken
that was pecking for seeds.

"Peep!" cried the frightened chicken. She ran home
to her mother. "Mother, mother," said the frightened
chicken. "Something dreadful, round, orange, and scary
bumped into me."

The mother hen said, "Stay close beside me and do
not be afraid. Nothing can harm you." So the mother
hen sat down, ruffled out her feathers, and the little
chicken crawled underneath them and was no longer
afraid.

The round, round pumpkin kept rolling.

He rolley, rolley, rolley, rolled,
And rolley, rolley, rolley, rolled,
And rolley, rolley, rolley, rolled.

And the round, round pumpkin brushed past a fat puppy who put his tail between his legs and skittled home to his mother.

"Yipe!" cried the fat puppy. "Something dreadful, round, orange and scary almost ran over me."

The mother dog said, "Woof, woof, my little puppy. Lie down beside me and do not tremble so. I am your mother, you know, and nothing can harm you here."

And the fat puppy stopped trembling and shivering and shaking, and soon he was snoozing.

The round, round pumpkin kept rolling.

He rolley, rolley, rolley, rolled,
And rolley, rolley, rolley, rolled,
And rolley, rolley, rolley, rolled.

And he rolled right between a horse's tall legs. The horse was not scared at all. He said to himself, "Mmmmmmm! That is odd. I have never seen a pumpkin rolling along like that before."

The round, round pumpkin kept right on rolling.

He rolley, rolley, rolley, rolled,
And rolley, rolley, rolley, rolled,
And rolley, rolley, rolley, rolled.

Suddenly there was a pussycat right in the pumpkin's path. The pussycat's back went up. Her whiskers stuck out straight and she said, "Spit-spat, spit-spat!" But it did no good.

The round, round pumpkin just rolled on.

He rolley, rolley, rolley, rolled,
And rolley, rolley, rolley, rolled,
And rolley, rolley, rolley, rolled.

And he rolled right up to a farmhouse door, and there he stopped! Out came the farmer's wife and she picked up the round, round pumpkin.

"How fine!" she exclaimed. "This is the most nearly perfect pumpkin I have ever seen. I will use it for a table decoration with some bright autumn leaves."

So the round, round pumpkin, pleased with himself, sat in a very important place right in the middle of the table on Thanksgiving Day!

—L.B.S.

The children gain practice on the "r" speech sound in the words "round," "rolley," and "rolled." They may whirl their hands in imitation of a pumpkin rolling. The ending may be changed for use at Halloween, with the pumpkin becoming a jack-o'-lantern.

FRISKY PONY

Frisky Pony was a beautiful, high-spirited black pony with a soft brown-and-white mane and tail. Like all ponies, he enjoyed running and galloping, and, oh, he was SO frisky. That is why he was called Frisky Pony.

It was a delight to see Frisky Pony trotting about the barnyard, with his head held high and his silky tail waving, and then to watch him break into a brisk run.

But Frisky Pony, though there were many people around the farm, still did not have a master. It was no fun running without a master who could guide him here and there and enjoy the running, too.

Now Frisky Pony had heard the name Robert somewhere. He was not quite sure where he had heard it, but he had sharp ears that stood up to catch sounds. One day, as Frisky was listening to nothing in particular, he heard "Robert — Robert — Robert." (*Soft voice.*)

"What a good name!" remarked Frisky Pony. "That is the name I want for my master, and I think I will go looking for Robert right now."

138

Frisky Pony began to run. He ran, ran, ran, ran, ran! (*Children repeat.*) His four little hoofs went clickety-clack, but there was no Robert to ride on his back.

Frisky Pony said, "If I run over the hill on the other side of the mill, maybe I will find Robert." So he ran, ran, ran, ran, ran, ran, ran. (*Children repeat.*)

A bulldog came along. "Gurrrrrrr— growl," growled the bulldog. "You almost ran over me. Watch your heels, you frisky, risky pony."

Frisky Pony stopped still. "Oh, I *am* sorry," he apologized. "I am running to find a new master named Robert. Have you seen him?"

The bulldog replied, "Robert? Robert? Let me see! Robert's a very nice name to be. No, Robert does not occur to me." (*Children repeat.*)

Frisky Pony said, "I have four hoofs that go clickety-clack, and I must have Robert to ride on my back." (*Children repeat.*)

"Well," said the bulldog, "run, run, run, run, run, run, run. Run, Frisky Pony, run!" (*Children repeat.*)

Frisky Pony began to run. He ran, ran, ran, ran, ran, ran, ran. (*Children repeat.*)

He met a rooster. The rooster crowed, "Er, er, er, er, er, errrrrrr! Where are you going, Frisky Pony?"

"I am running to find a master named Robert," replied Frisky Pony. "Have you seen him?"

The rooster replied, "Robert? Robert? Let me see! Robert's a very nice name to be. No, Robert does not occur to me." (*Children repeat.*)

Frisky Pony said, "I have four hoofs that go clickety-clack, and I must have Robert to ride on my back." (*Children repeat.*)

"Well," said the rooster, "run, run, run, run, run, run, run. Run, Frisky Pony, run!"

Frisky Pony began to run again. He ran, ran, ran, ran, ran, ran, ran. (*Children repeat.*)

Frisky Pony had run for a long time, and he had to stop and rest under the shade of a tree. As he was resting, he heard a "hello" in the distance. His ears turned toward the sound, and there he saw a little boy running toward him. The little boy had a halter in his hand.

He said, "Hello, Frisky Pony. Would you like a master?"

"Oh, yes," said Frisky Pony. "I have four hoofs that go clickety-clack, but I have no Robert to ride on my back. (*Children repeat.*) Is your name Robert, by any chance?"

"Why, however did you guess?" asked Robert. "Of course my name is Robert."

"Then please climb on my back," said Frisky Pony, "and we will run, run, run, run, run." (*Children repeat.*)

Frisky Pony was happy that he had a master, especially one named Robert, and with Robert on his back Frisky Pony ran, ran, ran, ran, ran, ran, ran. (*Children repeat.*)

In the distance, a voice called, "Robert — Robert — Robert."

Frisky Pony heard the voice and so did Robert. But it was a sound Frisky Pony had heard before.

"My mother is calling," said Robert to Frisky Pony. "I will take you home as a surprise."

"What shall we do now?" asked Frisky Pony, knowing exactly what Robert would say.

Robert replied, "Run, run, run, run, run, run, run. Run, Frisky Pony, run!" (*Children repeat.*)

—L.B.S. AND J.J.T.

The repetition of *run* and *ran* provides practice on the "r" sound and also illustrates the correct past tense of the verb *run*. Some children at the primary level use *runned* as the past tense of *run*.

Songs about ponies are "My Pony" and "Circus Ponies," from *Singing Fun* and *More Singing Fun,* Lucille F. Wood and Louise Binder Scott, Webster Division, McGraw-Hill Book Company.

THE CURIOUS, FURIOUS LION

Once there was a Curious, Furious Lion, and there was a red ribbon tied upon his ear!

"Errrrrrr! Grrrrrrr-owl! Rrrrrrrr-ow!" (*Children imitate.*)

The Curious, Furious Lion had tied the big red ribbon on his ear all by himself, though I cannot imagine HOW. The big red ribbon was tied by the Curious, Furious Lion, but he had forgotten why. He had forgotten why he had tied the great big red ribbon on his ear — his left ear — and he had forgotten when. So the Curious, Furious Lion growled,

> "A ribbon, a ribbon! Oh, dear, oh, dear!
> Why IS this red ribbon on my left ear?"
> (*Children repeat.*)

The Curious, Furious Lion knew the red ribbon was there all right. He could feel it when he turned his head. He could see it in the looking-glass water when he went to the brook to have a drink.

This made the Curious, Furious Lion more and more curious and more and more furious, and the more curious and the more furious he became, the more fiercely he growled,

> "A ribbon, a ribbon! Oh, dear, oh, dear!
> Why IS this red ribbon on my left ear?"

"Perhaps someone has played a trick on me," said the Curious, Furious Lion. "It is possible that I did not tie the ribbon on my left ear at all."

So right away, he made up his mind to find out. And he skulked away muttering to himself,

> "A ribbon, a ribbon! Oh, dear, oh, dear!
> Who TIED this red ribbon on my left ear?"

As the Curious, Furious Lion ambled and scrambled along, he saw a mischievous monkey hanging by his long tail from the branch of a tall coconut tree.

"You mischievous monkey, you," growled the Curious, Furious Lion. "Have you been up to some monkey business? Did YOU put this great big red ribbon on my left ear?"

The mischievous monkey jumped to the ground and peered at the red ribbon. Then he said, "No! I tell you true. Tie a red ribbon on a lion's ear? Why, that I would NEVER do. If I am not telling you the truth, you may tie two red ribbons on my tail."

Strangely enough, the Curious, Furious Lion believed the mischievous monkey, and he skulked away trying to remember and muttering to himself,

"A ribbon, a ribbon! Oh, dear, oh, dear!
Why IS this red ribbon on my left ear?"

Then the growling, scowling, yowling lion — the Curious, Furious Lion — saw an elephant.

"Aha!" cried the Curious, Furious Lion to the lumbersome, cumbersome elephant. "You lumbersome, cumbersome elephant, did YOU tie this great big red ribbon on my left ear?"

The elephant felt the red ribbon with the tip of his long serpentine trunk and then said, "No! I tell you true. Tie a red ribbon on a lion's ear? That I would NEVER do. If I am not telling you the truth, you may tie three red ribbons around my trunk — my long serpentine trunk."

The Curious, Furious Lion believed the lumbersome, cumbersome elephant, and he skulked away saying to himself,

"A ribbon, a ribbon! Oh, dear, oh, dear!
Why IS this red ribbon on my left ear?"

As he was muttering and sputtering and mumbling and grumbling, he heard a song. The Curious, Furious Lion stood stock-still in his tracks and listened. Out of the bushes came his friends singing,

"Merry Christmas, good friend lion.
We are glad that you are here
To attend the Christmas party
With a ribbon on your ear."

And as the animals and birds and reptiles gathered around, the Curious, Furious Lion KNEW. And the Curious, Furious Lion was just FURIOUS at himself and awfully CURIOUS that he could possibly forget something as important as a Christmas party, especially when he had tied the great big red ribbon on his left ear to help him remember. But then he thought about Christmas, and he twitched his left ear and growled happily, "Errrrrr! Grrrrrr-owl! Rrrrrr-ow!" And that is exactly what lions are supposed to do.

—L.B.S.

Suggested figures for the flannelboard are a lion with ribbon on his ear, a monkey, an elephant, and any other jungle creatures the children may wish to draw, color, and back with adhesive. They may take turns placing figures on the board as the story is told. The repetition makes it easy for children to follow and join in the telling of the story. The clearly and simply described events lend themselves to almost immediate retelling or to creative dramatics.

ROBERT AND THE WOODPECKER

One day, Robert was sitting under a leafy tree thinking about the blue sky and the clouds that looked like vanilla ice-cream cones, when he saw a baby bird on the ground. It was a baby woodpecker that had fallen from its nest.

"Poor baby woodpecker," said Robert. "I wonder where your mother and father are?"

Robert watched and waited, but he saw no mother or father woodpecker, so he picked up the baby woodpecker and took it home with him. Robert gave it water with an eye dropper, and he found some grubs for it to eat. After a time, Robert saw by the red feathers on the little bird's head that it would be a father woodpecker. Robert named him Red-Head.

Now woodpeckers do not like to stay indoors or in a cage. They like to fly about freely, prop themselves on poles or trees, and peck for their food. So one day, when Robert came home from school, he discovered that his friend Red-Head was gone! Robert was unhappy even though he knew the woodpecker was happier not being a pet.

To keep himself from getting too lonesome for Red-Head, Robert drew a picture of a woodpecker and hung it in his room. But Robert found that a picture was a poor substitute for a real live woodpecker. Then one afternoon many weeks later, while Robert was thinking about his friend, he heard a noise:

> "Rat-a-tat-tat. Rat-a-tat-tat.
> RRRRRRRRR-at-a-tat-tat!"
> (*Children participate.*)

Robert looked out the window, and there was Red-Head drilling away at the bark of the tree. The chips flew as his bill went:

"Rat-a-tat-tat. Rat-a-tat-tat.
RRRRRRRR-at-a-tat-tat!"

"Red-Head! Red-Head!" called Robert. But the wood-pecker kept drilling:

"Rat-a-tat-tat. Rat-a-tat-tat.
RRRRRRRR-at-a-tat-tat!"

Woodpeckers, as you know, feed on bugs that harm trees. They are especially fond of beetles and grasshoppers. Sometimes they make a cupboard in a tree and put their food into it. Red-Head had a tongue that was about twice as long as his body, and that tongue ended in a sharp point with barbs on the sides of the point to help him spear food easily.

Actually Red-Head was now a father with responsibilities, and he was finding grubs for his baby woodpeckers. Even though he heard Robert's voice, he could not think of two things at once, and he kept right on drilling:

"Rat-a-tat-tat. Rat-a-tat-tat.
RRRRRRRRR-at-a-tat-tat!"

One Saturday several weeks later, Robert and his father and mother decided to have a picnic in the woods. It was a lovely warm day, and after the family had eaten lunch and had put out the campfire with some water from a nearby spring, they sat under a shady tree and rested. Robert slipped away to look for something — just anything interesting that he could take to school on Monday morning. He found dozens of acorns and stuffed his pockets full of them. Then he went farther into the woods chasing a butterfly that could fly much faster than Robert could run. Finally Robert gave up the chase.

As he was sitting on a log resting, Robert suddenly realized that he was LOST. Have you ever had that feeling? It is not a good feeling at all.

Robert sat for what seemed hours on the log trying to decide what to do, and then — and then — he heard a familiar sound:

> "Rat-a-tat-tat. Rat-a-tat-tat.
> RRRRRRRR-at-a-tat-tat!"

Oh, joy! It was Red-Head. Now Robert didn't feel alone anymore. What a wonderful sound!

> "Rat-a-tat-tat. Rat-a-tat-tat.
> RRRRRRRR-at-a-tat-tat!"

Red-Head flew from tree to tree, drilling on each one so Robert would hear him, and at last Red-Head led Robert out of the woods and into the clearing where his family was waiting.

Red-Head still didn't want to be an indoor pet, but often he would fly back to the tree just outside Robert's window and begin drilling, just to remind Robert that woodpeckers can be very special friends.

—L.B.S.

Ask the class to make the woodpecker sound each time it occurs in the story. To stimulate conversation, ask the children to tell what they have learned and know about woodpeckers.

$$\frac{1}{\underline{l}eaf}$$

MAKING THE SPEECH SOUND

Let the lower jaw drop down to the position for producing "ah." Raise the tip of the tongue to press lightly against the alveolar ridge behind the upper teeth. The vocal cords vibrate and the soft palate is raised. The width of the mouth opening will vary according to the vowel preceding or following the "l" speech sound. This sound is one of the three most frequently misarticulated speech sounds in the English language. Usual substitutions are "w" (*wamp* for *lamp*) and "y" (*yamp* for *lamp*). Certain oriental races substitute "r" for "l" or "l" for "r" (*right* for *light* and *lun* for *run*).

You may call "l" the "singing-wind," "elevator," or "telephone-wires" sound.

CORRECTING THE DEFICIENT SPEECH SOUND

First show, by example, where the tongue tip should be placed to produce "l." Ask the child to look into a mirror to note his own tip-of-tongue position. As soon as he has done this, ask him to say "lah" to feel the correct movement of the tongue. Lifting and lowering the tongue will increase agility and enable the child to blend smoothly from a consonant sound to a variety of vowel sounds, e.g., *lah, lee, lie, low, loo.* From those syllables, the child may then proceed to words such as *lamb, look,* and *leaf.* Defer practice on the *l* consonant blends, *kl* (cl), *bl, fl, gl, pl,* and *sl,* until the child is able to produce a clear "l" in combination with a vowel sound.

INSTRUCTIONS TO THE CHILD

"Can you see my tongue tip go up high and rest on the shelf behind my upper teeth? Try it. Look into this mirror to see if your tongue tip can rise high and touch your shelf. Hold your tongue tip there and making a 'singing' sound with me, 'Llllllll.' Now pretend your tongue tip is an elevator going up to the top floor."

My tongue is an elevator;
Here it comes.
It stays on the very top floor and hums.
"Llllllllllll."
My elevator tongue goes down to the ground;
Then it rises again and makes this sound.
"Llllllllllll."

—L.B.S.

"Pretend you are a mockingbird and say these funny syllables after me: *La-la, loo-loo, lee-lee, luh-luh, lay-lay, ull-ull, ill-ill, all-all, ell-ell, illy-illy, ellow-ellow.* Your pinky tongue had to work very hard to do that."

Note: Some children have difficulty in pronouncing the "l" speech sound in final position. Usual mispronunciations are *schoo* for *school, beh* for *bell,* and *haw* for *hall.* Be sure, however, that the child does not pronounce the "l" in isolation at the end of a word, e.g., *schoo-ul* and *haw-ul* for *school* and *hall.*

WORDS FOR PRACTICE

Initial	*Medial*	*Final*
lamb	yellow	bell
letter	sailor	will
lock	jelly	full
lump	children	hill
left	soldier	shell
light	ruler	seal

USING THE "I HEAR IT" DEVICE

The following "I Hear It" rhyme contains not only the speech sound which the child should be producing but also various speech sounds ("w," "r," and "y") which he may be substituting for "l." Distinguishing separate speech sounds from one another and identifying them in words are initial steps toward the correction of any articulation defect.

Read the selection slowly, pronouncing the speech sounds plainly. Ask the class or an individual child to make the isolated sound when it occurs. The second time the selection is read, ask the children to repeat each line after you have said it. Always prolong the speech sound whenever possible so that it may be identified more easily.

I HEAR IT

I hear it in *lag* but not in *wag*.
I hear it in *lake* but not in *wake*.
I hear it in *lead* but not in *weed*.
    I hear it in *lest* but not in *west*.
    I hear it in *let* but not in *wet*.
    My tongue tip goes up and it sits on the shelf;
    I can make a singing sound all by myself.
    "Lll— lll— lll."

I hear it in *lung* but not in *rung*.
I hear it in *lug* but not in *rug*.
I hear it in *long* but not in *wrong*.
　　I hear it in *lard* but not in *yard*.
　　I hear it in *least* but not in *yeast*.
　　My tongue tip goes up and it sits on the shelf;
　　I can make a singing sound all by myself.
　　"Lll— lll— lll."

—L.B.S.

ARE WE LISTENING?

See the explanations on how to use the "Are We Listening?" device, page 81.

1. *Larry* went to the circus. He saw a *clown* eat a *large lemon*. The clown pretended he was *lazy* and *leaned* against his pet *lamb*. The *clown* then *led* a *leopard* around the ring. He *led* a *lizard* tied to a string. Were we listening? Let's see! What did the clown eat? What animals did he lead around the ring? What animal was tied to a string? What did the clown do to the lamb? Who ate a large lemon? Who went to the circus?

2. *Sally listened* and *listened*. She *listened* to a *lark* sing. She *listened* to her mother say, "I *love* you, *Sally*." She *listened* to a *lady* at the *library* read a story. She *listened* to her baby brother *laugh*. Were we listening? Let's see! What bird sang to Sally? What did Sally's mother say to her? Who read a story to Sally? What did her baby brother do? Where was the lady who read a story to Sally?

3. One day, Mrs. *Lee* went to the attic and found some very *old* things. She found a big *loom* that wove *cloth*. She found a *lantern* hanging on a hook. She found a *language* book in an *old leather* case. She found some

letters that were written fifty years ago. Were we listening? Let's see! What kind of book did Mrs. Lee find? What things did she find that were written fifty years ago? Who went up to the attic? Were the things she found new? What did she find that wove cloth? Where did she find the language book?

—L.B.S.

ELEVATOR RIDE

The elevator goes up
To the very top floor.
 "Lllllllllllll!"
  (*Children prolong the sound.*)
It comes to a stop
And lets the people out the door.
Going down, going down,
Going down, please!
 "Lllllllllllll!"
Just step right inside,
But be careful not to squeeze!
 "Lllllllllllllll! (*Voice goes up.*)
 Lllllllllllllll!" (*Voice goes down.*)
  —L.B.S.

Remind the children that the tip of the tongue is held against the little shelf behind the upper teeth when they make the "l" speech sound.

TELEPHONE WIRES

From my house to your house to homes everywhere
The sound of our voices can speed through the air.
 "Lllll— lllll— lllll!"
Sing little wires, your story to tell.
Sing little wires. "Lllllllllll!"

Just pick up the telephone, dial, then wait.
Your call will go through whether early or late.
     "Lllll— lllll— lllll!"
     Sing little wires, your story to tell.
     Sing little wires. "Lllllllllll!"
Out over the wires that stretch near and far,
Your phone calls will follow wherever you are.
     "Lllll— lllll— lllll!"
     Sing little wires, your story to tell.
     Sing little wires. "Lllllllllll!"
And what fun to count, as we travel along,
The poles with the wires that sing your gay song.
     "Lllll— lllll— lllll!"
     Sing little wires, your story to tell.
     Sing little wires. "Lllllllllll!"

—J.J.T.

The children may join in on the refrain. The "l" sound should
be prolonged each time it occurs in order to give the children sufficient time to feel the correct placement of the tongue tip on the
ridge behind the upper teeth.

CLOWNS

A clown is very funny.
He wears such funny clothes.
ALL: La, la, lee,
      He wears such funny clothes.

He has a funny mouth
Beneath a funny nose.
ALL: La, la, lee,
      Beneath a funny nose.

Some clowns are very tall,
And some are very fat.
ALL: La, la, lee,
      And some are very fat.

And where their hair should be
Is a funny little hat.
ALL: La, la, lee,
        Is a funny little hat.

Clowns wear enormous shoes
That flip-flop up and down.
ALL: La, la, lee,
        That flip-flop up and down.

It's fun to be so funny.
I think I'll be a clown!
ALL: La, la, lee,
        I think I'll be a clown!

                                   —J.J.T.

Pantomime this rhyme with the children as you encourage them
to use their bodies freely. The children gain practice on the "l"
sound in "La, la, lee."

LITTLE WIND

Little wind blow on the meadow;
Little wind blow on the trees.
Little wind blow on the desert;
Little wind blow on the seas.
Little wind blow on the cities;
Little wind blow on the town.
Little wind blow on the orchard;
Little wind blow the leaves down!

                                   —L.B.S.

The two repetitive words, *little* and *blow,* contain the "l" sound.
To add variety to the use of this selection, let half the class accom-
pany the poem by singing the syllable "la." The children begin
on the first tone of the scale and ascend one step with each successive
line of the poem. The rest of the class recites the poem and then
takes a turn at singing.

LIZZIE WAS A LIZARD

Lizzie was a lizard who could not say her name,
A lizard, a lizard who could not say her name;
But Lizzie learned how with the looking-glass game,
The looking-glass, the looking-glass, the looking-
glass game.
She practiced and she practiced, and it was lots of fun,
And now she can say "Lizzie" as well as anyone!

—L.B.S.

After the rhyme has been read to the children, ask them to take turns looking in a mirror to see if they can say Lizzie's name. This type of observation invites practice and a desire to correct the deficient speech sound. Use other animals whose names have the "l" sound: *Leo* was a *lion* and *Leppy* was a *leopard*. Play the "looking-glass game" by asking individual children to name words which begin with "l" as they watch themselves in a mirror.

IN THE LOOKING GLASS

I see my face in the looking glass,
When I look, look, look
In the looking glass.
I look at my hair,
And I see my ears there,
On the left and the right,
For I have a pair
In the look-look-looking glass!

I see my face in the looking glass,
When I look, look, look
In the looking glass.
I see two round eyes
That are full of surprise,
One left and one right,
And bluer than skies
In the look-look-looking glass!

154

I see my face in the looking glass,
When I look, look, look
In the looking glass.
I see a small nose,
And I see my chin,
And I see a red mouth
Where the food goes in,
In the look-look-looking glass!

I see my face in the looking glass,
When I look, look, look
In the looking glass.
Sometimes I smile,
And sometimes I frown,
But a smile is a frown
Turned upside down
In the look-look-looking glass!

—L.B.S.

This rhyme is learned easily by rote because of the repetition of words like *look* and *looking glass* which provide practice on the "l" speech sound. Each child may describe himself as he looks in the looking glass.

WHAT IS LOW?

Low is my stool which has three legs;
Low is the nest where the duck lays her eggs.

Low is my voice when I talk with you;
Low is the sound of a black cow's moo.

Low is the gas when there's not very much;
Low you must bend when your feet you do touch.

Low are the books on my bookcase shelf;
Low is the bench that I made for myself.

Low is a pretty, soft lullaby;
Low is the opposite of high!

—L.B.S.

Ask the children to name something else that is low. Listen for the "l" sound in *low*. This rhyme may be used to teach the concepts *low* and *high*.

A YARN TOLD WITH YARN

Once upon a time there was a little old farm, and on that little old farm there was a little old animal. You must guess what the little old animal was.

Was it a little old goat
With a rough, shaggy coat?

CHILDREN: (*Respond negatively.*)

It had a little old head,
   (*Place oval of yarn on board.*)
But no little old horns.
It had little old ears,
   (*Add small circles of yarn to head for ears.*)
And it liked to eat corn!

It had a little old body
   (*Attach long strip to head to make animal's back.*)
That was sleek and long.

156

That little old animal
Was very strong.
   (*Add underneath part of body.*)

Was it a little old donkey
That makes a loud bray?

CHILDREN: (*Respond negatively.*)

No, not a little old donkey,
But it did like hay.

It had little old legs,
   (*Add four strips of yarn for legs.*)
Two eyes, of course,
   (*Add round circles for eyes.*)
And well, you have guessed!
It was a little old HORSE!
   (*Add strips for tail.*)
                —L.B.S.

Cut strips of heavy yarn of different lengths and let the children take turns putting them on the flannelboard to create the figure of the horse as the story is told. The children will enjoy making their own figures with yarn strips. The repetitive word *little* contains the "l" speech sound in initial and final position.

BALLOONS

Eight balloons . . . I'll sell them to you.
Red and yellow and green and blue;
An orange one, a brown one, a purple one, too;
And here is a black one . . . I'll sell them to you.

Who will buy my blue balloon, as blue as the heaven?
Take it away . . . now there are seven.

Who will buy my brown balloon, brown like many sticks?
Take it away . . . now there are six.
Who will buy my red balloon, a color so alive?
Take it away . . . now there are five.
Who will buy my purple balloon? There are not many
more.
Take it away . . . now there are four.
Who will buy my green balloon, as green as any tree?
Take it away . . . now there are three.
Who will buy my orange balloon? I have so very few!
Take it away . . . now there are two.
Who will buy my yellow balloon, as yellow as the sun?
Take it away . . . now there is one.
Who will buy my black balloon? Now we are done.
Take it away . . . now there are none.

—J.J.T.

Cut out construction-paper balloon shapes to place on the flannelboard as the rhyme is said by the class. Words which have the "l" speech sound are: *balloon, yellow, blue, purple,* and *black.* As you ask the question, one child replies, "I will buy your blue balloon." He then places it on the flannelboard.

THE LOVELIEST SOUNDS IN THE WORLD [2]

Out on the green, green grass in the sleepy, sleepy meadow, the animals, the birds, the snakes, and the insects were resting in the warm sun and listening to the sounds around them.

Oh, there were many sounds in that sleepy meadow. There were mooing sounds, hissing sounds, neighing sounds, quacking sounds, puffing sounds, murmuring sounds, quiet sounds, mysterious sounds, and sounds loud,

---

[2] From *Time for Phonics Paper-Bag Puppet Patterns,* Webster Division, McGraw-Hill Book Company, 1963.

medium, and small. And those sounds were not all. Not all by any means!

"Lllllll," sang the pretty wind as it blew through the leaves on the trees.

"Shhhhhhhhh!" said the goat with a shaggy coat.

"Shhhhhhhhh!" whispered the grasshoppers and beetles and fireflies.

"Quiet, quiet!" said the birds.

"Sssssssstill," said the snake.

"Lllllllll," sang the singing wind again.

Suddenly there appeared a pair of pointed, pointed shoes that sat right down on the green, green grass in the sleepy, sleepy meadow. (*Place shoes on board.*)

The animals, the birds, the snakes, and the insects grew very quiet. "How strange," they all said, "to see two pointed, pointed shoes sitting on the green, green grass in this sleepy, sleepy meadow."

"Lllllllll," sang the singing wind again, and simply out of NOWHERE there appeared two long, long legs that sat right down on the pointed, pointed shoes on the green, green grass in the sleepy, sleepy meadow. (*Place legs on board. Children say refrain with you.*)

"Oh, how VERY STRANGE!" they all whispered.

Then the wind sang again as it rustled the leaves on the trees. "Lllllllllll," it sang. And there appeared a short, short jacket that sat right down on the long, long legs on the pointed, pointed shoes on the green, green grass in the sleepy, sleepy meadow. (*Place jacket on board.*)

"How EXTRAORDINARY!" they exclaimed.

"Lllllllll," sang the pretty singing wind, and COMPLETELY out of nowhere there appeared two long, long sleeves that sat right down on the short, short jacket on the long, long legs on the pointed, pointed shoes on the green, green grass in the sleepy, sleepy meadow. (*Attach sleeves to jacket.*)

159

"How MARVELOUS!" they all whispered, and they wondered at what was happening.

"Lllllllll," sang the singing wind again, and out of nowhere, SIMPLY OUT OF NOWHERE, there appeared two helpful, helpful hands that sat right down on the long, long sleeves on the short, short jacket on the long, long legs on the pointed, pointed shoes on the green, green grass in the sleepy, sleepy meadow. (*Attach hands to sleeves.*)

"Oh!" said the animals, the birds, the snakes, and the insects softly, for they had no words with which to express themselves. Oh, the wonder of it all!

Once more the singing wind made a lovely sound: "Lllllllllll." It sang again. "Lllllllllll." (*Children imitate.*)

There appeared a jolly, jolly face that sat right down on the short, short jacket with the long, long sleeves, and the helpful, helpful hands, and the long, long legs, and the pointed, pointed shoes on the green, green grass in the sleepy, sleepy meadow. (*Place head on body.*)

Then as suddenly as it began, the wind stopped singing, and for a long time nothing moved or made a sound. The animals in the sleepy, sleepy meadow scarcely dared to breathe. It was SO quiet. It was so VERY quiet. It was quieter than quiet.

Then the goat with a shaggy coat broke the silence. "Who are you?" he asked the creature.

"I am an elf," it replied, bowing low. "My name is Soundie."

"That is a charming name," said the snake.

"How do you happen to have the name of Soundie?" asked the insects.

Soundie replied, "I am interested in sounds — all sounds everywhere. I like loud sounds and medium sounds and small sounds. That is why my name is Soundie. I have three pairs of ears, as you can see. They are quite helpful, as you will agree when I tell you that I use all three." And

160

Soundie laid three pairs of ears down on the green, green grass. (*Place three pairs of ears on the board.*)

Soundie went on. "Here are my tiny, tiny listening ears." (*Place them beside Soundie's head.*) "When I wear these tiny, tiny listening ears, I can hear the loudest sounds. I have to wear these ears because loud sounds would harm my big or medium-sized listening ears."

"Oh, yes," everyone agreed.

"With these tiny listening ears, I can hear a cannon on the Fourth of July and a big plane zoom across the sky. I can hear rumbles of thunder before the rain. I can hear the whistle on a streamlined train."

Soundie took off his tiny, tiny listening ears and put on his great big ones. (*Place large ears beside head.*)

Soundie said, "With my big listening ears, I can hear sounds far, far away on any kind of day. I can hear a fat worm crawling under the ground and the smallest insect making a happy sound. I can hear a baby chick inside its shell getting ready to hatch, and a little seed growing in a pumpkin patch. I can hear a whisper on top of a mountain a long way off, and I can hear a grasshopper sneeze and even cough. I can hear people blink their eyes, and I can even hear the tiptoeing of flies."

All of the animals and insects and birds and snakes took a deep breath and waited for Soundie to continue.

"With my middle-sized, everyday listening ears," said Soundie, "I can hear the loveliest sounds in the whole world." (*Place middle-sized ears beside head.*)

"Have you found the loveliest sounds in the whole world?" they asked.

"I have indeed," replied Soundie, "and if you will follow me, I will share those sounds with you."

So away went the animals, the birds, the insects, and the snakes, following Soundie across the meadow until they came to a school.

The animals, the birds, the insects, and the snakes peered through the window and they saw — CHILDREN. Thirty-one children! And those children were standing ever so quietly, and each child had his hand over his heart.

"What are they doing?" asked the goat curiously.

"They are getting ready to say the Pledge of Allegiance to the flag," said Soundie.

The children began, and they said the Pledge of Allegiance without missing a single word. I am sure that you can say the Pledge of Allegiance, too.

The snake said, "Why, the children are making many sounds — loud, medium, and soft sounds — but mostly medium sounds. And they are making high and low sounds, and some of the sounds are like music."

"Yes," said Soundie. "The children are speaking the English language, and it is a musical language. It has many sounds, and the sounds all blend together to form words — thousands of words that we use when we read and talk and write and spell. Words help us to communicate."

"COMMUNICATE?" they asked.

"That means," explained Soundie, "that we ask questions and give answers, and read poems aloud, and write messages, and tell stories, and whisper secrets, and listen. There are dancing-prancing words and singing-winging words and long-strong words and short words and serious and wise words and polite words. There are strange and unusual words and precious words. There are mad, sad, and glad words. We need words to communicate. Words are spoken or read from books or written on paper. And the words have many sounds."

"How many sounds?" they all asked.

"About forty," said Soundie. "Some day I will capture all of those sounds because they are so lovely. And I think I will start to gather the sounds now if you will excuse me."

162

So Soundie took his leave and went back to his golden toadstool in the meadow by the catnip bed. He found a bit of leather and he cut and stitched until he had made a little leather treasure bag to hold the sounds.

Then Soundie set about finding the sounds — the loveliest sounds in the world — the sounds that you and I make when we talk. What do YOU think was the first sound that Soundie put into his wonderful treasure bag?

—L.B.S.

This story may be used for the "l" sound, for relaxation, and to emphasize sensory perception. Let the children draw and cut out their own patterns for a flannelboard Soundie, or use the professional patterns available in the *Time for Phonics Paper-Bag Puppet Patterns,* Webster Division, McGraw-Hill Book Company, 1963.

THE LOST SONG

Little Girl sat all by herself on the porch step of the farmhouse in which she lived.

Her coat was torn,
And her shoes were worn.

Little Girl was sad because she had no song. No song at all.

"I want to sing," said Little Girl, "but I have forgotten how. I have forgotten how to sing."

The robin sang its song.

The thrush sang, too.

The wind sang softly, softly, softly as it whispered through the leaves of a tall cottonwood tree.

There were songs everywhere.

Yes, there were songs everywhere, except on the porch step of the farmhouse.

For Little Girl could not sing. She had forgotten how. She had forgotten how to sing!

Now, in a deep, dark part of the forest, Lovely Song could not find a place to belong. Lovely Song drifted here and there, among the forest trees, and as it went from place to place, it sang:

La   la la la   la

Loo loo loo loo   loo

But it was true as the sun and the moon and the forest trees that Lovely Song was lost.

Lovely Song indeed was lost.

Lost, lost, lost!

"Do I belong to you?" Lovely Song asked the sparkling brook that flowed nearby.

The brook listened to Lovely Song. (*Repeat song.*)

"No," replied the brook as it trickled over the smooth stones. "No, you do not belong to me. You are so lovely. I wish you did. I wish you were my lovely song."

Lovely Song drifted toward the meadow.

"Do I belong to you?" Lovely Song asked the meadowlark.

The meadowlark listened to Lovely Song. (*Repeat song.*)

"No," said the meadowlark. "No, you do not belong to me. You are so lovely, I wish you did. I wish you were my lovely song."

Lovely Song said sadly, "I am a song, so I must belong. I must belong to someone."

164

Lovely Song drifted from the meadow to the farm-house.

On the porch step sat Little Girl.

> Her coat was torn,
> And her shoes were worn.

"Do I belong to you?" asked Lovely Song.

Little Girl listened to Lovely Song. (*Repeat song.*)

Little Girl smiled. "Yes, you belong to me," she said. "I had forgotten how to sing. But you have helped me to remember. Yes, you belong to me, Lovely Song. Come into my heart."

Then Little Girl began to sing. (*Repeat song.*)

> Her coat was torn,
> And her shoes were worn,

But there was a song in her heart.

And as true as the sun and the moon and the forest trees, nothing else mattered. Nothing at all! (*Repeat song.*)

—L.B.S.

Ask the children to sing the song softly each time it is repeated in the story. The syllables *la* and *loo* provide practice on the "l" speech sound.

CHAPTER 7

The Two "Th" Speech Sounds

MAKING THE SPEECH SOUND

The lips are relaxed and slightly parted. The tip of the tongue, spread wide and thin, is placed against the inner edges of the upper front teeth or protrudes slightly between the upper and lower front teeth. The breath is forced gently out between the tongue and teeth. The vocal cords do not vibrate. The soft palate is raised.

The voiceless "th" speech sound is mispronounced frequently among pre-school and kindergarten children, e.g., *free* for *three, sum* for *thumb,* or *tum* for *thumb.* You may call "th" the "goose" or "revolving-door" sound.

CORRECTING THE DEFICIENT SPEECH SOUND

If "f" is being substituted for voiceless "th," e.g., *fum* for *thumb,* the child can be shown the difference between these two positions easily. Usually he can imitate both sounds in isolation as "ffff" and "th" (prolonged). However, pronouncing the sounds in words and in connected speech may be difficult, and enough time should be allowed for establishing correct articulation patterns.

INSTRUCTIONS TO THE CHILD

"Show me your white gate (teeth). Open it just a bit and pretend your tongue tip is a little mouse coming out of his hole to look for cheese. Now blow like Gray Goose on the farm when she sees a puppy. 'Th— th— th!' What number comes after two? Right. It is *three*. Make a good blow when you say *three*. Hold up your *thumb*. What did you just hold up? (*Children respond.*) Good! Your *thumb* is an important part of your hand, isn't it? Listen as I name some words. When you hear a word which begins with the 'goose' sound, hold up your thumb: *three, thank, think,* top, *thumb*. Make the goose sound with me as we say this rhyme."

"You can make a 'goose' sound.
Try it with me now.
You can make a 'goose' sound.
I will show you how: 'Th— th— th!'
Tongue tip out, and now you know!
You can make a 'goose' sound;
Blow, blow, blow: 'Th— th— th!' "

—L.B.S.

WORDS FOR PRACTICE

Initial	*Medial*	*Final*
thimble	Martha	north
thumb	python	moth
thin	birthday	teeth
thick	toothbrush	earth
Thanksgiving	bathtub	path
thunder	truthful	booth

167

I HEAR IT

Refer to the section on "s" for suggestions on using "I Hear It." The substitution of "s," "t," and "f" for voiceless "th" is illustrated in this listening activity.

I hear it in *thumb,* but not in *some.*
I hear it in *thank,* but not in *sank.*
I hear it in *thick,* but not in *sick.*

> I hear it in *thin,* but not in *tin.*
> I hear it in *thigh,* but not in *tie.*
> My tongue tip peeks out and the air comes through.
> I heard it in *through.* Did you? Did you?
> "Th— th— th!" *Through.*

I hear it in *three,* but not in *free.*
I hear it in *throw,* but not in *fro.*
I hear it in *thread,* but not in *Fred.*

> I hear it in *thrash,* but not in *trash.*
> I hear it in *thrill,* but not in *trill.*
> My tongue tip peeks out and the air comes through.
> I heard it in *through.* Did you? Did you?
> "Th— th— th!" *Through.*

—L.B.S.

ARE WE LISTENING?

1. Bill went to the store to buy some *things.* He bought a *thimble* for Auntie Sue. He bought some *thread* for Grandma, some mittens with *thumbs* for himself, and a *thermometer* for the bathroom medicine chest. When Bill arrived home, he found that he had left the *thimble* at the store. What things *did* Bill bring home? Were we listening? Let's see. For whom did Bill buy the *thimble?* What did he buy for Grandma? What did he buy that takes your temperature? What did Bill buy for himself?

2. Dottie took a walk down a *path* to the woods. She smelled the sweet *earth* after a *thundershower.* She

felt the cool wind coming from the *south*. She gathered some ferns to make a *wreath*. Were we listening? Let's see. Where did Dottie walk? Where did the wind come from? What did Dottie gather? What did she smell? What made the earth smell sweet?

3. On a lazy day in May, I heard a *thrush* sing. I heard *thunder* before a shower. I saw some *thirsty* cows drinking from a stream. A *thorn* caught in my coat and tore a hole. My sister mended my coat with needle, *thimble,* and *thread*. Have we been listening? Let's see. What did I hear one day in May? What kind of bird was it? What tore my coat? What did my sister use to mend my coat? Why were the cows drinking from a stream?

—L.B.S.

THE GOOSE SOUND

I told my goose to go and play,
But she just looked at me.
I said, "Why don't you find some corn?"
She made this sound at me:
    "Th— th— th!"
What should I do about that goose
When she just hangs around?
I said, "Why don't you join your friends?"
She made this funny sound:
    "Th— th— th!"

—L.B.S.

Ask the children to pantomime a goose by holding one arm in vertical position, bending the wrist, and moving the hand back and forth to imitate a goose's head and bill each time the "goose" sound is made.

THE REVOLVING DOOR

I live in an apartment house;
It is in Baltimore.

169

And oh, I like to turn around
In the big revolving door!
        "Th— th— th,"
        Around, around, around,
        "Th— th— th,"
        In a sort of hushy sound.
I ride the elevator down;
It stops at every floor.
And then I turn around, around
In the big revolving door.
        "Th— th— th,"
        Around, around, around,
        "Th— th— th,"
        In a sort of hushy sound.

—L.B.S.

Ask the children to let their tongue tips show between the teeth
when they make the quiet "th" sound. Ask them to tell about their
own experiences with elevators and revolving doors.

AUTUMN WALK

I walked down the road as slowly as could be,
And I saw three apples on a big apple tree.

CHILDREN: One, two, three,
            One, two, three,
            I saw three apples on an apple tree.

I walked down the road on a bright, sunny day,
And I saw three squirrels that decided to play.

CHILDREN: One, two, three,
            One, two, three,
            I saw three squirrels that decided to play.

I walked down the road on the way to town,
And I saw three leaves that had turned to brown.

CHILDREN: One, two, three,
One, two, three,
I saw three leaves that had turned to brown.

I walked down the road, and then, and then,
I turned right around and I walked back again.

CHILDREN: One, two, three,
One, two, three,
I turned right around and I walked back
again.

—L.B.S.

This rhyme provides practice on the voiceless "th" sound through repetition of the word *three*. Ask the children to make up their own verses by telling what they may have seen in one of their walking experiences.

BE THANKFUL

Be thankful for home,
Be thankful for food,
Be thankful for birds that fly.

Be thankful for sleep,
Be thankful for flowers,
Be thankful for clouds in the sky.

Be thankful for friends,
Be thankful for rain
And the rainbow that follows close by.

—J.J.T.

Ask the children to take turns telling what they are thankful for. Ask them to feel the tongue tip peek between the teeth when they say *thankful* or *thank you*.

WHAT IS THIN? [1]

TEACHER: Do you know what is thin? Let's see
How many thin things there can be!

SOLO 1: A mouse's tail is long and thin;

SOLO 2: So is a nail;

SOLO 3: So is a pin!

SOLO 4: A blade of grass, sweet-smelling green,
Is thin;

SOLO 5: So is a long string bean.

SOLO 6: Spaghetti, with its sauce and meat,
Is thin and slippery to eat.

SOLO 7: A stem is thin; so is number 1;

ALL: Why, wc have only just begun!

SOLO 8: A stick of candy red and white,

SOLO 9: The string upon your sailing kite,

SOLO 10: The whiskers on a dog or cat,

SOLO 11: The tall brown feather on your hat,

SOLO 12: A needle and a piece of thread,

SOLO 13: The cool white sheet upon your bed,

SOLO 14: A bit of paper, yard of silk,

SOLO 15: The straw through which you drink your milk,

SOLO 16: A bow to play a violin,

ALL: Why even PEOPLE can be thin!
So now you see, we just begin
To tell of things we know are thin.
Now if you like to play this game,
Perhaps some thin things YOU can name!

Let the children take turns saying the solos. Ask them to name other things which are thin. Listen for the voiceless "th" speech sound in the words *thin* and *things*. Ask the children to cut out pictures of thin things from discarded magazines and bring them in. Use this rhyme and the following one to teach the opposite concepts, *thick* and *thin*.

---

[1] Used by permission of *The Instructor*. Poem by Louise Binder Scott.

172

THICK

Thick is the mud between my toes,
Thick is the grass my daddy mows.

Thick is the dough when you bake a cake,
Thick is the clay for something you make.

Thick are the purple grapes in a bunch,
Thick is the sandwich in my noon lunch.

Thick are the soles of your shoes outside,
Thick is a big gray elephant's hide.

Thick is the ice where people can skate.
Thick is a log, and it also is straight.

Thick is the clover on top of the hill.
Thick is the fog, and it also is still.

Thick is the jam you spill on your chin.
Thick is the opposite of *thin!*

—L.B.S.

Ask the children to name other things which are thick and to listen for the "th" speech sound. After a first reading by the teacher, the children may supply the last word in each couplet.

YOUR THUMB

Your thumb helps you to put on your coat;
Your thumb helps you to pilot a boat.

Your thumb helps you to eat with a spoon;
Your thumb helps you to sail a balloon.

Your thumb helps you to put on your sock;
Your thumb helps you to wind up the clock.

173

Your thumb helps you to turn on TV;
Your thumb helps you to write *one, two, three.*

Your thumb helps you to paint and to draw;
Your thumb helps you to hammer and saw.

Your thumb helps you to open the door;
Your thumb helps you to sweep up the floor.

Your thumb helps you to build things in the sand;
Your thumb helps you to shake my right hand.

—L.B.S.

Ask the children to tell what their thumbs can do. For variety in the use of the rhyme, ask them to supply the last word in each couplet or pantomime the action. The "th" speech sound is repeated fourteen times with the word *thumb.*

THE ELEPHANT DANCE

In the jungle, one fine day,
An elephant went out to play.
A quiet little spot he found,
And there he danced and danced around.
  Thumpity, thump, thump!
  Thumpity, thump, thump!
He stomped and made the jungle shake;
He clumped and made the jungle quake.
Such fun it was to dance and grunt,
He called a second elephant.
  Thumpity, thump, thump!
  Thumpity, thump, thump!
In the jungle, one fine day,
Two elephants went out to play.
A quiet little spot they found,
And there they danced and danced around.
  Thumpity, thump, thump!
  Thumpity, thump, thump!

They stomped and made the jungle shake;
They clumped and made the jungle quake.
Such fun it was to dance and grunt,
They called another elephant.
Thumpity, thump, thump!
Thumpity, thump, thump!

Continue the rhyme, adding another elephant each time. When all elephants have finished dancing, close with the final stanza:

I hope some fine and sunny day
I'll find those elephants at play.
(*Repeat refrain.*)

—J.J.T.

THE RUDE GOOSE

In the barnyard lived the horse, the pig, the goat, and the cow. The horse said, "Neigh." The pig said, "Oink." The goat said, "Maa." And the cow said, "Moo." (*Children imitate animal sounds.*)

The animals all respected each other and rarely, if ever, was there a cross word.

Now one day the farmer brought a goose to the barnyard. The animals, who wished to be friendly and hospitable, came forward to greet the goose.

"Neigh, neigh," said the horse. "Good morning to you, and a how-do-you-do?"

"Th— th— th," hissed the goose *three* times, putting out the tip of her tongue. (*The children repeat the entire sentence.*)

"Oink, oink," said the pig. "Good morning to you, and a how-do-you-do?"

The goose put out the tip of her tongue and hissed, "Th— th— th," three times. (*Children repeat.*)

"Maa, maa," baaed the goat. "Good morning to you, and a how-do-you-do?"

Mrs. Goose hissed three times, "Th— th— th." (*Children repeat.*)

"Moo," said the cow. "What have we now? A new member of the barnyard family? Well, well. Good morning to you, and a how-do-you-do?"

"Th— th— th," hissed the goose three times. (*Children repeat.*)

When the goose went behind the corncrib to see whether she might find a few grains of spilled corn, the animals had a meeting.

"What can we do to help the goose?" asked the horse. "She just will not be friendly with us."

"It is sad," said the pig. "She puts out the tip of her tongue at us in a very rude way." Of course the pig never put out his tongue at anyone — ever.

But nobody seemed to know what to do about the goose who said, "Th— th— th," three times.

The barnyard animals took turns at being chairman when they had meetings, and one day it was the cow's turn. But when she called a meeting, the goose refused to attend. She just put out the tip of her tongue and hissed three times, "Th— th— th." (*Children imitate.*)

Thanksgiving was coming soon and, as we know, this is the time to give thanks for our blessings.

"Maybe," said the cow to the other animals, "we can help the goose to feel thankful, too. If we set an example of thankfulness and politeness, perhaps she will learn from us."

Thanksgiving Day arrived and, of course, all of the animals gathered to give thanks for their blessings. The goose just sat in a corner of the barnyard, put out the tip of her tongue, and said, "Th— th— th," three times.

The *thank you*'s began and each animal had something to be thankful for.

Horse:	"I am thankful for oats,"
All:	Said the pretty black horse,
Horse:	"And for the kind master Who feeds me, of course."

Pig:	"I am thankful for mud,"
All:	Said the little old pig,
Pig:	"And for a nice puddle To wallow and dig."

Goat:	"I am thankful for grass,"
All:	Said the furry white goat,
Goat:	"For my lovely long beard And my fine shaggy coat."

Cow:	"I am thankful for corn,"
All:	Said the lovely brown cow.
Cow:	"Come, then, all together, Let's give our thanks now!"

All:	"We are thankful, so thankful, At Thanksgiving time, And so we are telling Our *thank you*'s in rhyme."

The goose listened to the animals giving thanks. She thought and she thought, and suddenly a great shame came over her. She decided to try to make up for her rudeness. So she waddled over to where the animals sat with bowed heads and said softly, "Thank you. Thank you for trying to help me."

The goose said, "Thank you," to every animal in the barnyard, and they were delighted that she had learned politeness. They invited her to share their food on that

Thanksgiving Day, and ever since, when a goose puts out the tip of her tongue and says, "Th— th— th" three times, you will know that this is her way of saying, "Thank you."

—L.B.S.

Ask the children to tell why the goose decided to be more polite. Suggest that the class dramatize this story and play the parts of the animals. Sack puppets may be used effectively. For further practice on the "th" speech sound, provide a box of small objects and toys. Ask individual children to choose a toy and say "Thank you." Hold up a small mirror so that the children can see if the tongue tip is peeking out.

THUMPY

Thumpy Thumper was a fuzzy gray rabbit that lived in a cozy burrow in the meadow with Mrs. Thumper. One day, as he was hopping along, he heard a fluttering of wings. Thumpy's ears stood up straight and they turned in the direction of the sound. A little robin flew down.

"Cheer, cheer. Spring is here. Let me whisper in your ear," said the robin. And the robin whispered a secret into Thumpy's tall ear, which Thumpy turned to catch the secret.

"Thank you, thank you, for reminding me," said Thumpy, and he hopped quickly back to the rabbit burrow and Mrs. Thumper. He told her the secret. Then both Thumpy and Mrs. Thumper went to look at the calendar. Sure enough! The robin was right. It was spring, and it was Easter time.

"Oh, Mama," cried Thumpy. "I am supposed to be an Easter Bunny for the first time, but how can I be a good Easter Bunny when I have no eggs to hide for the children?"

Mrs. Thumper agreed. "But you still have a whole day," she said, "so you had best get started at once, without a minute's delay."

Thumpy kissed Mrs. Thumper good-by and started out looking for eggs to color for Easter. Now where to look was a problem, but since an owl is supposed to know a lot because of his round, wise-looking eyes, Thumpy decided to ask the owl to help him.

The owl winked and blinked and stared straight ahead and listened as Thumpy said:

> "I thought about some Easter eggs.
> (*Children participate.*)
> I thought they might be blue.
> I thought they might be yellow and red
> And orange and purple, too.
> I thought I'd ask my feathered friends
> To share their eggs with me.
> I thought that I would color them
> For boys and girls, you see."

The owl winked and blinked and stared straight ahead and said, "I think . . . I think . . ."

"Yes," interrupted Thumpy. "What do you think?"

The owl continued slowly and wisely, "I think owl eggs are too round to be good Easter eggs. Anyway, I doubt that my wife would spare even one, because she wants to hatch some baby owls."

"Thank you just the same," said Thumpy, and the owl said, "My, what a polite rabbit!"

Thumpy hopped away singing:

> "I try to say *thank you*
> As I go on my way.
> *Thank you, thank you*
> Are magic words to say."

Thumpy stopped to rest, and suddenly he heard what he thought was a helicopter. He glanced up, and what he saw looked something *like* a helicopter. But it was not a helicopter at all. It was a tiny hummingbird. She put her long bill into a honeysuckle and had a sweet drink. Her wings made a whirring, humming sound like this: "Hmmmmmmmmmmmmm." (*Children imitate.*)

"Do you have some eggs I could color for Easter?" asked Thumpy.

> "I thought about some Easter eggs.
> I thought they might be blue.
> I thought about some yellow and red
> And orange and purple, too.
> I thought I'd ask my feathered friends
> To share their eggs with me.
> I thought that I would color them
> For boys and girls, you see."

"Oh," said the hummingbird, suspended in the air as her wings continued to hum. "You would not want MY eggs at all. They are much too small. In fact, they are the smallest eggs with shells in the whole world."

"Thank you just the same," said Thumpy, and the hummingbird said, "What a polite rabbit!"

Thumpy hopped along singing:

> "I try to say *thank you*
> As I go on my way.
> *Thank you, thank you*
> Are magic words to say."

Suddenly it began to rain and Thumpy had to take shelter in the hole of the big tree which stood nearby. When the rain stopped, Thumpy ventured out on the grass. It was very wet, so Thumpy went back into his shelter until the smiling sun had dried out the grass.

Coming out of the hole, Thumpy saw a little robin pulling a worm out of the damp earth.

"Hello, Robin," greeted Thumpy. "Wasn't that a refreshing rain?"

"Indeed so," said the robin. "Look at the lovely rainbow."

Thumpy looked and the rainbow reminded him that he had to find eggs to color for Easter, so he said to the robin:

> "I thought about some Easter eggs.
> I thought they might be blue.
> I thought about some yellow and red
> And orange and purple, too.
> I thought I'd ask my feathered friends
> To share their eggs with me.
> I thought that I would color them
> For boys and girls, you see."

The robin said, "I am sorry, but my nest of twigs, grass, string, and hair from a horse's tail has just been completed. I plastered the nest with mud and now my mate is going to lay some eggs in the nest. But our eggs are already colored blue and, besides, they would be much too small for Easter eggs."

"Thank you just the same," said Thumpy, and the robin said, "What a polite rabbit!"

Thumpy hopped away singing:

> "I try to say *thank you*
> As I go on my way.
> *Thank you, thank you*
> Are magic words to say."

Thumpy hopped and hopped, and soon he came to a zoo. There was a huge ostrich with a large feathered tail and a great long neck.

The ostrich was looking at a huge egg she had just laid.

Thumpy said:

> "I thought about some Easter eggs.
> I thought they might be blue.
> I thought about some yellow and red
> And orange and purple, too.
> I thought I'd ask my feathered friends
> To share their eggs with me.
> I thought that I would color them
> For boys and girls, you see."

The ostrich stretched her long neck down to Thumpy's ear and she said, "My egg is the biggest egg in the whole world. Even just one of my eggs would be too heavy for you to carry."

"You are right," said Thumpy. "Thank you just the same." And the ostrich said, "What a polite rabbit!"

Thumpy hopped along singing:

> "I try to say *thank you*
> As I go on my way.
> *Thank you, thank you*
> Are magic words to say."

Thumpy sat down to think. He thought and he thought and he thought. Then up he jumped and hopped fast to the henhouse where he KNEW he could find the right-sized eggs to color for Easter.

An old white hen fluffed out her feathers and sat down on the nest.

Thumpy said:

> "I thought about some Easter eggs.
> I thought they might be blue.
> I thought about some yellow and red
> And orange and purple, too.

I thought I'd ask my feathered friends
To share their eggs with me.
I thought that I would color them
For boys and girls, you see."

The hen got up from the nest. "That is indeed an excellent idea, Thumpy," she said. "Here are some eggs. There are exactly ten, and you may have them all, if you like. I am glad that you came before I began to sit on the eggs, for had I sat on them three weeks, they would have hatched some baby chickens, you know."

"Oh, thank you, thank you," said Thumpy happily, and the hen said, "What a polite rabbit!"

Thumpy hopped quickly back to the burrow to tell Mrs. Thumper that at last there were some eggs to color. Since the hen was a white hen, of course the eggs were white. Mrs. Thumper helped Thumpy carry the eggs back to the burrow, but not before they had both thanked the hen again for sharing so many eggs. They sang:

"We try to say *thank you*
As we go on our way.
Thank you, thank you
Are magic words to say."

Mrs. Thumper mixed the colors and Thumpy dipped each egg into the bright mixture. They came out five different colors. Can you name the colors? (*Children tell the colors Thumpy named in the poem.*) Thumpy colored two eggs blue, two eggs yellow, two red, two orange, and two purple, and that makes ten, doesn't it?

Thumpy was very tired from coloring eggs, but he knew he could not stop work. He had to look for good places to hide the eggs so that they would not be too easy for the children to find. Then back to the burrow he went — hop, hop, hop! After Mrs. Thumper had given him a nice carrot top for his supper, Thumpy dropped right off to sleep.

The next morning, Thumpy was awakened by Mrs. Thumper, who said, "Wake up, wake up! We have an Easter present."

And Mrs. Thumper was RIGHT, because there were three little *new* Thumpies who didn't even have their eyes open.

Thumpy was overjoyed.

"Now I will have three Thumpies to help me hide Easter eggs next year! I will teach them good rabbit manners, and they will be ever so polite."

As soon as the baby rabbits were ready to learn, Thumpy taught them the magic song:

> "I try to say *thank you*
> As I go on my way.
> *Thank you, thank you*
> Are magic words to say."

Do you agree that *thank you* is a magic thing to say? Why?

—L.B.S. AND J.J.T.

Ask the children to say the refrain each time with you as you read the story. You may ask the children to draw and cut out egg shapes from colored construction paper and back them with bits of flannel or flocking for the flannelboard. They may then take turns placing the shapes on the board as the story is read. The story not only helps the children learn colors but also presents arithmetical concepts in counting the pairs of colored eggs by two's.

THE LOST THIMBLE

Theodora Kitten liked to sew. She carried a little silk purse which held a needle, a thimble, and some thread.

One day, as she was getting ready to make herself a new bonnet, she found that her thimble was not in her purse.

"Deary me," sighed Theodora Kitten, "I simply cannot sew fine seams in a new bonnet without my thimble."

She searched under the divan, under the hassock, behind the grandfather clock, under the stair, and under three chairs. She searched everywhere, but still she could not find her thimble.

Theodora Kitten remembered that she had called upon several of her Mother Goose friends the week before, and she thought that by chance she might have left her thimble in someone's home. Perhaps one of her Mother Goose friends had seen the thimble. So she decided to visit each one of them again.

Theodora Kitten put on her almost worn-out bonnet and set out.

She tapped on Mother Hubbard's door.

Mother Hubbard opened the door and peered over her glasses at Theodora Kitten.

"What a nice surprise!" she said. "Come right in Theodora, and have some tea. I have just baked three thimbleberry tarts and I want to share them with you."

"Thank you," replied Theodora Kitten. "But speaking of thimbleberry tarts reminds me that I have lost my *thimble*.

> I have lost my thimble, (*Children participate.*)
> My shiny thimble.
> I need my thimble so.
> I have lost my thimble,
> My shiny thimble.
> Where is it? Would you know?"

Mother Hubbard replied, "Perhaps you left your thimble in the living room. I may have picked it up and put it into my cupboard for safekeeping." She looked in the cupboard but it was bare, save for the thimbleberry tarts.

Theodora Kitten said, "Thank you, Mother Hubbard.

> For my thimble (*Children participate.*)
> I will look
> In every corner,
> In every nook.
> Many places I must go.
> And if I find it, I'll let you know."

"I wish you luck," said Mother Hubbard.

After tea, Theodora Kitten thanked Mother Hubbard and went on her way. Soon she came to a haystack where Boy Blue was asleep. "Kerchoo!" sneezed Theodora Kitten, for a wisp of hay had tickled her little button nose.

The sneeze woke up Boy Blue, who began to blow his horn. When he saw Theodora Kitten, he apologized for making so much noise. "Excuse me, dear friend," said Boy Blue. "Sit down and have a friendly chat with me. You look very worried. Whatever is wrong?"

Theodora said:

> "I have lost my thimble,
> My shiny thimble.
> I need my thimble so.
> I have lost my thimble,
> My shiny thimble.
> Where is it? Would you know?"

Boy Blue said, "When you came to visit me last week, you may have left your thimble near the thornbush at the edge of the meadow where I was tending the sheep." So they went down to the thornbush and searched carefully, but no thimble was there.

186

Theodora Kitten said:

> "Thank you, Boy Blue.
> For my thimble I will look
> In every corner, in every nook.
> Many places I must go.
> If I find it, I'll let you know."

Almost as soon as she had said good-by to Boy Blue, Theodora Kitten came to the home of the Old Woman who lived in a shoe.

"Mercy me," exclaimed the Old Woman. "My house is all topsy-turvy. I wish I had known you were coming. I have so many children I do not know what to do. They keep things in an uproar most of the time."

"I understand," said Theodora Kitten.

> "I have lost my thimble,
> My shiny thimble.
> I need my thimble so.
> I have lost my thimble,
> My shiny thimble.
> Where is it? Would you know?"

The Old Woman replied, "You may have left it down in the toe of the shoe where we had the quilting party last week. But the shoe is so cluttered it may take us some time to find it." They looked and they looked and they looked but they could not find the thimble.

Theodora said:

> "Thank you, Old Woman in the shoe.
> For my thimble I will look
> In every corner, in every nook.
> Many places I must go.
> If I find it, I'll let you know,"

Theodora went to call upon Miss Muffet. She said to Miss Muffet:

> "I have lost my thimble,
> My shiny thimble.
> I need my thimble so.
> I have lost my thimble,
> My shiny thimble.
> Where is it? Would you know?"

Miss Muffet replied, "Weren't you sitting on my tuffet last week when you came to visit me?"

"Indeed I was," said Theodora.

"Then we will go to look under the tuffet right now," said Miss Muffet. But no thimble was there.

Theodora thanked Miss Muffet. By now Theodora was so tired and hungry that she decided to go home for lunch. After she had eaten, she would look for her thimble again.

Theodora went into her neat little house and took a cup from the cupboard. She poured herself some milk and as she was about to drink it, she heard a hoarse, noisy, "Caw, caw, caw!"

Theodora went to the open window, and there sat Inky Crow perched right on the windowsill. He held something shiny in his beak.

"My thimble! My thimble!" cried Theodora Kitten. "You have found my thimble! Oh, thank you! Thank you!"

Inky set the precious thimble on the windowsill.

"You are welcome indeed," he said. "You must have dropped your thimble in the yard when you were sewing under the elm tree. Well, you know how crows love shiny things. I picked up the thimble to take to my nest to add to my collection of shiny things. But when I examined the thimble closely, I saw your initials engraved inside it. I returned it to you just as soon as I knew you were home."

188

Theodora Kitten was SO grateful. "Thank you a thousand times," she said. Then she asked Inky Crow to stay for lunch, and she made some very special sunflower-seed cakes for him. She also gave him a sparkling silver bead to add to his collection of shiny things.

As soon as Inky Crow had flown back to his nest, Theodora Kitten sat down. She took out her needle and thread. She put on her thimble and she began to sew presents for each of her Mother Goose friends who had tried to help her. She made an apron for Mother Hubbard, a comforter to cover up Boy Blue while he slept under the haystack, and a small satin pillow for Miss Muffet's tuffet. Then she made a kerchief for each of the Old Woman's girl children and a tie for each of her boy children. And she made a bright new bonnet for herself.

So the story ended quite happily, and Theodora Kitten sang a new song:

> "I have my thimble,
> My shiny thimble.
> I need my thimble so.
> I have my thimble,
> My shiny thimble.
> I'll keep it wherever I go."

—L.B.S.

The children join in each time Theodora Kitten says either of her poems. The two refrains emphasize the voiceless *th* speech sound in the word *thimble*. Afterward, the children may dramatize the story, adding additional Mother Goose characters. It is also suggested that some of the Mother Goose rhymes be reviewed. Below is a recommended list:

Old Mother Hubbard	Little Miss Muffet
Bobby Shaftoe	The Old Woman in the Shoe
Little Boy Blue	Mary, Mary, Quite Contrary
Little Jack Horner	Humpty Dumpty
Peter, Pumpkin Eater	

A family of jackrabbits lived in a burrow on the wide, wide prairie.

One day, trip, trip, tripping and skip, skip, skipping and thump, thump, thumping and leap, leap, leaping came the Threap. And the Threap cried:

"I am so thin; I must not get thinner.
I need three jackrabbits for my dinner!"

But three prairie dogs barked, "Weep, weep, weep!" And the Threap became frightened and stole away into the dusk of the evening.

The next day, trip, trip, tripping and skip, skip, skipping and thump, thump, thumping and leap, leap, leaping came the Threap.

And the Threap cried:

"I am so thin; I must not get thinner.
I need three jackrabbits for my dinner!"

But three king snakes crawled out from under three speckled rocks and hissed, "Sssssssssssssss!" The Threap became frightened and stole away into the dusk of the evening.

Now this Threap was an odd-looking creature with pobbly toes and a wobbly nose and a most EXCRUTIAT-INGLY thin body. And across the prairie he would come trip, trip, tripping and skip, skip, skipping and thump, thump, thumping and leap, leap, leaping. Again the Threap cried:

"I am so thin; I must not get thinner.
I need three jackrabbits for my dinner!"

But three squawking prairie chickens flew at the Threap and pecked at him crying, "Cawk, cawk, cawk!" And the Threap became frightened and stole away into the dusk of the evening.

"Oh, what can we do," sighed the family of jackrabbits. "We do not fear the Threap because he is much too measly and too EXCRUTIATINGLY thin to harm us. He IS a beastly bother though, for he will keep tripping and skipping and thumping and leaping across the prairie unless something is done to stop him."

The three barking prairie dogs and the three king snakes and the three prairie chickens said, "Yes, it is true. The Threap is a beastly bother." Then they asked, "Shall we catch him and tie him up from his beastly ears to his pobbly toes? Shall we put a muzzle on his wobbly nose? Shall we tie his mouth together with soap weeds?"

The family of jackrabbits thought carefully about all of these suggestions, and then they said, "No. It would not be right to do this. The Threap wants to eat US and not you. We thank you for offering advice, but we will take care of the Threap ourselves."

All went well for several days and nothing was heard from the Threap. But one day, trip, trip, tripping and skip, skip, skipping and thump, thump, thumping and leap, leap, leaping came the Threap. And the Threap cried:

> "I am so thin; I must not get thinner.
> I need three jackrabbits for my dinner!"

And then — and then — the jackrabbits did a most ASTONISHING thing. They invited the Threap into their burrow. Wasn't that EXTRAORDINARY?

"Poor Threap," said the jackrabbits. "How hungry you must be! No wonder you are so measly and so EX-CRUTIATINGLY thin. Come and have some cactus salad and some purple-flower stew with us."

Then suddenly a most amazing thing happened. Slowly the Threap began to fade away and in his place appeared a lovely chameleon who had as many colors as a rainbow in a western sky after a thundershower.

The three prairie dogs and the three king snakes and the three prairie chickens marvelled at what had happened.

"How wonderful!" they said softly.

Then the chameleon explained, "Weeks ago, a wicked desert imp became angry with me because I would not do his bidding. The wicked imp turned me into a Threap and told me that unless someone showed me a great act of kindness I would remain a Threap and gradually become thinner and thinner and fade away into nothing. Your act of kindness saved me and now I am a chameleon again."

From that time on the lovely chameleon, with as many colors as a rainbow in a western sky after a thundershower, lived happily with the other desert creatures, and to this day nobody has ever seen a Threap. And we hope nobody ever will!

—L.B.S.

This allegory contains repetition of the voiceless "th" speech sound in the words *Threap, thin, thinner,* and *three.* Discuss with the class the lesson gained from the story. This story lends itself effectively to dramatization.

th
(Voiced)

them

MAKING THE SPEECH SOUND

The voiced "th," as in *this,* is made like the voiceless "th," as in *thumb,* except that the vocal cords vibrate. The sound is commonly misarticulated, e.g., *dem* for *them* and *mudder* for *mother.*

You may call voiced "th" the "fire-siren" or "electric-razor" sound.

CORRECTING THE DEFICIENT SPEECH SOUND

The process for correction is much the same as for the voiceless "th." Tell the children to let the tongue tip protrude between the teeth and to place their fingers on the front of the throat, or Adam's apple, and feel the voice motor hum. The sound should be prolonged.

INSTRUCTIONS TO THE CHILD

"When Daddy shaves, his electric razor makes a low hum like this: 'th— th— th.' To make a good humming-buzzing 'electric-razor' sound, the tongue tip has to peek out a wee bit and the voice motor must work. Try it with me. Open your white gate and let the tip of your tongue peep out. Say with me: *they, this, that, these, those. (Prolong the 'th' sound.)* Here is a nonsense poem you can learn very quickly if you are wearing your wide-awake listening ears."

This, that, these, those.
Here are my fingers; here is my nose.
This, that, these, those.
Watch me touch clear down to my toes.
   (Prolong the "z" sound at the end of nose and toes.)

—L.B.S.

WORDS FOR PRACTICE

Initial	*Medial*	*Final*
that	mother	bathe
this	father	breathe
these	brother	clothe
them	weather	smooth
those	feather	lathe
they	rhythm	soothe

FIRE SIREN

Five brave firemen are standing with pride.
   (Hold up five fingers.)
Zip, zip, zip, down the pole they slide,
   (Rub palms together.)
Jump on the engine, and away they ride. *(Clap.)*
      "Th— th— th— th,
         (Imitate siren and move finger in a spinning motion.)
      Th— th— th— th!"
Don't let the house burn! Go, go, go! *(Clap to rhythm.)*
Hurry, brave firemen! Oh, oh, oh!
Make that fire siren blow, blow, blow!
      "Th— th— th— th,
      Th— th— th— th!"
"Well, we put out the fire," the firemen said.

Then they jumped on the truck and away they sped,
To return to the firehouse and hop into bed.
      "Th— th— th— th,
      Th— th— th— th!"

                                              —L.B.S.

The voiced "th" speech sound may be prolonged as one continued sound as the children imitate the siren.

INDIAN FEATHERS

Indian feathers I will wear,
Indian feathers for my hair,
One feather, two feathers, three and four.
Don't you think I should have more
Fine red feathers in my hair —
Feathers like the Indians wear?
Five feathers, six feathers, seven, eight, nine —
Each feather has its Indian sign.
Now, I wear upon my head
Nine tall feathers painted red.
Watch the feathers that I wear;
Watch the feathers in my hair.
Nine tall feathers move and sway
When I dance in an Indian way.

THOOM-pah! THOOM-pah! THOOM-pee-ay!
THOOM-pah! THOOM-pah! THOOM-pee-ay!

                                              —J.J.T.

This rhyme will give the children a chance to repeat the voiced "th" sound many times in *thoom* and in *feathers*. In the final two-line refrain, use a slow, rhythmic beat with a heavy accent on each *thoom* to imitate the sound of an Indian drum. Follow this activity with "How Many Feathers?" by Lucille F. Wood and Louise Binder Scott, from *Singing Fun,* Webster Division, McGraw-Hill Book Company.

195

There's a story-book animal who lives in a zoo;
We don't know what he is, but we call him a *thoo.*
  (*Voiced "th."*)

Refrain: Yes, we call him a thoo,
            And he lives in a zoo,
            And if you'll talk nicely,
            He'll talk nicely, too!

His neck, which is slender, turns this way and that;
On his face there are whiskers just like a tomcat.

Refrain: (*Children repeat lines 3, 4, 5, and 6.*)

His head, which is wobbly, turns this way and that,
And his fur is as soft as a little brown bat.

Refrain: (*Children repeat.*)

His tail — it is long and turns this way and that,
And his ears are so small they belong on a rat.

Refrain: (*Children repeat.*)

His eyes, which are round, can turn this way and that,
And if you're not careful, he'll eat up your hat!

Refrain: (*Children repeat.*)

Besides some of this, that, these, them, and those,
A thoo at a zoo has a very flat nose.

Refrain: (*Children repeat.*)

And so I've described him so plainly for you,
Now perhaps you can draw a good story-book thoo!

                                        —L.B.S.

Some children substitute voiced "th" for "z," e.g., *thoo* for *zoo.*
This nonsense rhyme uses both the correct pronunciation *zoo*
and the substituted *thoo* in the refrain so that the children gain
practice in hearing and pronouncing both sounds. The phrase "this
way and that," which occurs four times, offers added practice with
voiced "th." Ask the children to draw their impressions of a story-
book *thoo.*

CHAPTER 8

The "F" and "V" Speech Sounds

MAKING THE SPEECH SOUND

The upper front teeth are pressed lightly against the lower lip and air is forced out between the teeth and the lip. The soft palate is raised and there is no vibration of the vocal cords. The *f* speech sound sometimes is misarticulated as "p" or "th," e.g., *pour* for *four* or *thour* for *four*.

You may call "f" the "angry-kitten" sound.

CORRECTING THE DEFICIENT SPEECH SOUND

Ask the child to bite the lower lip gently and blow out his breath at the same time. Ask him to hold up the palm of his hand and feel the air blow against it as he produces the "f" sound.

197

INSTRUCTIONS TO THE CHILD

"When I say *four,* what do my teeth do? (*Response.*) Can your teeth do the same? Can they bite down on your lower lip gently? Try it. Watch in the mirror to see if your teeth and lip are working together to make this quiet sound. That is the 'angry-kitten' sound. What comes after three? What comes after four? Did you hear the 'angry-kitten' sound when you said both of those numbers? Here is a counting rhyme. I will say it. Then you can say it after me."

One, two, three —
Three fuzzy kittens by my tree.
One, two, three, four —
Four fuzzy ducklings near my door.
One, two, three, four, five —
Five fuzzy bees are in their hive.

—L.B.S.

WORDS FOR PRACTICE

Initial	*Medial*	*Final*
face	waffle	giraffe
fence	safety	calf
fish	Africa	roof
farmer	rifle	wolf
fox	fifty	chief
fire	sofa	leaf

Consonant Blends:

*f*resh	*f*lag	le*ft*	scar*f*	el*f*
*f*rame	*f*lake	so*ft*	dwar*f*	wol*f*

198

I HEAR IT

See the section on "s" for instructions on using this exercise. The usual speech-sound substitutions, "p" and voiceless "th" for "f," are included here.

I hear it in *fall* but not in *Paul.*
I hear it in *fast* but not in *past.*
I hear it in *fat* but not in *pat.*
    I hear it in *Fred* but not in *thread.*
    I hear it in *free* but not in *three.*
    I bite on my lip and the air comes through.
    I hear it in *four* and *five.* Do you?
    "F, f, f!" *Four* and *five.*
    You can do it, too!
I hear it in *fig* but not in *pig.*
I hear it in *fine* but not in *pine.*
I hear it in *feel* but not in *peal.*
    I hear it in *fin* but not in *thin.*
    I hear it in *first* but not in *thirst.*
    I bite on my lip and the air comes through.
    I hear it in *four* and *five.* Do you?
    "F, f, f!" *Four* and *five.*
    You can do it, too!

—L.B.S.

MY LITTLE BLACK KITTEN

My little black kitten has velvety fur;
When she is happy, her motor will purr.
When she is angry, her tail will stand up;
Then she will talk to our little brown pup:
    "F, f, f, f, f!" (*The children make the sound.*)

—L.B.S.

TEN FLUFFY KITTENS

One fluffy kitten was sleeping in a shoe.
His sister woke him with a purr,
And then there were two.
Two fluffy kittens were invited out to tea.
A striped kitten joined them,
And then there were three.
Three fluffy kittens playing on the floor.
A gray one came to have some fun,
And then there were four.
Four fluffy kittens were sitting in the drive.
A stray alley cat came by,
And then there were five.
Five fluffy kittens were doing foolish tricks.
They asked a friend to help them,
And then there were six.
Six fluffy kittens took a trip to Devon.
They brought a little cousin home,
And then there were seven.
Seven fluffy kittens slept till very late.
A black one came to waken them,
And then there were eight.
Eight fluffy kittens sat right down to dine.
A neighbor came to call on them,
And then there were nine.
Nine fluffy kittens were playing in the den.
A baby sister came along,
And then there were ten.
Ten fluffy kittens curled up in a heap.
They purred a happy little song
And soon were fast asleep.

—L.B.S.

This rhyme is effective when acted out in pantomime or used as a finger play or flannelboard activity. The word *fluffy* begins with the *fl* consonant blend.

FALLING STAR

I saw my falling star one night.
It gave a light — a twinkling light,
And oh, it was a splendid sight!
It was so very bright.

CHILDREN: My falling star,
             My falling star
             Was falling fast
             And falling far!

I wondered where my star would fall.
Upon a stately fir tree tall?
Upon my home? Upon a stall?
Upon a pond so small?

CHILDREN: My falling star,
             My falling star
             Was falling fast
             And falling far!

I wonder, but I do not know —
Somebody told me long ago
That falling stars are wishes — oh,
It surely must be so!

CHILDREN: My falling star,
             My falling star
             Was falling fast
             And falling far!

—L.B.S.

The children say the refrain, which repeats the "f" speech sound in the words *falling, fast,* and *far.* Ask individual children whether they have ever wished upon a star as they saw one falling, and let them tell their wishes.

FOUR LITTLE BIRDS

Four little birds
  Without any home —
    One, two, three, and four.
    Four little birds,
      All in a row,
        Sat beside my door!

Four little birds
  With feathers brown
    Shivered in the snow.
    Four little birds,
      All in a row,
        Had no place to go.

Four little birds
  Had no nest
    Where birdies ought to be.
    Four little birds
      Left their tree
        And came to live with me!

—L.B.S.

The "f" speech sound is repeated seven times in the word *four*. Let the children draw the birds, back them with flannel, and place them on the flannelboard as the poem is said. The poem is easily learned by rote.

FROSTY LITTLE FELLOW

A frosty little fellow
Came to visit us last night.
He painted all the flowers
And everything in sight.

CHILDREN: Frosty little fellow;
           In the night he came.
           Frosty little fellow;
           Can you guess his name?

His icy fingers painted
Silver phantoms on each tree,
And he left his feathery footprints
For all of us to see.

CHILDREN: Frosty little fellow;
In the night he came.
Frosty little fellow;
Can you guess his name?

He worked until the morning,
And oh, to our delight
We saw that fields and fences
Were frosted sparkling white.

CHILDREN: Frosty little fellow;
In the night he came.
Frosty little fellow;
Jack Frost was his name!

—L.B.S.

The refrain gives practice on two words beginning with the
"f" speech sound, *frosty* and *fellow*. Ask children in second or
third grade to paint pictures of their impressions of the scenes
Jack Frost left behind. Let the children begin by telling what they
think he painted. Check the children's comprehension of the word
phantoms.

SIGNS OF WINTER

On a big gray cloud away up high,
Sat a soft little snowflake in the dark sky.
"I must fall," said the snowflake white.
"I must fall down to the earth tonight!"
      Fluttery, fluttery, fluttery, fly,
      Fluttery, fluttery, down from the sky!

Said the big gray cloud, "Oh, please don't go,
For something might happen to you, you know."
But the little snowflake with a tear in his eye,
Said, "Good-by, good-by, I am leaving the sky."
      Fluttery, fluttery, fluttery, fly,
      Fluttery, fluttery, down from the sky!

Then off he went, and he floated down
Till he came to a quiet New Hampshire town.
And there on the hard brown earth he lay.
The next day, some children came out to play.
      Fluttery, fluttery, fluttery, fly,
      Fluttery, fluttery, down from the sky!

They said, "A snowflake has come to say
That winter at last is on its way.
Good-by to summer, good-by to fall,
Good-by to little leaves one and all."
      Fluttery, fluttery, fluttery, fly,
      Fluttery, fluttery, down from the sky!

That day, from the clouds came snowflake mothers
And snowflake fathers and sisters and brothers.
Oh, hundreds of snowflakes came fluttering down,
Covering rooftops all over the town!
      Fluttery, fluttery, fluttery, fly,
      Fluttery, fluttery, down from the sky!

The children laughed, for they had a plan!
From mounds of snow, they would make a man!
Then all that day they worked very hard,
And they made a snowman out in the yard.
    Fluttery, fluttery, fluttery, fly,
    Fluttery, fluttery, down from the sky!

—L.B.S.

The children say the refrain. Let them pantomime the action
of snow falling by raising the hands high, moving the fingers gently,
and lowering the arms slowly on each line of the refrain. Ask individual children to retell the story idea presented in the poem.

THE HALLOWEEN KITTEN

Flossie was a witch who lived near Foggy-Boggy Lake
in a crooked house that had crooked walls and halls,
crooked floors and doors, and a crooked roof with a
crooked chimney.

Everything about Flossie's house was crooked, except
for the broomstick on which she rode into the sky away
up high.

Now Flossie knew that Halloween was just "a hoot
and a holler" away, and there was much work to be done
before she could ride into the sky away up high. But most
important of all, Flossie needed a black cat. The cat that
had ridden on Flossie's broomstick for many a Halloween
had been adopted by a family, and she was no longer interested in Halloween.

Now one evening, there was a meeting of all the
ghosts, goblins, bats, owls, and spooks on Eerie Rock near
Foggy-Boggy Lake. At this meeting, all Halloween plans
were to be discussed.

Gooley Goblin was the chairman, and he called the
meeting to order. He rapped on the rock and asked in a
quavering voice, "Are there any Halloween problems?
Hmmmmmmmm?"

Flossie Witch climbed upon the rock and said, "Mister Chairman, it is almost Halloween, when spooky sights are seen. But I have no black cat to ride with me."

"Are there any suggestions? Hmmmmmm?" asked Gooley Goblin.

Hooty Owl fluttered his feathers and waited to be recognized by the chair. Then he said, "I suggest that Flossie Witch advertise for a black cat in the *Moonlight Nooz*."

Flossie thanked Hooty Owl for his suggestion and put an advertisement in the *Moonlight Nooz.*

> **Wanted:** *A black cat to ride on a broomstick on Halloween night. Apply to Flossie Witch, Crooked Lane, Foggy-Boggy Lake.*

The day before Halloween, Flossie was dusting cobwebs from one of her crooked chairs near the crooked stairs when she heard a small "Mew."

She opened the crooked door and peered over her glasses at a little black kitten sitting on the doormat.

"Have you come in answer to my advertisement in the *Moonlight Nooz?*" asked Flossie Witch.

"Yes, yes," replied the little black kitten. "I want more than anything to be a Halloween cat. Will you choose me, please?"

Flossie took a long look at the little black kitten. "Well," she said. "I don't know. You *are* small to be a Halloween cat and your voice sounds rather weak, but I suppose you must start sometime. Before I make a final decision, I must ask you some questions. Can you stick out your whiskers and look fierce? Can you fluff out your tail as big as two? Can you make an angry sound: 'f, f, f, f, f'?"

"I'll try," said the little black kitten.

"You appear to be a smart kitten," said Flossie Witch, "so I'll give you a chance."

"Oh, thank you," said the little black kitten happily.

"Then let's practice," ordered Flossie Witch.

> "Hump your back, (*Hand imitates hump.*)
> Fluff your tail,
>   (*Raise arm and wiggle fingers.*)
> Stick out your whiskers,
>   (*Hold pointer fingers beside upper lip.*)
> Meow and wail,
> And say, 'F, f, f, f, f!' "
>   (*Children imitate sound.*)

Black Kitten humped her back. She fluffed her tail. She meowed and wailed. But she just could not say, "F, f, f, f!"

"Dear me," sighed Flossie Witch. "This will never do. A good Halloween cat must make an angry sound. Please try again."

So Black Kitten humped her back, she fluffed her tail, she stuck out her whiskers, and she meowed and wailed. But she simply could not say, "F, f, f, f!"

Flossie Witch said, "Perhaps if you were to take a ride on my broomstick into the sky away up high, you might *feel* more like a Halloween cat. Come with me and we shall see. Hop on the back of my broomstick, and away we will go."

The balloon moon was full as they rode into the sky away up high. Black Kitten sat up very straight, perched on the broomstick behind Flossie Witch.

As they passed a brown bat, Flossie said,

> "Now is the time.
> Hump your back,
> Fluff your tail,
> Stick out your whiskers,
> Meow and wail,
> And say, 'F, f, f, f!' "

And as the broomstick whizzed along, Black Kitten humped her back, she fluffed her tail, she stuck out her whiskers, and she meowed and wailed, but she could not say, "F, f, f, f!"

Flossie Witch was most annoyed.

"Fiddle-faddle," she said. "We may just as well go back to Foggy-Boggy Lake." Which is just what they did, and they went to bed for the rest of that night.

But Black Kitten could not sleep. She twisted and turned on the crooked floor trying to get comfortable. Finally she got up and padded out the door and down the crooked walk away from Foggy-Boggy Lake.

The round balloon moon made shadows along the path as Black Kitten pit-patted along. All at once, she saw something standing in front of her. It was Gooley Goblin. Of course, Little Black Kitten had never seen Gooley Goblin, so she humped her back, she fluffed her tail and stuck out her whiskers, and she meowed and wailed, but when she tried to say, "F, f, f, f!" she could not do so.

"Ho, ho," laughed Gooley Goblin. "Aren't you the new kitten that belongs to Flossie Witch?"

"Yes," replied Black Kitten faintly.

"Then all I can say is you're a fraidy cat — or rather, a fraidy *kitten*," said Gooley Goblin jumping over a fence and disappearing.

Now "fraidy cat" is a dreadful thing to say to anyone, and particularly to a dear little kitten who wants to be a Halloween cat. It was enough to make Black Kitten want to cry.

Down from the tree flew Hooty Owl. "What's wrong?" he asked.

"Oh," cried Black Kitten, "I can hump my back, fluff my tail, stick out my whiskers, and meow and wail, but I cannot make a special angry sound I need to be able to ride on Flossie Witch's broomstick."

"Well, why can't you make the special angry sound?" asked Hooty Owl.

"I don't know," replied Black Kitten. "I've never really thought about it."

"Then think about it now," said Hooty Owl. "You want to be a Halloween Kitten. In order to do so, you must make an angry kitten sound. You must practice until you CAN do it. It is as simple as that."

Black Kitten tried and tried, but she could not say, "F, f, f, f!"

"I suppose it is not your fault," said Hooty Owl. "Perhaps nobody has ever showed you how. It's easy as can be. Just bite with your front teeth on your lower lip and let a puff of air come through. I have a beak and no teeth, so I cannot show you. Anyway, I'm not supposed to make that sound."

Black Kitten did as Hooty Owl said, and she let a puff of air come through, "F!" Then she let two puffs of air come through, "F, f!"

She became so excited about it that she made five puffs of air come through, "F, f, f, f, f!" She practiced and she practiced. Then she went to Looking-Glass Brook to try to see her reflection in the water as she said, "F, f, f, f!"

When she returned to the crooked house near Foggy-Boggy Lake, Flossie Witch was hurrying around getting breakfast.

"Hmmmm," she said. "I suppose you have been out for a prowl. Tonight is Halloween, you know, and there are many things to be done before we can ride away up high in the sky."

She gave Black Kitten a dish of milk and cooked a breakfast of toasted corn silks for herself.

The day passed quickly and soon the orange balloon moon rose and night noises began. Crickets chirped. Fireflies lighted their lanterns and frogs croaked in Foggy-Boggy Lake.

Flossie Witch locked the door of the crooked house and climbed on her broom.

"It is time," she said to Black Kitten. "It is time to fly away up high into the sky."

Black Kitten sat on the broomstick behind Flossie Witch.

And all at once she said, "F, f, f, f!"

Flossie Witch laughed loudly. "Good Black Kitten! Brave Black Kitten! Fierce Black Kitten," she said. "For many a Halloween you shall ride with me into the sky away up high. And you will —

> Hump your back,
> Fluff your tail,
> Stick out your whiskers,
> Meow and wail,
> And say: 'F, f, f, f!' "

It happened just that way. And if you do not believe me, ask the big orange balloon moon.

—L.B.S.

The children pantomime the action each time the refrain is said. Suggest that they dramatize the story with paper-bag puppets or flannelboard figures.

LITTLE FIREFLY

Little Firefly was exploring among the thick clumps of moss by the brook when a dewdrop fell down upon his head.

"Oh!" cried Little Firefly. "My head is hurt— hurt— hurt!"

Little Firefly went right home to tell his mother what had happened and his mother, Mrs. Firefly, kissed the bump on Little Firefly's head to help make it well. (Can you tell me, now, just how big is a bump on the head of a tiny, tiny firefly?) Mrs. Firefly made a blanket of leaves and covered Little Firefly with some soft spider webs to make him warm and comfortable. Then Mrs. Firefly knelt beside his bed and rubbed his wings and said soothing things to him, and soon Little Firefly stopped trembling.

Little Firefly's mother made him some soup from three poppy seeds and served it to him in the smallest acorn cup that ever was. And Little Firefly appreciated this very much — oh, VERY much.

Little Firefly's mother said,

"We love you, Little Firefly.
We hope you'll feel fine by and by."

As Little Firefly lay with his hurt head, some fairies came to call and brought wild fern that had a special sweet fragrance. And Little Firefly appreciated this very much — oh, VERY much.

The fairies said,

"We love you, Little Firefly.
We hope you'll feel fine by and by."

Mrs. Ladybug, dressed in an orange-and-black polka-dot dress and a little perky bonnet, brought a bit of dandelion fluff to put under Little Firefly's head so he would be more comfortable. And Little Firefly appreciated this very much — oh, VERY much.

Mrs. Ladybug said,

"We love you, Little Firefly.
We hope you'll feel fine by and by."

Mrs. Bee came with a small jar of honey and fed some to Little Firefly to help him feel stronger. And Little Firefly appreciated this very much — oh, VERY much.
Mrs. Bee said,

"We love you, Little Firefly.
We hope you'll feel fine by and by."

Mrs. Wasp brought a book called *Delicious Snapdragon Recipes for Insects*. And Little Firefly appreciated this very much — oh, VERY much.
Mrs. Wasp said,

"We love you, Little Firefly.
We hope you'll feel fine by and by."

Mrs. Butterfly brought some peach juice in a nut shell and held Little Firefly's head while he drank the juice down to the last drop. And Little Firefly appreciated this very much — oh, VERY much.
Mrs. Butterfly said,

"We love you, Little Firefly.
We hope you'll feel fine by and by."

Mrs. Moth brought some maple pudding made from the sap of a maple tree, and she fed a big spoonful of it to Little Firefly. And Little Firefly appreciated this very much — oh, VERY much.
Mrs. Moth said,

"We love you, Little Firefly.
We hope you'll feel fine by and by."

After a while, Little Firefly grew stronger and he stopped hurting and finally he didn't hurt anymore at all because his heart was filled with friendship. So out of bed he jumped and he said, "My heart is so full of appreciation and friendship that I must show kindness in some way to all my friends. The forests and rivers are dark at night, and all creatures need light."

So Little Firefly lit a lantern and flew all night long to light the way for his friends and guide them on their way.

When you see a firefly with his lantern, you will know that he is on his way to do kindness for someone and to give light in the darkness.

—L.B.S. (Based upon an old legend.)

This story provides repetition of the "f" speech sound in the words *firefly, feel,* and *fine.* The "v" speech sound is repeated in the words *love* and *very.* Ask the children to repeat the refrain used by Little Firefly's friends each time it occurs. The children may dramatize the story and discuss the values of returning kindness for kindness and showing appreciation.

MAKING THE SPEECH SOUND

This speech sound is produced like "f," except that the vocal cords vibrate for "v." The *v* speech sound frequently is misarticulated as "b," e.g., *balentine* for *valentine* or *seben* for *seven.* Children of Spanish-American background in particular may mispronounce the sound this way in both initial and medial position in words. Often the voiceless sound "f" is substituted for "v," e.g., *haf* for *have*. Sometimes children who are learning English as a second language have difficulty hearing the difference between "f" and "v."

You may call "v" the "fly" sound.

CORRECTING THE DEFICIENT SPEECH SOUND

Use the same techniques as for "f." Ask the children to feel the voice-motor vibrations by placing one hand on the larynx area or beside the nose as they say *vine*. Ask them to say the following words in order to hear and feel the difference between *f* and *v: fine—vine; fast—vast; fee—V; face—vase.* (Note: If *vase* is pronounced as *vahz* in your area, do not use the word.)

INSTRUCTIONS TO THE CHILD

"Bite your lower lip gently and let your voice motor hum as you make the sound with me: 'Vvvvvvvvvvv.' Did you feel what happened? Look into the mirror and see if your upper teeth are touching your lower lip: 'Vvvvvv-vvvvv.' Now let's say some words that begin with this buzzing sound: *valentine, voice, violets, violin. (Prolong the 'v' sound.)* What was the first sound that you heard when you named those words? Here is a rhyme about the fly that makes that 'vvvv' sound. Say the 'fly' sound with me."

I saw a fly upon the wall.
I could not hear him crawl at all.
I wondered why he didn't fall!
And then that fly began to zoom: "Vvvvvvvvv."
He buzzed and buzzed around the room. "Vvvvvvvvv."
He paused a second on the floor. "Vvvvvvvvv."
And then he zoomed right out the door. "Vvvvvvvvv."

—L.B.S.

214

WORDS FOR PRACTICE

Initial	*Medial*	*Final*
valentine	navy	glove
vine	seven	stove
voice	beaver	wave
velvet	river	sleeve
van	eleven	five
vest	oven	move

I HEAR IT

See the section on "s" for instructions on using this listening activity. Attention is called to the unwanted substitution of "b" for "v" in the following exercise.

I hear it in *veil* but not in *bail.*
I hear it in *very* but not in *berry.*
I hear it in *van* but not in *ban.*

I hear it in *vee* but not in *bee.*
I hear it in *vase* but not in *base.*
I bite on my lip and let the air through.
I used my voice motor. Did you and you?
"Vvvvvvv— vvvvvvvv!"

I hear it in *veep* but not in *beep.*
I hear it in *vend* but not in *bend.*
I hear it in *vest* but not in *best.*

I hear it in *vote* but not in *boat.*
I hear it in *vow* but not in *bow.*
I bite on my lip and I let the air through.
I used my voice motor. Did you and you?
"Vvvvvvvvv— vvvvvvvvvv!"

—L.B.S.

NAUGHTY FLY

The little fly
Goes sailing by.
Oh, he is sly,
That naughty fly.
    "Vvvv— vvvv!"

He likes to plot
And tease a lot.
But I *cannot*
Give him a swat!
    "Vvvv— vvvv!"

He bites my toe.
He's pesky. Oh!
But this I know,
I love him so.
    "Vvvv— vvvv!"

That fly is bound
To be around,
And I have found
I *need* his sound.
    "Vvvv— vvvv!"
        —L.B.S.

Ask the children to make the "vvv" sound each time it occurs. The sound should be prolonged.

I WILL MAKE A VALENTINE

I will make a valentine,
    A valentine of red.
I will give the valentine
    To a boy named Fred.

I will make a valentine,
  A valentine of blue.
I will give this valentine
  To a girl named Sue.

I will make a valentine,
  A valentine of yellow.
I will give this valentine
  To a friendly fellow.

I will make a valentine,
  A valentine of green.
I will give this valentine
  To a girl named Jeanne.

I will make a valentine,
  A valentine of pink.
I will give this valentine
  To a boy named Link.

I will make a valentine,
  Of red and white and blue.
I will give this valentine
  To no one else but you.

—J.J.T.

The children may cut different colored valentines from construction paper and hold them up as the rhyme is said. Various lines may be used as solos.

VALENTINES, VALENTINES!

Valentines, valentines,
Fifty-five or more —
Why, you can find valentines
In almost any store!

Valentines with violets,
Valentines with lace,
Valentines with glitter,
Or with a cupid's face.

Valentines with verses
That say, "I love you true."
Valentines all trimmed with red
Or silver, green or blue.

Valentines, valentines,
Fifty-five or more —
Why, you can find valentines
In almost any store!

—L.B.S.

This poem may be learned easily by rote because of its repetitive nature. Words containing the "v" speech sound are *valentines, five, violets, verses,* and *silver.* The various lines describing valentines of a particular design or style may be assigned as solos.

THE VENTURES AND THEIR ADVENTURES

Mr. and Mrs. Venture lived in a pretty cottage covered with vines. The cottage was in a village. Now Mr. and Mrs. Venture had no children, but they did have a happy pet housefly named Lovey.

Lovey buzzed here and there singing her joyful song: "Vvvvvvvv!" (*Children participate.*)

One day, the Ventures decided to go to the fair. As they started out the door of the cottage, Lovey buzzed: "Vvvvvvvvvv!"

"Be quiet, you noisy fly," said Mr. Venture with annoyance. The Ventures did not know that Lovey was trying to warn them that a match had not been blown out and was burning away in a basket of old papers. So the Ventures went to the fair and, while they were gone, their

218

pretty cottage burned to the ground. The fire department could not save one single stick of their little cottage.

The Ventures, of course, had to set about looking for a new home, and Lovey buzzed along right behind them: "Vvvvvvvvv!" That night the Ventures slept under a tree. In the middle of the night they were awakened by angry voices. Peering from behind the tree, the Ventures saw two robbers who were fighting over a bag of gold.

"The gold is MINE!" shouted one robber.

"No! The gold is MINE!" shouted the other.

Then Lovey flew out from behind the tree where the Ventures were hiding and buzzed right in the robbers' ears. "Vvvvvvvvvv!"

"Help!" cried the robbers, and they dropped the bag of gold and ran away.

The Ventures looked at the bag of gold.

"Shall we keep it?" asked Mr. Venture.

"Shall we take it to the Mayor?" asked Mrs. Venture.

They were both so excited about the gold that they forgot all about thanking their pet housefly or giving her credit for chasing away the robbers.

The Ventures wound up by taking the gold to the mayor, who took it to the city council. After a time, the mayor came back, thanked the Ventures and gave them a reward of ten pounds. As the Ventures resumed their walk down the road, Lovey buzzed along behind them: "Vvvvvvvvvvv!" On their way, they met a man with a violin.

"Please buy my violin," pleaded the man. "It is a good violin, but I have had no violin lessons and I cannot play it."

"Vvvvvvvvvvv," buzzed the housefly. She tried to tell the Ventures that they could not play a violin either — that they would, in truth, be wasting their money. But the Ventures did not listen. They gave the man their ten pounds — all the money they had — and took the violin.

Mr. Venture played the violin rather badly, for what else could he do with a bow that had only two slender hairs. And poor Mrs. Venture sang a very sad song. The screechy, screechy tune and the squeaky, squeaky song were heard by a man with a vacuum cleaner. The vacuum cleaner needed a new cord, but of course the man would say nothing about this, for he wanted to get rid of it.

"I adore your music," said the man with the vacuum cleaner. "Would you be willing to trade that violin for this fine vacuum cleaner?"

"Well," said Mr. Venture. "We will certainly need a vacuum cleaner when we find a home."

"Vvvvvvvvvv!" buzzed Lovey. She tried to tell the Ventures that they were getting no bargain. But the Ventures said crossly, "Be quiet, noisy fly," and they traded their violin for the vacuum cleaner.

A third man came along. He was wearing a yellow polka-dot vest. "Oh," cried Mr. Venture. "I have wanted a polka-dot vest for a long time. Will you trade your vest for this vacuum cleaner?"

Now the vest had a big hole in the back and the man was anxious to get rid of it. Besides that, he was an electrician and he was sure that he could fix the vacuum cleaner as good as new. So the trade was made.

"Vvvvvvvvvv!" buzzed Lovey. But, of course, it was too late to tell the Ventures anything.

Along the road came a little girl carrying a valentine.

"Oh," cried Mrs. Venture happily. "What a beautiful valentine! Would you trade it for this yellow polka-dot vest, little girl?"

"Vvvvvvvvvv!" buzzed Lovey, but the warning went unheeded.

The little girl liked to dress up in old clothes so she agreed to trade her valentine for the vest. She found that the vest fit her to a T, even though there was a hole in back, and she went off down the road skipping and singing.

The Ventures carried the valentine and took turns admiring it, but a wind came along and whisked the valentine right out of Mrs. Venture's hand. It went sailing out of sight to nobody knew where.

So the Ventures had nothing to show for any of their trades, and they were as penniless as when they started.

As they walked along, they began to think about all that had occurred. Finally Mr. Venture said, "We have been very foolish. Now we must begin to do something useful with our lives."

"That is indeed true," agreed Mrs. Venture. "What shall we do that is useful?"

Mr. Venture did not really know, but as the two of them rested under a tree, with Lovey buzzing quietly nearby, Mr. Venture had an inspiration and a thought. He pulled a notepad and pencil out of his pocket and began to write a poem.

There were really a great many verses, but there is not time to read them now. Mr. Venture sent the verses to a magazine and he won first prize. Mr. Venture became a famous poet who traveled all over the country with Mrs. Venture, giving lectures on poetry to large audiences.

Lovey, the pet housefly, buzzed right along behind them: "Vvvvvvv!"

Mrs. Venture decided to try her hand at writing, too, and she wrote a children's book called *Lovey, the Pet Housefly*. The book won the "best literature" award for that year! The Ventures never, never told Lovey to be quiet again, and all their lives were full of peace and happiness.

—L.B.S.

The children join in saying the "Vvvvvvv" refrain each time it occurs in the story. Words which contain the "v" sound are *Ventures, adventures, Lovey, violin, vacuum, vest, valentine, vines, lives, very,* and *verses.*

CHAPTER 9

The "Sh" and "Zh" Speech Sounds

MAKING THE SPEECH SOUND

When the *sh* speech sound is produced, the sides of the tongue are pressed against the teeth and gums while the body of the tongue is arched toward the hard palate. The lips are protruded and drawn in slightly at the corners. The teeth are slightly separated. The soft palate is raised, and there is no vibration of the vocal cords. Air is forced out between the teeth in a wide path to make the voiceless sound of "sh." This is a continuant sound.

You may call "sh" the "seashell" or the "quiet" sound.

CORRECTING THE DEFICIENT SPEECH SOUND

This speech sound frequently is misarticulated if the child retracts the lips in a smiling position. He may substitute "s," "t," or "ch" for "sh," e.g., *seep* for *sheep, teep* for *sheep,* or *cheep* for *sheep.* Conversely, the child also may substitute "sh" for "ch," e.g., *sheep* for *cheep.* Air may slip over the sides of the tongue, causing a lateral lisp.

Asking the child to protrude the lips as he watches himself in a mirror is the first step in correction after he has heard the sound correctly and is able to differentiate it from the incorrect sound he is producing.

INSTRUCTIONS TO THE CHILD

"I will make a quiet sound: 'sh.' (*Prolong the sound.*) Did you hear it? The voice motor does not hum. Push out your lips like a piggy nose. Good! Now make the air rush out: 'sh— sh— sh.' Let's name some words that begin with the quiet sound: *shoe, shell, shade, shelf.* Here is a rhyme about a seashell that makes the sound of the sea. When you hear the quiet sound of the sea, make it with me."

> Little seashell by the sea,
> Whisper your pretty sound to me.
> "Sh— sh— sh!"
> Now I know what I will do!
> I'll whisper your sound right back at you!
> "Sh— sh— sh!"
>
> —L.B.S.

WORDS FOR PRACTICE

Initial	Medial	Final
shoe	seashore	fish
ship	threshers	sash
shelf	wishing	bush
shadow	squashes	wash
sheep	usher	dish
shell	cowshed	brush

223

I HEAR IT

Refer to the section on "s" for suggestions on using "I Hear It." This selection includes the "ch" and "s" sounds commonly substituted for "sh."

I hear it in *share* but not in *chair.*
I hear it in *sheaf* but not in *chief.*
I hear it in *sheep* but not in *cheep.*
    I hear it in *sheet* but not in *cheat.*
    I hear it in *shin* but not in *chin.*
    I push out my lips and I make them round
    When I make this very quiet sound.
    "Sh— sh— sh!" (*Prolong each sound.*)
I hear it in *show* but not in *so.*
I hear it in *shore* but not in *sore.*
I hear it in *shoot* but not in *suit.*
    I hear it in *shoe* but not in *Sue.*
    I hear it in *shock* but not in *sock.*
    I push out my lips and I make them round
    When I make this very quiet sound.
    "Sh— sh— sh!"

—L.B.S.

ARE WE LISTENING?

1. At the *seashore,* I had a wonderful time with my friend. The sun was *shining* warm and bright and casting *shadows* on the sand. We ate *shrimp* at a restaurant. We bought some *shells* at a little *shop.* Are we listening? Let's see! Where did I go? What was the sun doing? What did we buy? Where did we buy it? What did we eat?

2. Out on a lonely hillside, stood a *shepherd.* He was tending his *sheep.* When evening came, he herded the *sheep* back to the farm and they went into a *shed.* The next morning, he *sheared* the *sheep* and sold the wool

to make cloth. Are we listening? Let's see! Who stood on the hillside? What was he doing? When evening came, what did he do? What happened to the *sheep* the next morning? Where did the *sheep* sleep?

3. What do we do at my house in the morning? My daddy *shaves* and goes to work. My sister *shampoos* her hair and takes a *shower*. My mother finds me a clean *shirt*. I tie my *shoes* and get ready for school. Are we listening? Let's see! What does Daddy do? What does Sister do? What does Mother do? What do I do? Which of these things are done at your house in the morning?

—L.B.S.

THE SOUND OF "SH"

"Sh!" the trees whisper
    when the wind passes near.
"Sh!" sings the seashell
    when it's held near your ear.
"Sh!" says your mother
    if the baby's asleep.
"Sh!" the waves echo
    from the ocean deep.

—J.J.T.

Ask the children to make the "quiet" sound each time it occurs in the poem.

SKATING

Let us go skating over the ice;
    Swish, swish, swish!
The air is crisp and the weather is nice.
    Swish, swish, swish!
My hands are warm and my feet are, too;
    Swish, swish, swish!

225

I have a red scarf and my skates are new.
    Swish, swish, swish!
Oh, let us go skating over the ice!
    Swish, swish, swish!
And what if we do fall once or twice?
    Swish, swish, swish!

—L.B.S.

The children say the refrain which emphasizes the "sh" sound at the end of *swish*. The "sh" sound can be prolonged to imitate the sound of skate blades gliding across the ice.

THE WHISPERING TREES

In the back of my yard are the whispering trees,
And they sway very quietly in the warm breeze.
CHILDREN: "Sh— sh— sh!" (*Prolong the sound.*)
            "Sh— sh— sh!"

They whisper their secrets only to *me,*
And only *I* know what their secrets can be.
CHILDREN: "Sh— sh— sh!"
            "Sh— sh— sh!"

If you hear the trees whisper, please answer them, do!
And I know they will share many secrets with you.
CHILDREN: "Sh— sh— sh!"
            "Sh— sh— sh!"

—L.B.S.

Ask individual children to tell what they might hear the trees whisper.

SH! SH! SH!

"Sh, sh, sh!" I hear galoshes in the snow,
        galoshes in the snow,
        galoshes in the snow.

"Sh, sh, sh!" I hear galoshes in the snow,
And the snow is where I play!

"Sh, sh, sh!" I hear the seashell in the sand,
        the seashell in the sand,
        the seashell in the sand.
"Sh, sh, sh!" I hear the seashell in the sand,
And the sand is where I play!

"Sh, sh, sh!" I hear the squishy-wishy mud,
        the squishy-wishy mud,
        the squishy-wishy mud.
"Sh, sh, sh!" I hear the squishy-wishy mud,
And the mud is where I play!

"Sh, sh, sh!" I hear a cricket near my bed,
        a cricket near my bed,
        a cricket near my bed.
"Sh, sh, sh!" I hear a cricket near my bed,
And its music makes me sleep!

—L.B.S.

This poem can be learned easily by rote because of the repetition of words and phrases. The children make the "sh" speech sound each time it occurs. Ask them to tell what else makes the "sh" sound. Words containing this sound are *galoshes, seashell, squishy-wishy.*

THE SEASHELL

One day at the beach, the wind blew fiercely. The waves dashed high on the rocks. Swish— swish— swish— swash! (*Children imitate words and prolong the final "sh."*)

A little seashell from the ocean deep
Was suddenly awakened from his sleep.

The angry ocean tossed the little seashell back and forth, back and forth. The little seashell was frightened and cried, "What is happening to me?" Then with one big SWISH, a huge wave tossed the little seashell out on the beach. And there he lay, too afraid to move.

Then everything was still. The waves stopped dashing and splashing. The wind made a soft whispering sound. The bright sun came out and smiled down on the trembling little seashell. The whisper made by the wind was just like a soft lullaby. Here is what the wind sang:

> "Shhhhh, little seashell
> Lying on the sand.
> Do not be afraid,
> For you have friends on the land.
> Shhhhh!"
> (*Children repeat refrain each time.*)

The waves murmured softly,

> "Shhhhh, little seashell
> From the ocean deep,
> Listen to my lullaby,
> And soon you'll be asleep."
> (*Children repeat.*)

The sun said nothing, but it shone radiantly down on the little seashell and made him feel all warm and comfortable and safe.

Suddenly, the little seashell was picked up off the beach and tossed high into the air. The little seashell heard a boy say, "Oh, this is just an old seashell. It is not worth anything. I don't want it." And the boy threw the seashell down in the sand.

The frightened little seashell again lay on the beach.

But the ocean whispered,

"Shhhhh, little seashell,
Just lie very still.
Nothing can bother you.
Nothing will!
Shhhhh!" (*Children imitate.*)

The breeze sang,

"Shhhhh, little seashell,
Be calm and still.
Nothing can harm you.
Nothing will." (*Children repeat.*)

Then a tired little boy came to where the seashell was lying so very calm and still. And the little seashell knew that the tired little boy had been crying because he was lost from his father and mother.

The little seashell forgot his own problems because he was so sorry for the tired little boy. The seashell thought, "Perhaps — perhaps, if I whisper the quiet sound, the little boy will hear me and stop crying."

So the seashell whispered the song of the ocean and the wind, "Sh— sh— sh— sh— sh!" (*Children repeat and prolong the sound.*)

Surely enough, the tired little boy did stop crying and he looked all around to see where the lovely quiet sound was coming from.

Then he saw the little seashell.

"What a pretty seashell," said the tired little boy.

The seashell whispered, "Sh— sh— sh— sh!" (*Children imitate.*)

"The seashell is talking to me," said the little boy. He picked it up and held it close to his ear and listened, "Sh— sh— sh— sh!" (*Children imitate.*)

Soon the tired little boy's mother and father came along, and they were very, very glad to see that their little boy was safe and was not crying. The father picked up his tired little boy, who held the seashell in a hand that had grown limp. In fact, the tired little boy's whole body had become limp, for he was now fast asleep.

They all went home together, the mother, the father, the tired little boy, and the seashell. And all night long, the seashell lay on the shelf in the tired little boy's room. The little seashell sang and sang happily all the night long, "Sh— sh— sh— sh!" (*Children imitate.*)

The little seashell was so happy because he knew that he had helped a tired little boy by singing the lovely quiet song that the ocean and the wind had taught him. "Sh— sh— sh— sh!" (*Children imitate.*)

—L.B.S.

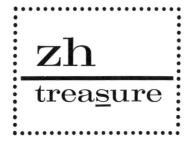

MAKING THE SPEECH SOUND

This sound is made like "sh," except that the vocal cords vibrate. The "zh" speech sound is one of the last sounds acquired by the child in normal speech development, since it is found in so few of his early vocabulary words. This sound occurs only medially and finally in words, and the sound is never spelled by the letters *zh* in a word. In standard fourth grade dictionaries, "zh" is listed as the symbol for the *s* in *television*.

230

You may call "zh" the "space-ship," the "hair-clippers," or the "vacuum-cleaner" sound.

CORRECTING THE DEFICIENT SPEECH SOUND

Correction should follow the techniques for the "sh" speech sound. Ask the children to place their fingers on the front of the throat and hum "zh," prolonging the sound.

INSTRUCTIONS TO THE CHILD

"When you say *television,* do you hear a 'zh' sound inside the word? Say the word with me: *television.* Did you hear the sound? Name these words after me and listen for the 'zh' sound: *measure, treasure, explosion.* Did you hear the 'zh' sound in those three words? Here is a rhyme about a vacuum cleaner that says 'zh— zh' when it cleans the room."

The vacuum cleaner hums and hums
As it picks up dirt and crumbs.
"Zh— zh— zh!"
It is so nice to know it can
Keep my room all spick-and-span.
"Zh— zh— zh!"

—L.B.S.

WORDS FOR PRACTICE

Initial	Medial	Final
——	pleasure	garage
	division	rouge
	invasion	barrage
	leisure	mirage
	television	prestige
	explosion	loge

HELICOPTER

The helicopter on the ground
Makes a very noisy sound.
    "Zh— zh— zh!"

Now it is warming up to fly,
And soon I will be in the sky.
    "Zh— zh— zh!"

It needs no runway like a plane;
It lands and goes straight up again.
    "Zh— zh— zh!"

Now tell me, why do you suppose
It never even bumps its nose?
    "Zh zh— zh!"

            —L.B.S.

THE "HAIR-CLIPPERS" SOUND

Benny sits very tall in the big barber chair,
And he listens to the clippers as they cut off his hair.
    "Zh— zh— zh!"
    "Zh— zh— zh!"

The clippers trim so carefully all the way around.
Oh, Benny likes to listen to the "hair-clippers" sound.
    "Zh— zh— zh!"
    "Zh— zh— zh!"

"Thank you, Mister Barber," Benny says. "Now I
   will pay
For the haircut that your hair clippers gave me today."
    "Zh— zh— zh!"
    "Zh— zh— zh!"

            —L.B.S.

The children make the "zh" speech sound each time it occurs
in the rhyme.

232

MEASURING MYSELF

I measured my arm,
I measured my toes,
I measured my fingers,
I measured my nose,
I measured my neck,
I measured my chest,
I measured my waist,
And now I will rest!

—L.B.S.

The "zh" sound is used medially in the word *measured*. The poem may be pantomimed as the children say it in unison.

BOUND FOR A STAR

"Zh———!" goes the rocket
Bound for a star.
"Zh———!" goes the rocket
Traveling afar,
          Past meteors,
          Past rainbows,
          Past comets at play.
          The rocket zooms on
          To a star far away.
"Zh———!" goes the rocket
Bound for a star.
"Zh———!" goes the rocket
Traveling afar.
"Zh—————!"
     (*Voice gets softer.*)

—J.J.T.

This poem presents the "zh" sound in isolation. Have the children prolong the sound whenever it occurs. The poem can be used as motivation for the story which is included at the end of this section.

Artemus, the astronaut, walked toward his rocket. He was the youngest astronaut in the whole world. But young as he was, this was still not his first trip into space. He couldn't even remember how many times before he had soared through the air in the nose of a huge rocket.

Now he was almost ready for another trip. He climbed inside the big rocket and settled into his specially built seat to wait for the countdown and blast-off. He switched on his air-conditioning unit. "Zh———!" sounded the motor quietly. He checked his safety straps to be sure each was fastened. Then he turned on the small television set that would let him see what was happening outside the rocket. The motor of the air conditioner made a quiet sound: "Zh———!"

Artemus checked the dials in front of him. There were large round dials and small square dials. Right inside the rocket there was a dial that would measure how fast he was going and a dial that would measure how many miles he had traveled in space.

From deep inside the big rocket came the sound of its motor starting. "Zh———!" it went. "Zh———!" It wasn't a very loud noise now, but Artemus knew that soon it would burst into a tremendous roaring noise that would fill his ears with its sound. "Zh———!" said the rocket motor as it waited to start its trip into space.

Artemus began to turn other switches that controlled the machines and motors that would make it possible for him to carry on his job when he was zooming through space at thousands of miles an hour. His little compartment slowly began to fill with sound.

"Zh———!" (*Softly.*)

"Zh———!" (*A little louder.*)

"Zh———!" (*With a loud voice.*)

The countdown was about to begin. Artemus would just have time to take a look inside his special treasure box and think about each of the treasures he kept there. He reached down under his seat and pulled out a box. It was made of metal and had a hinged lid.

His eyes sparkled as he lifted each treasure gently and placed it back inside the box. There was the ring that he had found on his visit to the zoo and the round sand dollar from his trip to the seashore last summer. There were two small, square magnets from a rocket motor, a pencil flashlight, a souvenir pennant from the County Fair, a shiny rock that looked like gold, and a tiny plastic dog that someone had given him for Christmas.

Perhaps he would find something to add to his collection of treasures on this trip through space. Some comet dust perhaps? Or a shooting star?

He closed his treasure box and placed it under the seat again. It was time to start the countdown. He listened. His equipment was in fine order. "Zh———!" sang the motors. "Zh———!" echoed the machinery. "Zh———!" answered all the instruments inside the big rocket. "Zh———!"

Now, the countdown had started. Ten — nine — eight — seven — six —— Suddenly, Artemus heard a voice that interrupted the countdown.

"Artemus! Artemus!" called the voice.

Five — four — three — two — the countdown continued.

"Artemus!" It was his mother calling.

"Come, now, and get cleaned up for supper."

The countdown stopped.

The trip through outer space in the great rocket ship would have to be postponed until after supper.

Artemus climbed slowly out of the big cardboard box that he called his rocket and walked across his backyard to the house. The sound of the rocket motor seemed to follow him across the yard. "Zh———!" it went. "Zh———!" until the back door closed behind Artemus.

—J.J.T.

As the story is read, the children should be encouraged to make the "zh" sound each time it occurs. Have them prolong the sound for best effect. If desired, let the children suggest items that Artemus might have included in his treasure box. You may wish to have the children listen for words in which the "zh" sound occurs, i.e., *measure, treasure, television*.

CHAPTER 10

The "Ch" and "J" Speech Sounds

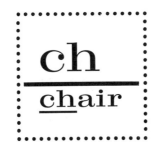

MAKING THE SPEECH SOUND

This sound is a combination of "t" and "sh." In producing it, the tongue, lips, and teeth move rapidly from the "t" position to the "sh" position. The tongue tip is pressed firmly against the entire gum ridge, holding the air inside the mouth. As the tongue assumes the position for "sh," the air is released suddenly and explosively as the "ch" sound. The lips are squared or drawn in slightly at the corners and protruded. The soft palate is raised, and there is no vibration of the vocal cords. This speech sound is misarticulated frequently.

You may call "ch" the "train," the "engine," or the "sneezing" sound.

CORRECTING THE DEFICIENT SPEECH SOUND

As pointed out above, this speech sound is a combination of two sounds, "t" and "sh." It is the transition from one sound placement to another that causes much of the difficulty. It is hard for the child to make the rapid movements needed to produce the explosive "ch" as in *chin.* Therefore, "t" may be substituted for "ch," e.g., *tair* for *chair;* or the child may find it easier to make only the last part of the sound and say *share* for *chair.* Both the latter substitution and reversed pronunciation (*chair* for *share*) are common among Spanish-American children, who confuse these two sounds by saying, "I will sit in a *share* and tie my *choose.*"

Occasionally, air may spill over the sides of the tongue, causing a lateral lisp.

Ear training should be provided for "sh" and "ch." Here is a suggested list of word pairs for practice:

shoe — chew	sheep — cheap	dish — ditch	wish — witch
ship — chip	shin — chin	wash — watch	hash — hatch

INSTRUCTIONS TO THE CHILD

"To make a good 'sneeze' sound, it is important to hear the sound properly. Clap when you hear me say a word that begins with 'ch' as in *chicken: children, chimney, cherry,* fan, *cheese.* Did you hear it plainly? Good! I will open my mouth just wide enough for you to see my tongue tip go up and touch the little shelf behind my upper teeth. Did you see it? Let me see your tongue tip do the same. Now I will put my tongue tip up again and drop it down for 'sh.' I will do this several times: 't—sh, t—sh, t—sh.' Try this with me. Now I will do it fast: 'Ch, ch, ch, ch.' That sounded like an engine, didn't it? Let's start our engines very slowly: 't—sh, t—sh, t—sh, t—sh, ch, ch, ch.' Let's make our trains go 'choo-choo-choo-choo.' Here is a counting rhyme in which you can make that engine sound with me."

238

ENGINES

Engine, engine, number one,
Take me with you just for fun!
"Ch, ch, ch! Ch, ch, ch!"
Engine, engine, number two,
I like everything you do.
"Ch, ch, ch! Ch, ch, ch!"
Engine, engine, number three,
Make your engine sound for me.
"Ch, ch, ch! Ch, ch, ch!"
Engine, engine, number four,
Let's go faster, I implore.
"Ch, ch, ch! Ch, ch, ch!"

Engine, engine, number five,
Be sure to stop when we arrive.
"Ch, ch, ch! Ch, ch, ch!"
Engine, engine, number six,
I can hear your clickety-clicks.
"Ch, ch, ch! Ch, ch, ch!"
Engine, engine, number seven,
It's twenty minutes to eleven.
"Ch, ch, ch! Ch, ch, ch!"
Engine, engine, number eight,
Hurry now, and don't be late.
"Ch, ch, ch! Ch, ch, ch!"

Engine, engine, number nine,
Toot your whistle. That is fine!
"Ch, ch, ch! Ch, ch, ch!"
Engine, engine, number ten,
Let us make that sound again.
"Ch, ch, ch! Ch, ch, ch!"

—L.B.S.

This rhyme may be used as a chant for jumping rope. The word
engine contains medial "j," the voiced cognate of "ch."

WORDS FOR PRACTICE

Initial	*Medial*	*Final*
chimney	hatchet	match
chocolate	teacher	witch
check	peaches	coach
chain	Richard	watch
Charles	kitchen	sandwich
chick	woodchuck	hutch

I HEAR IT

The common substitutions, "t" and "sh" for "ch," are emphasized in the following drill. See the unit on "s" for instructions for using the "I Hear It" selection.

I hear it in *chair* but not in *share*.
I hear it in *cheat* but not in *sheet*.
I hear it in *cheer* but not in *shear*.
> I hear it in *chew* but not in *shoe*.
> I hear it in *chip* but not in *ship*.
> I raise up my tongue to make a *t,*
> And it drops down for "sh" as you can see.
> "T—sh, t—sh, t—sh, ch!"

I hear it in *chub* but not in *tub*.
I hear it in *chop* but not in *top*.
I hear it in *chin* but not in *tin*.
> I hear it in *chap* but not in *tap*.
> I hear it in *chalk* but not in *talk*.
> I raise up my tongue to make a *t,*
> And it drops down for "sh" as you can see.
> "T—sh, t—sh, t—sh, ch!"

—L.B.S.

ARE WE LISTENING?

1. When I went to the woods, first I saw a *chipmunk*. It went, *"Chatter-chatter,"* as it ran up the tree. I saw little squirrels *chasing* among the bushes. Are we listening?

Let's see! Which animals were *chasing* among the bushes? Who said, *"Chatter-chatter"*? What was the first animal I saw in the woods? What were the squirrels doing?

2. *Charles* went to a restaurant. He ate fried *chicken.* Then he had a toasted *cheese sandwich.* His mother had *cherry* pie for dessert. His father had *cheese* cake. For dessert, *Charles* had *chocolate* ice cream. Are we listening? Let's see! What kind of *sandwich* did *Charles* have? What did his mother have for dessert? What did his father have for dessert? What did *Charles* have for dessert? Who went to the restaurant? What fried food did *Charles* eat?

3. In the living room, we have a TV set. We turned it on. The *channel* was 10. We saw a show about Indians. In the show, a big *chief* called his braves together and they had a pow-wow. Daddy *watched.* He sat in his big leather *chair.* Grandpa played *checkers* with Mother. Are we listening? Let's see! What station did we turn on? Who called his braves together for a pow-wow? Where did Daddy sit? What game did Mother and Grandpa play?

—L.B.S.

SONG OF THE TRAIN

"Ch! Ch! Ch-ch-ch!"
That is the song of the train.
"Ch! Ch! Ch-ch-ch!"
Through the sunshine and rain.

"Ch! Ch! Ch-ch-ch!"
Clicking over the track.
"Ch! Ch! Ch-ch-ch!"
With a red caboose at the back.

Coal cars,
Freight cars,
Oil cars, too!
Chugging,
Chugging!
All night through.

"Ch! Ch! Ch-ch-ch!"
With a red caboose at the back.
"Ch! Ch! Ch-ch-ch!"
Clicking over the track.

"Ch! Ch! Ch-ch-ch!"
Through the sunshine and rain.
"Ch! Ch! Ch-ch-ch!"
That is the song of the train.

—J.J.T.

The "ch" sound is presented in isolation in this poem. The concept of loudness as one aspect of vocal nuance can be taught through having the children make the train disappear into the distance. The volume of their voices is reduced as the "Ch! Ch! Ch-ch-ch!" becomes softer and softer and finally fades away.

THE LITTLE TRAIN

The little train goes,
"Choo, choo, choo!"
It blows its whistle
Too, too, too!
"Ch, ch, ch! Choo, choo, choo!
Ch, ch, ch! Choo, choo, choo!"

The little train runs
Down the track.
It turns around and
Comes right back!

"Ch, ch, ch! Choo, choo, choo!
Ch, ch, ch! Choo, choo, choo!
Whoo—oo—oo—oo!"

—L.B.S.

Ask the children to rub sand blocks or the palms of their hands together as they make the sound of the train. The poem may be acted out as the class forms coaches and an engine and runs around the room. One group of children may make the "ch" sound throughout the poem.

THE SNEEZES

TEACHER: If I ever catch a cold
                   And have the sniffles, too,
                   I may have to sneeze and sneeze.
CHILDREN: Ker-choo! Ker-choo! Ker-choo!
                   Ker-choo! Ker-choo!
                   I have to sneeze.
                   Ker-choo! Ker-choo!
                   Excuse me, please!

TEACHER: And I must use my handkerchief
                   To keep the sneeze from you.
                   I cover up my mouth and nose.
CHILDREN: Ker-choo! Ker-choo! Ker-choo!
                   Ker-choo! Ker-choo!
                   I have to sneeze.
                   Ker-choo! Ker-choo!
                   Excuse me, please!

—J.J.T.

When this selection was tried out in the classroom, one second grader suggested that each member of the class hold up a handkerchief before his nose and mouth as the sneezes were taking place. Used in this way, the poem provides an effective lesson in good health habits.

243

I'M A TRUCK

I'm a truck,
I'm a truck,
I work hard every day.
I'm a truck,
I'm a truck,
I travel on the big highway.
     "Ch, ch, ch, ch, ch, ch!"
     I travel on the big highway!

I'm a van,
I'm a van,
And I work with all my might.
I'm a van,
I'm a van,
Moving furniture in the night.
     "Ch, ch, ch, ch, ch, ch!"
     Moving furniture in the night!

I'm a bus,
I'm a bus,
Come along and take a ride.
I'm a bus,
I'm a bus,
I have thirty-two seats inside.
     "Ch, ch, ch, ch, ch, ch!"
     I have thirty-two seats inside!
               —L.B.S.

Suggest that the children make up a tune for the poem. Remind them that the lips must be "pushed out" to make a good "ch-ch" sound.

THE CHERRY TREE

Robin Redbreast lived in a cherry tree.
"Cherrily, cherrily, cheer-up," said he.

"Who will eat ripe cherries today with me?
Cherrily, cherrily, chee!"

A little brown chipmunk came by that way.
"Chattery, chattery, chatter," said he.
"I will eat some cherries with you today.
Chattery, chattery, chee!"

Some happy children came out to play.
"We are so hungry for cherries," said they.
"May we share some cherries with you today?"
Said Robin, "Of course you may."

"Cherrily, cheer-up, cherrily chee.
Come, children, eat some ripe cherries with me!
There are plenty of cherries for all," said he.
"Cherrily, cherrily, chee!"

—L.B.S.

Ask the children to tell what they know about robins.

CHEE-CHEE-A-ROO

TEACHER: Each morning when the sun comes up,
I feel just like a bird.
I sing and sing a happy song;
It's something I have heard.

CHILDREN: Chee-chee-chee-a-ree,
Chee-chee-chee-a-roo,
Chee-a-ree, chee-a-roo,
Chee-a-ree-a-roo.

TEACHER: I don't know where I heard the song,
Or how it came to be,
Unless the robin made it up
Especially for me.

CHILDREN: Chee-chee-chee-a-ree,
             Chee-chee-chee-a-roo,
             Chee-a-ree, chee-a-roo,
             Chee-a-ree-a-roo.

TEACHER: I like to sing chee-chee-a-roo,
             Because I feel so gay,
             And people want to listen to
             My cheerful song all day.

CHILDREN: Chee-chee-chee-a-ree,
             Chee-chee-chee-a-roo,
             Chee-a-ree, chee-a-roo,
             Chee-a-ree-a-roo.

                                              —J.J.T.

This selection may be used for a special program as well as for practice on the "ch" speech sound.

CHOO-CHOO ENGINE [1]

Once there was a little steam engine named Choo-Choo who lived in Santa's workshop at the North Pole. Now Choo-Choo was a pretty little engine, for Santa's seventeen elves had made bright, shiny wheels, a red cab, and a black smokestack for him. They even made a fine whistle that went, "Toot-toot! Toot-toot!"

The elves gave Choo-Choo a special engine sound, too: "Ch, ch, ch, ch, ch, ch, ch!" (*Children imitate.*) In fact, Choo-Choo liked his engine sound so much that he practiced it over and over very carefully: "T—sh, t—sh, t—sh, t—sh, t—sh!" (*Children imitate by placing tongue tip up for "t" and dropping it down for "sh."*) "Ch, ch, ch, ch, ch, ch, ch, ch, ch, sh—!" (*Say "ch" sounds fast, gradually slowing down to a stop with "sh."*)

_____

[1] From the *Listening Time Records, Album 3,* by special permission of Bowmar Records. Story by Louise Binder Scott.

It was just one day until Christmas Eve and there were letters coming from boys and girls all over the world — letters in every language asking for toys. It kept Santa busy just opening the letters, to say nothing of filling all of the orders for toys. Whoosh! Down Santa's chimney came thousands of letters, one following the other. It fairly made Santa's head spin trying to keep up with them.

Mary wanted a dancing doll with yellow curls and silver slippers. Terry wanted an army of marching soldiers beating drums. Lisa wanted a velvet bunny with a powder-puffy tail and long floppy ears. But not one boy or girl asked for Choo-Choo.

Choo-Choo knew this, and he felt so disappointed and so sad when Santa Claus said, "You are a splendid engine, Choo-Choo, but perhaps my seventeen elves should not have made you. Children seem to want streamlined trains these days. You are a bit old-fashioned." But when Santa saw that he had hurt Choo-Choo's feelings, he said, "Never mind, Choo-Choo. Perhaps someone will ask for you after all. Just keep yourself in trim. One of these days, someone will ask for you, I am sure."

All that long day before Christmas Eve, Choo-Choo sat on the toy shelf and practiced and practiced his engine sound so he would be ready just in case a letter came asking for him. "Ch, ch, ch, ch, ch, ch." (*Children imitate.*)

At last Christmas Eve arrived. There was much commotion in the workshop. Santa brushed the fur on his coat as he prepared for the long journey, and Mrs. Santa mended his mittens.

"Now, let me see!" said Santa. "I wonder if I have everything. A top for Gary, a doll for Marie, a truck for Larry, and a jeep for Lee. A ball for Billy, a game for Ned, a dollhouse for Milly, and a bike for Ted. Well, I believe we are all ready," said Santa, pulling on his boots and fastening his belt. "My reindeer are anxious to start on this long trip. I wonder if I have forgotten anything?"

Yes, there *was* something. It was Choo-Choo. But nobody had asked for him, so what was Santa to do? Choo-Choo just sat in a corner making a sad choo-choo sound, "Ch, ch, ch, ch, ch, ch." (*Children imitate slowly.*)

Then suddenly, whoosh! Down the chimney came a letter. It came just as Santa was about to go out the door.

"Botheration!" said Santa. "I have no time to fill these last minute orders for toys. I should have been on my way three minutes ago." Santa sat down to think and, as he did so, he noticed Choo-Choo. His eyes brightened.

"Maybe," said Santa hopefully, "just maybe some boy or girl wants Choo-Choo. I'd better open the letter and read it to be sure." So he quickly opened the letter and read:

Dear Santa:

Please may I have a little steam engine? My grandfather is an engineer on a big engine that pulls a long freight train across many states. I want an engine just like his — one that makes a fine engine sound. That is all I want. Thank you, Santa.

Love,
Billy

"Hooray," cried Santa. "Billy wants Choo-Choo!"

Zip! Into Santa's bag went Choo-Choo. Zip! Into the sleigh went the bag! Zip! Over the housetops went the sleigh! Zip! Right onto Billy's rooftop coasted the sleigh! Zip! Down the chimney went Choo-Choo. Zip! Under the tree went Choo-Choo!

The next morning, Billy and his grandfather had a merry time watching Choo-Choo run around the tree and you can bet that Choo-Choo was the happiest little engine ever, for he now belonged to a very special little boy with whom he could share his fine engine sound. "Ch, ch, ch, ch, ch, ch." (*Children imitate.*)

One day, Chip went for a ride on the bus. *Chug, chug, chug, chug, chug!* (*Children repeat.*)

Along the highway went the bus. *Zippety-zip! Zzzzzzoom! Honk, honk! Chug, chug, chug, chug, chug!* (*Children repeat.*)

It was a lovely day and there were lots of things to see from the window. There were lots of things to see inside the bus, too. Mostly people!

Chip looked at the people. People, people, people! So many kinds of people there were! There were thin ones and fat ones. Some were men and some were women and some were boys and girls of all ages. There were dark skins and light skins and black, brown, and yellow hair. All of the people were going somewhere and Chip was going somewhere, too. *Chug, chug, chug, chug, chug, chug!* (*Children imitate.*)

Chip got tired of watching the people, so he looked out the window for a while. When he got tired of looking out the window, he watched the people again.

Scratch, scratch, scratch! What was THAT?

Chip listened. He could see nothing, but he could hear something. "Cheep, cheep, cheep, cheep!" (*Children repeat.*)

What do you think it was? (*Children guess.*)

Right behind Chip, sat a pretty little girl with blue eyes and blond hair. On her lap was a basket. The basket had a cloth cover.

Scratch, scratch, scratch! "Cheep, cheep, cheep, cheep!" (*Children imitate.*)

Chip did not want to stare at the basket on the little girl's lap. That would have been too impolite. But Chip was so curious it HURT.

Chip felt a tap on his shoulder and he looked around. It was the pretty little girl.

"Would you like to see what is in my basket?" she asked.

"Oh, would I!" said Chip eagerly, jumping to his knees on the seat and peering over the back of the seat.

The pretty little girl lifted the cloth on top of the basket.

"Cheep, cheep, cheep, cheep!" (*Children repeat.*)

Chip took a peek. There were six baby chicks! "Cheep, cheep, cheep!" (*Children repeat.*)

Chip smiled. The pretty little girl said, "I visited my grandfather's farm and he gave me these chicks to take home. Isn't this a lovely Easter present?"

Chip agreed and said so. He continued to smile and smile. Can you guess why? No? Chip was going to a farm that day himself, and the bus was taking him to a town where he would be met by *his* grandfather.

That very morning, Grandfather had called and said, "Chip, are you big enough to ride on the bus by yourself? Then come to visit me this weekend and see the new baby chicks that have just hatched out in the brooders."

So now you know why Chip was riding on the big bus that went *zippety-zip, zzzzzzzoom, honk, honk,* and *chug, chug, chug, chug, chug.* (*Children repeat.*)

Maybe — just maybe — Grandfather would give Chip one of the new baby chicks — or at least let him hold it for a little while.

—L.B.S.

Ask the children to imagine different endings for this story.

j
___
jeep

MAKING THE SPEECH SOUND

This sound is made like "ch," except that less pressure is exerted and the vocal cords vibrate. It is a combination of "d" and "zh," that is, the tongue tip rises to press against the alveolar ridge for "d," but the complete action or explosiveness does not occur. The tongue drops down for "zh" and the result is the "j" speech sound as in *jump*. The "j" sound is usually mispronounced by children who are also having difficulty with "ch."

You may call "j" the "jeep," the "trolley," or the "jumping-jack" sound.

CORRECTING THE DEFICIENT SPEECH SOUND

Ask the child to make "d" and then "zh" separately several times. Then try to combine the sounds in rapid succession. Ear training is important when the child is saying *dump* or *zhump* for *jump*. Air may spill over the sides of the tongue in a lateral lisp. Use the following word pairs to help the child discriminate between *ch* and *j*:

Jane — chain   joke — choke   jump — chump   Jill — chill

INSTRUCTIONS TO THE CHILD

"I am going to make a new sound, so listen carefully: 'j, j, j.' Did you hear it plainly? It sounds almost like the 'engine' sound, doesn't it? We will call it the 'jeep' sound, because the word *jeep* begins with that sound. Now I will name some words that have the 'jeep' sound at the end: *fudge, cage, budge.* Did you hear the 'jeep' sound? Raise your tongue tip and let it press against the shelf behind your upper teeth. Say 'd' with me. Now say 'zh' with me. Try to say the 'jeep' sound: 'j, j, j.' Fine! Let's make that 'jeep' sound as we say some words: *jeep, jam, jump.* Here is a poem about a jeep sound. Make the 'jeep' sound each time you hear it."

> Make a jeep sound with me now.
> Watch and I will show you how.
>> "J, j, j, j, j!"
> My tongue tip goes up high for "d,"
> And then drops down for "zh," you see!
>> "J, j, j, j, j!"
>
> —L.B.S.

WORDS FOR PRACTICE

Initial	Medial	Final
jam	magic	badge
judge	pigeon	bridge
jar	Dodgers	cage
jeep	major	hedge
joke	imagine	range
jay	engine	fudge

I HEAR IT

The "d" and "ch" sounds, common substitutions for "j," are emphasized in this "I Hear It" drill. For added instructions, refer to the "s" unit.

> I hear it in *jeep* but not in *cheap.*
> I hear it in *Jill* but not in *chill.*
> I hear it in *jest* but not in *chest.*

I hear it in *jug* but not in *dug*.
I hear it in *jolly* but not in *dolly*.
I raised my tongue tip up for *d,*
And dropped it down for "zh," you see.
"J, j, j."
I hear it in *junk* but not in *chunk*.
I hear it in *joke* but not in *choke*.
I hear it in *Jane* but not in *chain*.
I hear it in *just* but not in *dust*.
I hear it in *jump* but not in *dump*.
I raised my tongue tip up for *d,*
And dropped it down for "zh," you see.
"J, j, j."

—L.B.S.

THE JIGGLING TROLLEY CAR

Climb aboard,
And take a ride.
We will not start
Till you're inside.

Jiggle, jiggle, jum, jum!
Jiggle, jiggle, jum, jum!
Jiggle, little trolley car,
Jiggle on your track!

We pass many houses,
Both old and new.
Familiar places
Are gone from view!

Jiggle, jiggle, jum, jum!
Jiggle, jiggle, jum, jum!
Jiggle, little trolley car,
Jiggle on your track!

253

Red light says, "Stop!"
Green light says, "Go!"
Traffic is moving
Fast and slow.

Jiggle, jiggle, jum, jum!
Jiggle, jiggle, jum, jum!
Jiggle, little trolley car,
Jiggle on your track!

The trolley sways
And rocks me so.
Soon it's off
To sleep I go.

Jiggle, jiggle, jum, jum!
Jiggle, jiggle, jum, jum!
Jiggle, little trolley car,
Jiggle on your track!

—J.J.T.

This rhyme presents the "j" sound in a rhythmic nonsense phrase. The rhythm of the rhyme should convey the rocking and jiggling motion of a trolley. Have the children sway back and forth with gentle hip action, holding the back straight. Fists may turn in counter-clockwise motion to represent wheels.

THE JEEP

One day, I tried to start my jeep.
The motor turned around.
It went, "J, j, j, j, j,"
A most strange sort of sound.
"I just can't go, (*Slowly.*)
I just can't go!
Oh, jiggle, jiggle, jee.
I just can't go,
I just can't go!
What can the matter be?"

I said, "Oh, you have told me now!
I know just what you mean
When you say, 'J, j, j, j, j.'
You need some gasoline."
        "Now I can go, (*Faster.*)
        Now I can go!
        Oh, jiggle, jiggle, jee.
        Now I can go,
        Now I can go!
        I'm on my way, you see!
          'J, j, j, j, j,'
            Jiggle, jiggle, jiggle."
            (*Faster and faster as the voices*
            fade into a whisper.)
                        —L.B.S.

Let the children act out the poem. Call attention to the "j"
sound. Tongue tip touches the ridge behind the upper teeth and
drops down for "zh." Words which begin with the "jeep" sound
are *jeep, jiggle, jee,* and *just.* The word *strange* ends with the "j"
sound.

THE BIG, BIG BULLFROG

A big, big bullfrog sang, "Jug-a-rum,"
And his deep voice sounded like a big bass drum!
        "Jug-a-rum, jug-a-rum,
        Jug-a-jug-a-jug-a-jug-a,
        Jug-a-rum!"

255

The big, big bullfrog sang, of course,
In a low gruff voice that was rather hoarse.
    "Jug-a-rum, jug-a-rum,
    Jug-a-jug-a-jug-a-jug-a,
    Jug-a-rum!"

The big bullfrog was especially fond
Of little old insects that lived near the pond.
    "Jug-a-rum, jug-a-rum,
    Jug-a-jug-a-jug-a-jug-a,
    Jug-a-rum!"

The big, big bullfrog croaked all night;
He croaked and he croaked as any frog might.
    "Jug-a-rum, jug-a-rum,
    Jug-a-jug-a-jug-a-jug-a,
    Jug-a-rum!"

—L.B.S.

One child may play a guiro as the class says the refrain. The guiro is a hollow gourd which has notches cut on one side of it. The guiro is played by scraping a stick back and forth over the notches.

THE JOLLY, JOLLY JACK-O'-LANTERN

A jolly, jolly jack-o'-lantern sat upon a fence, all happy and proud because it was Halloween.

> Oh, he was so happy! (*Children repeat.*)
> He had a round face
> With a zig-zag grin,
> And some candle wax
> Was upon his chin.

There was a bright candle inside the jolly, jolly jack-o'-lantern, and the candle had melted a bit and dropped a little pin-point of wax on the jolly, jolly jack-o'-lantern's chin right below his grin. But the wax on his chin made the jolly, jolly jack-o'-lantern look, well — *distinguished!*

Of course, the jolly, jolly jack-o'-lantern was glad that he had a light to shine on Halloween night so that he could look scary. He said:

> "I'm a jolly, jolly jack-o'-lantern,
>   (*Children repeat.*)
> And my name begins with *J*.
> I'll play some jokes this Halloween
> On anyone who comes my way!"

All of the jet-black cats with stiff whiskers and jeweled eyes, and all of the jet-black witches who rode in the sky, and all of the brown bats that went flying by were scared of the jolly, jolly jack-o'-lantern when they heard him say:

> "I'm a jolly, jolly jack-o'-lantern,
>   (*Children repeat.*)
> And my name begins with *J*.
> I'll play some jokes this Halloween
> On anyone who comes my way!"

But all at once — WHOOSH! A wind came along and blew out the jolly, jolly jack-o'-lantern's candle. Now I ask you, what good is a jack-o'-lantern without a light on Halloween night? How could he look scary and how could he play jokes if he didn't look scary? The jolly, jolly jack-o'-lantern was no longer jolly and he no longer sang. But his name still began with *J*, and for that he was thankful.

The jet-black cats with the stiff whiskers and jeweled eyes, the jet-black witches who rode the skies, and the brown bats that went flying by were not a bit scared now.

The jet-black cats screamed, "MEE-OW!"

The jet-black witches laughed, "Hee-hee!"

The little brown bats whispered, "Look at us," as they swooped down and tried to knock the jack-o'-lantern off the fence.

But finally, they all grew tired of their teasing and disappeared into the night, leaving the jack-o'-lantern all alone on the fence. The candle wax was still upon his chin, but Mr. Jack-o'-lantern did not look quite so *distinguished*.

Suddenly, he felt something on his face, just below the bit of wax on his chin. The something moved. From the way it moved, the jack-o'-lantern knew it was a little bug, and he was SO glad to have company.

"Welcome, little bug," said the jack-o'-lantern.

"Oh, Mr. Jack-o'-lantern," said the little bug. "I am so cold, for the air is chill and the ground is covered with frost. I have nowhere to go." And the little bug began to cry.

"There, there," comforted the jack-o'-lantern. "Just crawl through my crooked mouth. Inside of me it is cozy and warm. There is a lot of heat left from the candle that was burning inside me before the wind blew it out."

"Thank you, thank you," said the little bug as it hurriedly crawled through the jack-o'-lantern's mouth and settled down for a nap.

The wind blew — WHOOSH! The air was chill. And the ground was covered with frost. But the little bug was warm inside the jack-o'-lantern, and although the jack-o'-lantern had no light to shine on Halloween night, he once more was happy deep down inside. After all his name did begin with *J* and he still had that pin-point of wax on his chin that made him look distinguished in an odd sort of way. But best of all, he had helped a little bug feel safe and warm.

—L.B.S.

The children gain practice on the "j" speech sound as they say the refrain. The story lends itself to creative dramatics.

JOHNNY JUMPER

Johnny Jumper was a rabbit that lived in a meadow with his mother and father. Since he was the only little rabbit in the family, often Johnny Jumper was very lonely. When this happened, Mother and Father Rabbit would try to find something interesting for Johnny Jumper to do. It might be counting carrot seeds. It might be playing a game called "Hide the Lettuce Leaf." There seemed to be no end to the number of things Johnny's mother and father could think up for him to do.

One day, when Johnny Jumper was lonely as could be, there was nobody around to help him think of interesting things to do. Mother Rabbit had gone to the village, and Father Rabbit had gone to have his whiskers trimmed at the barbershop.

Johnny Jumper said, "I know! I'll find someone to play with me." So Johnny Jumper hopped away and met a chicken.

> "My name is Johnny Jumper,
>   (*Children join in.*)
> And I am here to see
> If you would dance a jolly jig
> Or jump awhile with me."

But the chicken, who was scratching busily in the garden, said:

> "I'm sorry, Johnny Jumper.
>   (*Children join in.*)
> That's what I'd like to do,
> But you are larger than I am,
> So I cannot jump with you."

Next, Johnny Jumper met a spotted dog with drooping ears.

"My name is Johnny Jumper,
And I am here to see
If you will dance a jolly jig
Or jump awhile with me."

But the dog, who was busily chasing his tail, said:

"I'm sorry, Johnny Jumper.
That's what I'd like to do,
But I must find my master, George,
So I cannot jump with you."

Johnny Jumper understood why the dog could not play with him, so he went on his way. Some squirrels were jumping from branch to branch in an oak tree nearby. They jumped to the ground and began to chase one another to a bridge which crossed over a little brook. Johnny Jumper called to the squirrels:

"My name is Johnny Jumper,
And I am here to see
If you would dance a jolly jig
Or jump awhile with me."

The squirrels called from the bridge over the little brook:

"We're sorry, Johnny Jumper.
That is what we'd like to do,
But we are playing on this bridge,
So we cannot dance with you."

By now, Johnny Jumper was tired of looking for play-mates who would jump with him, so he sat down to think. Finally he went to sleep, and he had a dream in which he heard a robin say:

"Cheerily-chee! One playmate, two, or three,
Will be waiting at your door, so please go there to see."

Johnny Jumper woke up. He remembered what the robin in his dream had said, so he hurried home fast. There waiting on the doorstep were three little rabbits just his size, with tall ears and little pink eyes.

"My name is Johnny Jumper,
And I am here to see
If you would dance a jolly jig
Or jump awhile with me."

Then the three little rabbits, whose names were Jack, Jill, and Joan, chorused:

"Why, Johnny Jumper, yes we would!
That's what we'd like to do.
We'd like to dance a jolly jig
And jump awhile with you."

And from that time on, you may be sure that Johnny Jumper was never lonely again.

—J.J.T.

This story can be used effectively with a flannelboard or as a creative dramatics activity. For a listening activity, ask the children to name words that contain the "j" speech sound.

OLD JEREMY

Old Jeremy was a very old man whom all people, children in particular, loved dearly.

One reason why everybody loved Old Jeremy was that he went about the country in his rickety old jeep doing kindnesses for others. Always and always, Old Jeremy thought of people's needs.

One day, Old Jeremy said, "It is time to take a trip in my old jeep. I must find a job helping someone." So he got into his rickety old jeep and went down the road:

261

Jiggle-ty, jiggle-ty, jog, jog, JOLT!
Jiggle-ty, jiggle-ty, jog, jog, JOLT!
(*Children participate.*)

There was forlorn Kitten Cat, sitting beside the road. "Why are you sitting there, Kitten Cat?" asked Old Jeremy, stopping his old rickety jeep with a screech.

Little Kitten Cat mewed sadly and replied:

"I am just a kitten cat,
A kitten cat, but oh,
Nobody seems to want me,
And I have nowhere to go."

"There, there, Kitten Cat," said Old Jeremy kindly, "Jump into my jeep and join me. I must find a job helping someone. Perhaps you can be of help, too. Would you like that, Kitten Cat?"

"Mee-ow!" cried Kitten Cat, jumping into the old jeep and perching herself right beside Old Jeremy. And away they went:

Jiggle-ty, jiggle-ty, jog, jog, JOLT!
Jiggle-ty, jiggle-ty, jog, jog, JOLT!

There beside the road sat Pug-Nosed Puppy, whining to himself. Old Jeremy stopped the jeep and asked, "Why are you whining, Pug-Nosed Puppy? Isn't the world treating you right, and if so, why not?"

Pug-Nosed Puppy lifted his sad little head and replied:

"I am just a pug-nosed puppy,
A pug-nosed puppy, but oh,
Nobody seems to want me,
And I have nowhere to go."

"I want you, Pug-Nosed Puppy," said Old Jeremy. "Jump into my rickety old jeep and join the two of us, Kitten Cat and me. I must find a job helping someone. Perhaps you can be of help, too."

The pug-nosed puppy needed no second invitation, for he loved Old Jeremy at once. Though dogs usually do not care for cats, even Kitten Cat did not bother him. Away they all went:

Jiggle-ty, jiggle-ty, jog, jog, JOLT!
Jiggle-ty, jiggle-ty, jog, jog, JOLT!

They saw Mrs. Scratchy Hen right in their path, and Old Jeremy turned the jeep quickly to avoid hurting her.

What are you doing here, Mrs. Scratchy Hen?" asked Old Jeremy. "Can I be of assistance to you?"

Poor Mrs. Scratchy Hen looked at Old Jeremy and said:

"I am just a poor old scratchy hen,
A scratchy hen, but oh,
Nobody seems to want me,
And I have nowhere to go."

"That can be fixed in a hurry," said Old Jeremy. "Jump into my old rickety jeep and join me. I must find a job helping someone. Perhaps you can be of help, too."

Mrs. Scratchy Hen flew right into the jeep and away they went:

Jiggle-ty, jiggle-ty, jog, jog, JOLT!
Jiggle-ty, jiggle-ty, jog, jog, JOLT!

Just as Old Jeremy was about to turn a bend in the road, he saw Wattles Rooster sitting beside the road.

263

Wattles Rooster was completely silent because he was so unhappy.

Old Jeremy stopped his rickety old jeep and asked, "Why are your feathers drooping, Wattles Rooster? May I help you in some way?"

Wattles Rooster ruffled his droopy feathers and replied in a slow and very sad voice:

> "I am just a wattles rooster,
> A wattles rooster, but oh,
> Nobody seems to want me,
> And I have nowhere to go."

"Your worries are over," said Old Jeremy. "Jump into my rickety old jeep and join the four of us. I must find a job helping someone. Perhaps you can be of help, too."

So Wattles Rooster flew into the rickety old jeep and jumped up on Old Jeremy's shoulder, and away they went:

> Jiggle-ty, jiggle-ty, jog, jog, JOLT!
> Jiggle-ty, jiggle-ty, jog, jog, JOLT!

At long last they came to a cottage with green shingles on the roof. Old Jeremy stopped the rickety old jeep and said, "Maybe this is the place to stop and be of service."

So they all got out of the rickety old jeep and went to the door. Old Jeremy knocked, and a very tiny woman came to the door.

"May we help you?" Old Jeremy asked the very tiny woman.

"Oh, indeed, yes," she cried. "My humble cottage is overrun with mice. My alarm clock will not work. And robbers have taken my food. It is five miles to the nearest store, and I have no way to get there to buy more food."

264

Then, just as you would suppose, Old Jeremy, Kitten Cat, Pug-Nosed Puppy, Mrs. Scratchy Hen, and Wattles Rooster set about helping the very tiny woman.

Kitten Cat caught all of the mice.

Scratchy Hen laid an egg a day.

Wattles Rooster crowed each morning so the very tiny woman needed no alarm clock.

Pug-Nosed Puppy barked and kept the robbers away.

And Old Jeremy drove the rickety old jeep into town to buy food:

> Jiggle-ty, jiggle-ty, jog, jog, JOLT!
> Jiggle-ty, jiggle-ty, jog, jog, JOLT!

As it happened, each one had a job to do. But one day, it was time to go on their way.

Kitten Cat would not leave.

Pug-Nosed Puppy would not leave.

Mrs. Scratchy Hen would not leave.

And Wattles Rooster would not leave.

They would not leave the very tiny lady who needed them. But Old Jeremy had to leave, because there were other people who needed his help. There were lots of jobs to do.

"Very well, my little friends," said Old Jeremy. "It is good that you want to stay and help the very tiny woman. But I must be on my way."

So after fond good-bys were said, Old Jeremy drove his rickety old jeep down the road:

> Jiggle-ty, jiggle-ty, jog, jog, JOLT!
> Jiggle-ty, jiggle-ty, jog, jog, JOLT!

—L.B.S.

The children may participate in helping tell the story almost immediately, since the refrain is so easily learned. The refrain contains the "j" speech sound.

CHAPTER 11

The "T" and "D" Speech Sounds

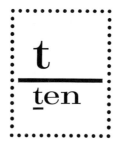

MAKING THE SPEECH SOUND

The tongue tip is pressed lightly against the gum ridge (alveolar) behind the upper teeth, and air is held inside the mouth. When the tongue tip is lowered quickly, the air is released suddenly and explosively as the "t" speech sound. The soft palate is raised. The vocal cords do not vibrate, and the lips and teeth are parted.

You may call "t" the "ticking" or the "watch" sound. Some teachers like to use both names and call "t" the "ticking-watch" sound.

CORRECTING THE DEFICIENT SPEECH SOUND

Children have little difficulty in pronouncing this sound, but if it is omitted or distorted, ask the child to touch the little "shelf" behind his upper teeth with his tongue tip and use a mirror for observation. He may hold the back of his hand in front of his mouth to feel the explosion of air as it is emitted.

INSTRUCTIONS TO THE CHILD

"When you make a 'ticking-watch' sound, your tongue tip touches up high like this: 'T, t, t.' Did you see what my tongue tip did? Can your tongue tip do the same as mine? Listen as I say a word: *ca-t.* Did you hear the last sound? What was it? Was it a quiet sound? That sound is at the beginning of some words we say. Name the words after me and feel what your tongue tip does: *ten, toe, tie, top.* Here is a poem. In this poem, you will hear the ticking sound. When you hear it, make it with me."

> I wind and wind my yellow top,
> So it will spin around.
> And when I wind my yellow top,
> It makes a "ticking" sound.
> "T, t, t, t, t, t."
>
> —L.B.S.

WORDS FOR PRACTICE

Initial	*Medial*	*Final*
table	cattle	boot
tooth	atom	rat
towel	Atlantic	feet
tub	letter	kite
toad	motor	coat
tank	oatmeal	meat

Consonant Blends:

*tr*ee	*tw*elve	sle*pt*	sa*lt*	hea*rt*	pa*st*
*tr*ain	*tw*ins	ke*pt*	fe*lt*	pa*rt*	*st*op

I HEAR IT

Refer to the explanation on pages 80-81 for using the "I Hear It" rhyme.

I hear it in *tack* but not in *sack*.
I hear it in *tail* but not in *sail*.
I hear it in *tell* but not in *sell*.
 I hear it in *too* but not in *chew*.
 I hear it in *time* but not in *chime*.
 I raise my tongue tip and touch the shelf.
 And I can do this all by myself.
 "T, t, t, t!"
I hear it in *tank* but not in *thank*.
I hear it in *tick* but not in *thick*.
I hear it in *tie* but not in *thigh*.
 I hear it in *take* but not in *shake*.
 I hear it in *toe* but not in *show*.
 I raise my tongue tip and touch the shelf.
 And I can do this all by myself.
 "T, t, t, t!"

           —L.B.S.

CLOCKS

"Tick-tock, tick-tock," (*Low voice and slowly.*)
Said the grandfather clock so tall.
"Tick-tock, tickety-tock,"
 (*High voice and quickly.*)
Said the kitchen clock on the wall.
"Tickety-tickety-tickety-tick," (*Fast.*)
Said the very small clock by the bed.
And, "T, t, t, t, t, t," (*Whisper.*)
Is the tick that my little watch said.

        —L.B.S.

The children enjoyed being the different clocks when this rhyme was tried out in the classroom. Let various children make the sounds of the clocks while the rest of the class says the narrative lines in unison.

BIRTHDAY CLOCK

Tick-tock, tickety-tock,
  (*Children say refrain each time.*)
Tickety-tickety-tock!
Tick-tock, tickety-tock!
That is the sound of my birthday clock!

There is a birthday party at one!
Tickety-tock! Oh, what fun!
An invitation is here for you!
Tickety-tock! Count to two!

Tick-tock, tickety-tock, (*Children say refrain.*)
Tickety-tickety-tock!
Tick-tock, tickety-tock!
That is the sound of my birthday clock!

Lots of presents there will be.
Tickety-tock! Count to three.
There is someone at the door!
Tickety-tock! Count to four.

(*Children repeat refrain.*)

My friends are starting to arrive.
Tickety-tock! Count to five.
We will have some games and tricks.
Tickety-tock! Count to six.

(*Children repeat refrain.*)

Soon the hour will be eleven.
Tickety-tock! Count to seven.
The birthday clock says, "Don't be late!"
Tickety-tock! Count to eight.

(Children repeat refrain.)

On chocolate ice cream we will dine.
Tickety-tock! Count to nine.
The doorbell's ringing now again.
Tickety-tock! Count to ten.

(Children repeat refrain.)

Guests are coming. There are seven.
Tickety-tock! Count to eleven.
Let's blow out the candles soon.
Tickety-tock! It is noon!

(Children repeat refrain.)

There is a birthday party at one!
Tickety-tock! Oh, what fun!
Seven candles you can see.
Happy Birthday now to ME!

(Children repeat refrain.)

—L.B.S.

THE LADYBUG PARADE

Tick-tack, tick-tack, *(Children say refrain.)*
See them go —
Dainty little ladybugs
Marching in a row!

Red ones and yellow ones,
Spotted ones and black,
Plain ones and fancy ones,
With round and shiny backs.

Tick-tack, tick-tack, (*Children say refrain.*)
See them go —
Dainty little ladybugs
Marching in a row!

With tiny heads and short legs
And gauzy wings to fly,
With shiny little wing covers
To keep them safe and dry!

(*Children repeat refrain.*)

Aphids in the orange grove,
Gobbling all that grows;
Tick-tack, tick-tack,
Now what do you suppose?

(*Children repeat refrain.*)

Tick-tack, tick-tack,
The ladybugs have come!
What happened to the aphids?
They were eaten, every one!
—VIRGINIA SYDNOR PAVELKO

Let the children strike rhythm sticks together to represent the ladybugs walking. The selection may be divided into solo parts, with the entire class saying the refrain.

TOMMY AND HIS WHISTLE

Tommy has a whistle;
He made it just today.
And when he toots his whistle,
The whistle goes this way:
      Tootily-tootily-tootily-toot!
      Tootily-tootily-tootily-toot!

Tommy made his whistle
From a slender river reed.
When Tommy blows his whistle,
It makes quite a sound indeed!
 Tootily-tootily-tootily-toot!
 Tootily-tootily-tootily-toot!

Oh, Tommy likes his whistle
That blows a tootily-toot!
He calls his little whistle
A flutily-flutily-flute.
 Tootily-tootily-tootily-toot!
 Flutily-flutily-flutily-flute!

—L.B.S.

The children say the refrain each time it occurs. Tell them
that "wide-awake" tongue tips can touch the shelf behind their
upper teeth rapidly.

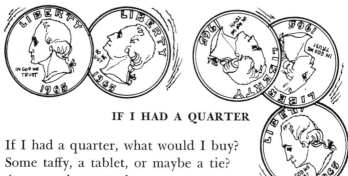

IF I HAD A QUARTER

If I had a quarter, what would I buy?
Some taffy, a tablet, or maybe a tie?
A toy truck or a tank
Or a ten-gallon hat?
A trap that would help me
Catch mice for my cat?
Some tinsel to decorate
My Christmas tree?
Or maybe a toy tent or Indian tepee?
Some turnips or tenpins?
A tangerine, too?

Two raspberry tarts,
One for me, one for you?
There are so many things that my quarter would buy.
I can't make up my mind. Won't you please help me try?

—J.J.T.

Ask each child to add something beginning with the "t" sound. Suggest this sentence pattern: "My quarter would buy a _____." The children may want to make pictures to illustrate this rhyme and use the pictures on a flannelboard as the rhyme is recited.

WHAT IS TALL?

Tall is an oak or a black walnut tree;
Tall is my daddy, who stands beside me.

Tall is a horse that sleeps in a stall;
Tall is our grandfather clock in the hall.

Tall is a giraffe in a circus or zoo;
Tall is a house with a tall chimney flue.

Tall is a ladder with steps I can climb;
Tall is a haystack at warm haying time.

Tall are the ears on my bunny so sweet;
Tall are the stilts that I wear on my feet.

Tall is a skyscraper high in the sky;
Tall you will grow and you won't have to try!

—L.B.S.

Ask the children to name other things which are tall. This rhyme may be used to teach and contrast the opposite concepts *tall* and *short*. After the rhyme has been read a few times, the children will be able to add the last word in each couplet.

273

THE TINY, TINY PEOPLE

The tiny, tiny people
Whose name begins with *T*
Are much smaller than your finger or your thumb!
They dine on food as we do,
But the portions, don't you see,
Are really not much bigger than a crumb!
The tiny, tiny people
Whose name begins with *T*
Look very much like you and you and me;
But you'll never, never see them,
For they live in fairyland,
Where such tiny, tiny people ought to be.

The tiny, tiny people live on the side of a molehill.

There is Mr. Tiny. He is the father. There is Mrs. Tiny and she is the mother. They live in a tiny, tiny house no bigger than a little jewel box, but it is quite large enough for the Tinies and their eight children.

On the front of the tiny, tiny house is a tiny, tiny door. There is a door in back, too. Tiny, tiny windows let in the sunlight. Mrs. Tiny made curtains for the windows from a scrap of thin white cloth that was torn from a dress hem caught on a sharp rosebush thorn. Mrs. Tiny starched and ironed the tiny bit of cloth and made curtains for every single window in the tiny, tiny house — enough curtains for ten windows! Think of that!

On top of the tiny, tiny house is a tiny, tiny chimney, because in the tiny, tiny living room there is a tiny, tiny fireplace. One toothpick would make enough fire for that tiny, tiny fireplace to burn six or seven hours.

As I said before, there are eight tiny, tiny children. Each of the children is one year younger than the next one. Now if the oldest is ten, the youngest would have to be three. Isn't that correct? (*If some pupils have difficulty understanding this, list the ages of the children in the story on the chalkboard: 10, 9, 8, 7, 6, 5, 4, 3. Then let the class count them.*)

So there are ten tiny, tiny people who live in that house which is as small as the smallest jewel box, upstairs and all. There are five tiny, tiny bedrooms, so actually nobody ever feels crowded at all.

The tiny, tiny people
Whose name begins with *T*
Are much smaller than your finger or your thumb!
They dine on food as we do,
But the portions, don't you see,
Are really not much bigger than a crumb!
Oh, the tiny, tiny people
Whose name begins with *T*
Look very much like you and you and me;
But you'll never, never see them,
For they live in fairyland,
Where such tiny, tiny people ought to be.

There is Tim, whose nickname is short for Timothy. He is ten. There is Tom, whose nickname comes from Thomas. He is nine. There is Theodore, whose nickname is Teddy, and he is eight. There is Tammy, and that is her one and only first name. She is seven. There is Tina, whose nickname comes from Katrina, and she is six. There is Tish, whose name is short for Patricia, and she is five. Next there is Terrance, whose nickname is Terry. He is four. And last, there is Trudy, whose nickname comes from Gertrude, and she is three. Trudy is the baby in the tiny, tiny family and she will be the baby until a new baby comes to live with the Tinies.

You may wonder why everyone's name begins with *T*. The tiny, tiny postman, whose name is Mr. Gum, wondered, too. One day he asked, "Why does everyone's name begin with *T?*"

"Why not?" replied Mr. Tiny, and of course the tiny, tiny postman had no answer to that question.

He counted out the packages and mail for the Tinies and said, "Well, *T* is an important alphabet letter. I wish my name began with *T*, but I suppose I shall just have to be content with G."

Mr. Tiny said, "Why, there is nothing wrong with G. Our baby's name is Gertrude. So her name begins with G. We call her Trudy for short."

The tiny, tiny postman handed three letters to Mr. Tiny. Of course, those letters were not alphabet letters. They were letters from friends.

Oh, there is SO much more I might say about the Tinies, but perhaps you would like to make up some stories about them yourself. You could do it, I am sure, if you set your mind to it.

Now the tiny, tiny people want their home kept a secret, so please don't tell anybody about it. Big folks might get curious and, in doing so, might get careless along with it. One never knows what could happen. Someone might accidentally step on one of the children or knock earth out from under the tiny, tiny house that is no bigger than the smallest jewel box.

The tiny, tiny people
Whose name begins with *T*
Are much smaller than your finger or your thumb!
They dine on food as we do,
But the portions, don't you see,
Are really not much bigger than a crumb!
Oh, the tiny, tiny people
Whose name begins with *T*
Look very much like you and you and me;

But you'll never, never see them,
For they live in fairyland,
Where such tiny, tiny people ought to be!

—L.B.S.

Miniatures delight children, who enjoy feeling bigger than the characters. The poem is repeated three times to make it easy for child participation. Suggest that individual children make up episodes about the Tinies; write down their dictated stories for use as wall charts. Call attention to words which begin with the "t" speech sound.

TICKER-TEE

Ticker-Tee was a tiny watch that lived in a clock shop where dozens of clocks sang a merry tune morning, night, and noon. Ticker-Tee made a soft little tick-tick like this: "T,t,t,t,t." (*Children imitate.*) The tick was so soft that you had to put your ear very close to hear it. Can you make Ticker-Tee's sound close to MY ear right now? Let me hear YOUR tick. . . . Good!

"How I wish that I could tick loudly and boldly like tall Grandfather Clock," sighed Ticker-Tee.

Grandfather Clock ticked — so — slowly — like — this: "Tock, tock, tock, tock-a-tock. I am a reliable Grandfather Clock. Tock, tock, tock, tock. I am a reliable Grandfather Clock!" (*Children repeat.*)

"Oh, how I wish that I could tick ever so quick like the little kitchen clock," sighed Ticker-Tee.

Kitchen Clock went: "Tick, tick, tick, tick, tick, tick. My ticks are quiet. My ticks are quick!" (*Children imitate.*)

"Oh, how I wish that I could tick like the bedroom clock," sighed Ticker-Tee.

Bedroom Clock went: "Tick-a-tick — a — tick — a — tick. Time to get up! Time to get up!" (*Children imitate.*)

277

"Oh, how I wish, I wish, I wish," sighed Ticker-Tee as he made his soft little tick: "T,t,t,t,t,t." (*Children imitate.*)

It was Christmas time and everyone was scurrying here and there, buying presents for people they loved. Mrs. Happy came into the clock shop, hoping to find some nice gifts and especially ONE gift for somebody SHE loved very much.

The shopkeeper said, "Perhaps I can help you."

Mrs. Happy told the shopkeeper that she really would appreciate some help. She said, "I want to find a present for a special little boy. He belongs to me. He is special because I chose him."

Now Ticker-Tee could think of nothing more pleasant than belonging to a special little boy, so he ticked as loudly as he could, hoping that Mrs. Happy would notice him: "T,t,t,t,t,t,t,t." (*Children imitate.*)

Mrs. Happy picked up one clock after another, listening to the tick, tick, tick of each one. "All of these ticks are much too loud or too fast or too slow," said Mrs. Happy. "None of these are right for my special little boy."

Ticker-Tee ticked and ticked and ticked: "T,t,t,t,t,t,t." (*Children imitate.*)

Then — oh, then — Mrs. Happy SAW Ticker-Tee.

"What a darling little watch!" she exclaimed. She held Ticker-Tee to her ear. Ticker-Tee ticked and ticked and ticked: "T,t,t,t,t,t,t." (*Children imitate.*)

Mrs. Happy said, "Please wrap this little watch in your prettiest Christmas paper. I know that my special little boy will be pleased, because he wants a watch just like this one more than anything else in the world."

Ticker-Tee kept on ticking inside his package all the way home with Mrs. Happy: "T,t,t,t,t,t,t,t,t,t." (*Children imitate.*)

And on Christmas morning he ticked for a special little boy, too: "T,t,t,t,t,t,t,t,t,t,t." (*Children imitate.*)

—L.B.S.

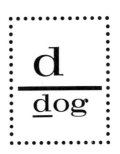

d
dog

MAKING THE SPEECH SOUND

This speech sound is made like "t," except that slightly less pressure is exerted and there is vibration of the vocal cords. The quickly lowered tongue tip causes air to be released suddenly and explosively as the "d" sound.

You may call "d" the "drip-drop," the "typewriter," or the "drum" sound.

CORRECTING THE DEFICIENT SPEECH SOUND

Use the same techniques as for the "t" speech sound. When pronouncing the "d" sound in isolation, an unwanted vowel sound is sometimes added. It is wise to use the speech sound in final position in a word at first so that the child can hear it more definitely. The teacher should be cautious, however, that a schwa sound is not added to the "d" sound in initial or final position in words, e.g., *duh-id* for *did,* or *be-duh* for *bed.*

INSTRUCTIONS TO THE CHILD

"Can you see what my tongue tip does when I say 'do-do-do'? Did it go up high and did it touch the little shelf and bounce down? Listen for the sound at the end of *re-d. (Emphasize, but do not distort, the final "d.")* Did you hear it? Can you say the word with me? *Re-d.* Clap

279

when you hear a word that ends with this sound: *red, good, food*, car, *head, lid*. Did every word end with the 'drip-drop' sound? Which one did not? (car) Name these words after me and feel what the tip of your tongue does: *doll, dish, dog, duck*. What did your tongue tip do? Say the lines of this little rhyme after me."

My pajamas are *re-d, re-d, re-d*.
I sleep inside a *be-d*.
I have a pillow for my *hea-d*.

—L.B.S.

WORDS FOR PRACTICE

Initial	Medial	Final
dance	lady	add
donkey	riddle	bed
deer	paddle	seed
dinner	medal	food
doll	tadpole	card
dog	reindeer	mud

I HEAR IT

Refer to the section on "s" for suggestions for using the "I Hear It" rhyme.

I hear it in *day* but not in *they*.
I hear it in *Dan* but not in *than*.
I hear it in *den* but not in *then*.
I hear it in *dough* but not in *no*.
I hear it in *do* but not in *new*.
My tongue tip goes high and it sits on the shelf;
My voice motor hums inside of myself.
"D, d, d." Did YOU do it? Yes?

I hear it in *dot* but not in *not.*
I hear it in *dip* but not in *nip.*
I hear it in *deer* but not in *near.*
I hear it in *doze* but not in *those.*
I hear it in *dare* but not in *there.*
My tongue tip goes high and it sits on the shelf;
My voice motor hums inside of myself.
"D, d, d." Did YOU do it? Yes?

—L.B.S.

RAINDROPS

The rushing rain helps thirsty crops.
The sun comes out; the cool rain stops!
Dud, dud, dud!
Dud, dud, dud!

Rain makes a puddle on the ground
With such a quiet drip-drop sound.
Dud, dud, dud!
Dud, dud, dud!

I like the rain best when it stops;
But I still can hear the drip-drip-drops.
Dud, dud, dud!
Dud, dud, dud!

—L.B.S.

It is impossible to pronounce the "d" speech sound in isolation without adding a vowel sound. Rather than pronounce it as "duh," add a short *oo* sound (as in *book*). The isolated sound is useful only for introducing production and discrimination of the speech sound. The sound should be used in words and in connected speech as soon as possible.

Ask the children to feel what the tongue tip does when they make the "d" sound.

LEARNING TO TALK

My brother Danny is so small,
He can't do very much at all.
He cannot run. He cannot walk.
But Baby Danny likes to "talk."
     Da, da, da, da, da, da, da!
     Da, da, da, da, da, da, da!

My brother Danny wears a bib,
And takes his nap inside a crib.
When he's awake, he talks to me.
With what he says I quite agree.
     Da, da, da, da, da, da, da!
     Da, da, da, da, da, da, da!

My brother Danny cannot say
The words that we use every day.
But our relationship is great,
Because we can COMMUNICATE!
     Da, da, da, da, da, da, da!
     Da, da, da, da, da, da, da!

—L.B.S.

Ask the following questions: Do you have a baby at home? How does your baby talk? Do you listen? What do you say to your baby? Why is it important to listen when your baby talks?

It is important to listen and talk to a little baby because that is the way he will learn to talk. He imitates speech. When he says, "Da, da, da," he is using his tongue tip just as you use yours.

Discuss the meanings of the words *relationship* and *communicate*.

THE SOUND OF THE DRUM

Dum-dum-dum is the sound of the drum
As the soldiers march along,
Dum-dum-dum, diddle-dum-dum-dum,
As the soldiers march along.

Dum-dum-dum is the sound of the drum
For the soldiers brave and strong.

Dum-dum-dum is the sound of the drum
As the flag goes floating by,
Dum-dum-dum, diddle-dum-dum-dum,
As the flag goes floating by.
Dum-dum-dum is the sound of the drum
For the colors floating high.

Dum-dum-dum, diddle-dum-dum-dum!
Dum-dum-dum, diddle-dum-dum-dum!
   (*Softer voice.*)
Dum-dum-dum, diddle-dum-dum-dum!
   (*Softer still.*)

                                    —J.J.T.

The "d" speech sound occurs in initial and medial position in the words that imitate the sound of the drum, and as part of the *dr* consonant blend in the word *drum*. Ask one group of children to make the sound of the drum continuously as the rhyme is said.

WHAT GOES DOWN?

Down goes the soup to my "tummy" in me;
Down go the stairsteps, one, two, and three.

Down comes the rain with its drip, drip, drops!
Down comes my umbrella when the rain stops!

Down comes the plane on the airport runway;
Down to the rooftop comes old Santa's sleigh.

Down comes the ball when I toss it way up;
Down goes the milk that I drink from my cup.

Down goes the duck when she dives for a bug;
Down goes the worm in the tunnel it dug.

Down flies the hummingbird to a bright flower;
Down falls the rain in a lovely spring shower.

—L.B.S.

Ask the children to name other things that come or fall down.
Ask them to listen for the "d" speech sound in *down*. Use the rhyme
to introduce a discussion of the "opposite" words *up* and *down*.
After a few readings, the class will be able to supply the last word
in each couplet.

CHAPTER 12

The "K" and "G" Speech Sounds

MAKING THE SPEECH SOUND

The back of the tongue is raised and pressed against the soft palate, holding the air inside the mouth. The soft palate is raised to keep the air from escaping through the nasal cavity. When the back of the tongue is lowered quickly, the air is released suddenly and explosively with a "coughing" sound. The tip of the tongue usually is on the floor of the mouth and the lips and teeth are parted slightly. The vocal cords do not vibrate.

You may call "k" the "cough" or the "crow" sound.

CORRECTING THE DEFICIENT SPEECH SOUND

The child may substitute "t" for "k," e.g., *tum* for *come*. The tongue position is not easy to see and imitate because it occurs at the back of the mouth. Though the motivation for correcting this sound is largely one of aural discrimination, the teacher may demonstrate a technique devised by Miss Frances C. Hunte, Speech Specialist, Garvey School District, California. Miss Hunte holds her left hand in front of her with palm up and fingers curved back from the second joint. She asks the children to pretend that the finger nails are lower front teeth and the palm of the hand is the bottom, or floor, of the mouth. The right hand and forearm together represent the tongue. She places the finger tips of her right hand in the palm of the left hand, then flexes the right elbow quickly as she says, "K, k, k." She then asks the children to demonstrate with their hands and arms this activity, and repeat the "k" speech sound each time the elbow kicks back.

INSTRUCTIONS TO THE CHILD

"When I made the 'k' sound, did you hear a little cough? It is a quiet cough, isn't it? Try it with me: 'k, k, k.' We do not turn on our voice motors. I will name a word: *book*. Did you hear the 'cough' sound at the end of *book?* Let's see if we can hear the sound at the beginning of some words: *kitten, key, kind.* Repeat the words after me. Did you feel the little cough at the back of your throat? What did the back of your tongue do? Let's all open our mouths and look at each other's pinky tongue as it kicks back and makes the 'cough' sound. Here is a rhyme about the cough sound. When you hear the 'cough' sound, say it with me."

> I ate some cake.
> A crumb went down
> My "Sunday throat" and then
> I coughed, "K, k, k, k!"
> And coughed it up again!
>
> —L.B.S.

WORDS FOR PRACTICE

Initial	Medial	Final
candle	acorn	book
cork	checkers	clock
kangaroo	locket	sack
curtain	ticket	neck
cabbage	buckle	duck
king	doctor	chick

Consonant Blends:

*cl*oud	*cr*oss	si*lk*	fo*rk*	bo*x* (ks)	*Q*ueen (kw)
*cl*ass	*cr*ow	mi*lk*	ba*rk*	si*x* (ks)	*q*uack (kw)

I HEAR IT

Refer to instructions for using the "I Hear It" device in the "s" unit on pages 80-81.

I hear it in *cake* but not in *take*.
I hear it in *can* but not in *tan*.
I hear it in *cub* but not in *tub*.
    I hear it in *cold* but not in *told*.
    I hear it in *key* but not in *tea*.
    The back of my tongue is raised up high
    To make a cough sound, and now you may try:
    "K, k, k!"
I hear it in *kite* but not in *tight*.
I hear it in *cone* but not in *tone*.
I hear it in *cook* but not in *took*.
    I hear it in *car* but not in *tar*.
    I hear it in *call* but not in *tall*.
    The back of my tongue is raised up high
    To make a cough sound, and now you may try:
    "K, k, k!"

—L.B.S.

ARE WE LISTENING?

1. Danny has three pets: a *caterpillar,* a *calico cat,* and a *canary.* The *caterpillar* spun a *cocoon* and went to sleep. The *canary* liked to swing in its *cage.* The *calico cat* drank *cream.* Are we listening? Let's see! Name one of Danny's pets. Name another. Another. What did the *caterpillar* do? What did the *cat* drink? What did the *canary* like to do? Why do you think the *cat* is called a *calico cat?* Have you a *cat?* Tell us about it. Have you seen a *cocoon?* Tell about it.

2. Libby hears many sounds. She hears the *clapper* in the bell go ding-ding. She hears the *clang-clang* of the trolley. She hears a *cricket* chirp in the grass. Libby hears bees buzz in the purple *clover.* Are we listening? Let's see! What part of the bell helps it to ring? How does the trolley go? What chirps in the grass? Have you ever heard or seen a *cricket?* Where?

3. A *crow cries,* "*Caw, caw!*" A *cow* says, "Moo," to her *calf.* A *coyote* howls on the prairie. A *cocker* spaniel barks. A hen *clucks* and *cackles.* Are we listening? Let's see! What two things does a hen do? What animal howls on the prairie? What kind of dog barks? What mother moos to her *calf?*

—L.B.S.

THE "COUGH" SOUND

Some sounds are made a funny way;
I feel a "cough" sound when I say,
   "K, k, k!"

I cannot feel it in my nose;
But in my throat the "cough" sound goes,
   "K, k, k!"

It quite surprised me when I found
That in my throat I made this sound,
   "K, k, k!"

I hear the sound in *can* and *cake,*
And at the end of *book* and *make,*
   "K, k, k!"

So when I listen to a word,
I try to think if I have heard,
   "K, k, k!"

                                    —L.B.S.

Ask the child to place his fingers on the Adam's apple as he makes the cough sound. This is an explosive sound which can best be heard at the end of such words as *book, cake,* and *duck.*

THE CROW FAMILY

Five sly crows were as black as could be,
And they lived in the top of a sycamore tree.
   "Caw, caw, caw!"

Grandfather Crow sat out on a limb,
And he sang a song that was splendid for him.
   "Caw, caw, caw!"

Grandmother Crow flew low in the tree,
And she sang a song that was quite off key.
   "Caw, caw, caw!"

Black Mother Crow was perched on her nest,
And she sang a song that *she* knew the best.
   "Caw, caw, caw!"

Black Father Crow found a bright, shiny thing,
My gracious! You should have heard HIM sing!
   "Caw, caw, caw!"

Black Baby Crow, who was so wee and small,
Couldn't sing *his* song very well at all!
　　"Caw, caw, caw!"

Five sly crows were as black as could be,
And they lived in the top of a sycamore tree.
　　"Caw, caw, caw!"
　　　　　　　　　　—LOUISE BINDER SCOTT AND
　　　　　　　　　　VIRGINIA SYDNOR PAVELKO

Let the children cut out the crow family from black construction
paper and glue each crow to a tongue depresser. They may use
these puppets for acting out this rhyme. The repetitive "caw"
gives practice on the "k" speech sound. When dramatizing this
poem, encourage vocal variety as the children imitate the various
crows.

THE TINY, SHINY CRICKET

There's a tiny, shiny cricket
That I really want to see;
There's a happy-scrappy cricket
That would like to hide from me.
On his back are two fine covers
That protect his gauzy wings,
And he rubs those shiny covers
To make music when he sings.
　　Crrrrrrr-ick, crrrrrrr-ick, crrrrrr-ee!
　　My cricket sings to me!

One wing cover has a scraper
And the other has a file,
And he gaily serenades us
In his chirpy cricket style.
When the world is dressed in darkness
And the stars are twinkling bright,

290

Then my happy, snappy cricket
Comes to visit me at night.
  Crrrrrrr-ick, crrrrrrr-ick, crrrrrr-ee!
My cricket sings to me!

As he plays his crackly music,
I creep out of bed — and there
Is that tiny, shiny cricket
Sitting right behind my chair!
All the house is still at nighttime,
Gone to rest is everything,
But that happy, snappy cricket
Thinks it's time to dance and sing!
  Crrrrrrr-ick, crrrrrrr-ick, crrrrrr-ee!
My cricket sings to me!
     —VIRGINIA SYDNOR PAVELKO

The "k" speech sound is emphasized in the work *crick,* both in initial and in final position. The poem may also be used for drill on the "r" sound, which is prolonged in the refrain.

QUACK-QUACK

Five ducks went for a walk one day,
  Quack-quack! Quack-quack! Quack-quack!
The five ducks had some things to say.
  Quack-quack! Quack-quack! Quack-quack!
We'll wade through puddles on the ground,
And gobble up all the bugs around,
And make a loud quack-quacking sound.
  Quack-quack! Quack-quack! Quack-quack!
     —J.J.T.

Repetitive drill is provided for the initial *kw* consonant blend with the word *quack.* In saying the phrase "Quack-quack," the stress should be placed upon the second *quack.*

CHRISTMAS IS COMING

Christmas is coming,
Christmas is coming,
Christmas will soon be here.
Christmas is coming,
Christmas is coming,
It's the happiest time of the year.

It's almost time for Santa Claus
To load his sleigh with toys
And make a trip around the world
To visit girls and boys.

Christmas is coming,
Christmas is coming,
Christmas will soon be here.
Christmas is coming,
Christmas is coming,
It's the happiest time of the year.

I've written a letter to Santa;
It is just for old Saint Nick.
I'll seal my letter and stamp it,
And then I'll mail it quick!

(*Repeat refrain.*)

—J.J.T.

The *kr* consonant blend is presented in the word *Christmas,*
which also contains medial and final "s." Repetition of the phrase
"Christmas is coming" may inspire the children to set the words to
music.

CRICKETY CRICKET

Crickety Cricket was a tiny, shiny black cricket. Usually, he was a happy little cricket, but now fall days had

come and Crickety Cricket was cold — so cold that his chirps became slower — and slower — and slower.

> Cr-ick, cr-ick, cr-ee.
> Cr-ick, cr-ick, cr-ee.

Now Crickety Cricket didn't know it, but he was a fine thermometer. Yes, indeed. You really and truly could tell the temperature by the number of chirps he made. If you happened to have a stop watch or a watch with a second hand, by counting each chirp Crickety Cricket made in fifteen seconds, and adding the number forty to that number, you would know the temperature of out-of-doors places.

But Crickety Cricket didn't know about thermometers and he cared less because — *brrrrrrrr* — he was COLD! When a cricket is cold, he rubs his shiny wing covers together ever so slowly, as if he really didn't care about making chirps at all.

> Cr-ick, cr-ick, cr-ee,
> Cr-ick, cr-ick, cr-ee. (*Children join in.*)

When a cricket is warm and comfortable, he rubs his wing covers together briskly in snappy, happy chirps.

> Crick, crick, cree!
> Listen to me!
> Crick, crick, cree! (*Children join in.*)

Now being cold was bad enough, but having no home was worse. Crickety Cricket was the most homeless cricket this side of Insectville. So the tune of Crickety Cricket grew slower — and slower — and slower — and sadder — and sadder — and sadder until his music made you feel sad and lonely and homeless, too.

Crickety Cricket enjoyed scraping those wing covers together briskly. He was proud of his gauzy wings that helped him fly, and he was glad that he had hard wing covers to protect them.

Sitting in the shrubbery was fun, too, especially on a night that had a full moon. When everybody in the rambling farmhouse had gone to sleep, that was the time when Crickety Cricket began to rub the file of one wing cover against the scraper of the other wing cover.

> Crick, crick, cree!
> Listen to me!
> Crick, crick, cree!

And it was such fun to play in the insect orchestra with the other crickets on a warm summer night. But now those carefree days were over. The crickets were looking for snug places to hide from the sharp winds and seeking safe homes where they could spend the winter.

A shivery blast of wind whooshed the leaves about in a merry-go-round fashion, so that Crickety Cricket had to take refuge under a thick pile of damp leaves that could not be blown about. But he knew that the leaves would dry out, and so he found a big gray stone and crawled under it with a scurry. Soon black thunderclouds gathered and a torrent of rain descended. It made large puddles all around, and one big puddle even creeped under the gray stone where Crickety Cricket was hiding. The earth became wet and muddy, and finally Crickety Cricket had to pull himself out and look for another place to go. Luckily he saw a woodpile, and he jumped for that woodpile as quickly as you could say "crickle-crackle-crockle."

He found a crack between two pieces of wood, a nice snug crack that was the best home he had found so far that evening. How long he was there, he did not know, but he heard voices and the voices grew louder and louder. The voices belonged to two boys who were coming right toward the woodpile.

One boy said, "Let's bring this wood into the house, for a storm is coming up."

A second boy said, "Let's see who can carry the most."

Crickety Cricket felt the board on which he was resting lifted up, and he hung on for dear life.

The two boys carried the wood to the porch and put it into a woodbox. Then they took three of the larger sticks and carried them into the house and into the living room, where a fire was hissing in the fireplace.

After everyone had said "Goodnight" and had gone to bed, Crickety Cricket decided to go exploring, because he was so warm and happy. He began to chirp:

> "Cr-ick, cr-ick, cr-ee,
> Cr-ick, cr-ick, cr-ee."

He crawled along the braided rug and found a grain of popcorn that someone had spilled, and he nibbled at it happily. Then he crawled to the wood basket.

Suddenly, Crickety Cricket felt like playing some joyful music and he began to rub the file of one wing cover against the scraper of the other wing cover.

> Crick, crick, cree!
> Listen to me!
> Crick, crick, cree!

His chirps became so happy and lively that he woke up all the members of the family, who were certainly not expecting to hear a cricket. In their beds, they all listened to the snappy, happy music.

> Crick, crick, cree!
> Crick, crick, cree!

295

Grandma said to Grandpa, "Listen! There's a cricket downstairs."

Daddy said to Mother, "Listen to the cricket!"

And the two boys said, "We must have brought a cricket in with the wood."

But the family was glad that Crickety Cricket was there, for some folks say that a cricket in the house brings luck. They all went to sleep again as they listened to the cricket music.

> Crick, crick, cree!
> Listen to me!
> Crick, crick, cree!

Nobody knew better than Crickety Cricket that a home where a cricket sings is a happy home, so he stayed in the corner by the fireplace. And sometimes, when Mother was sweeping, she would see him there and she was careful not to bother him.

Sometimes the two boys would leave bits of buttered toast or scraps of lettuce or apple in a bottle top for Crickety Cricket.

And Crickety Cricket sang and sang and sang.

> Crick, crick, cree!
> Happy, happy me!
> Crick, crick, cree!

—L.B.S.

The children join in saying the refrains each time they occur. The story may be tied in with a unit on nature study.

CAW-CAW, THE CROW, PLAYS A TRICK [1]

Caw-Caw, the crow, sat on a fence watching the other crows eating in the cornfield and listening to their noisy

---

[1] By special permission of *The Grade Teacher*. Story by J. J. Thompson.

cawing. Caw-Caw usually was the noisiest crow of all. At the moment he was very, very quiet. Now when Caw-Caw gets very quiet, he is usually up to something. And he was!

"I'll play a trick on my pals," thought Caw-Caw. "I'll pretend that I lost my voice and can only say 'K, k, k' instead of caw-caw-caw. When they talk to me, I'll just look at them and say 'K, k, k.' "

He laughed loudly to himself as he thought about how angry his pals would be when he answered their questions with "K, k, k." Spreading his wings, he flew into the cornfield to join his pals, who were pecking away at the corn. Soon his head was bobbing up and down with the others, but, of course, he was very quiet.

The crows stopped eating and looked at Caw-Caw, who kept right on eating. "Caw-Caw," one asked, "why are you so quiet?" "Don't you feel well?" asked another.

Caw-Caw stopped eating then and replied, "K, k, k!"

"What kind of sound is that?" asked the astonished crows. "Crows are supposed to say caw-caw-caw. What's wrong with your voice?"

But Caw-Caw only looked at them again and coughed, "K, k, k!"

The crows were quite puzzled. This was not like Caw-Caw at all. "I'd better go get Dr. Crow," said one as he flew away for help.

The crows were so worried that they all stood around watching Caw-Caw gobbling up the corn. He would stop now and then to say "K, k, k!" He was having a real feast while they were standing there worrying about him.

When Dr. Crow arrived, he watched Caw-Caw, who kept right on eating. Then he asked, "Is there something wrong, Caw-Caw?"

Caw-Caw tried to look sad as he coughed, "K, k, k!"

Dr. Crow looked into Caw-Caw's eyes. He peered into Caw-Caw's ears. He asked Caw-Caw to open his beak, and he looked far down Caw-Caw's throat. "Say 'ah,' Caw-Caw," he ordered.

"Ahhhhh," said Caw-Caw, keeping his tongue very still.

"Now, say 'caw-caw-caw,'" again ordered Dr. Crow.

But Caw-Caw was not going to give up his trick yet. "K, k, k!" he coughed.

"Hmmmm," remarked Dr. Crow. "This is serious."

Caw-Caw gave Dr. Crow a strange look. Now he was worried. Did Dr. Crow really find something wrong?

"Caw-Caw," said Dr. Crow, "I've never seen such a case before, but I think I can help you. Sing this song:

> I make my tongue peek right,
> I make my tongue peek left,
> I make my tongue peck down and up.
> I make my tongue say 'K,'
> I make my tongue say 'Caw,'
> I make my tongue say 'Kit-cat-cup.'"
> (*Children repeat each line and do
> the tongue exercises.*)

Caw-Caw sang in a loud voice right along with the doctor. He was through singing before he realized that wise old Dr. Crow had tricked him. Before he could open his beak again, the doctor had wrapped a huge bandage of cornsilk around it.

"Mmph, gluph!" mumbled Caw-Caw.

"We'll keep that bandage on until tomorrow morning," said Dr. Crow. "I'm sure you will be fine by that time."

Caw-Caw wanted to tell the doctor that he was fine right now, but all he could do was mutter angrily as he watched his pals pecking hungrily away at the corn.

The other crows felt sorry for Caw-Caw because he had been caught in his own trick. They stopped eating long enough to untie Caw-Caw's beak and to sing this song to him:

"I make my tongue peek right,
I make my tongue peek left,
I make my tongue peek down and up.
I make my tongue say 'K,'
I make my tongue say 'Caw,'
I make my tongue say 'Kit-cat-cup.' "
    (*Children repeat each line and do
    the tongue exercises.*)

This story gives the children experience in making the "k" sound in isolation and in short monosyllables, i.e., *caw, crow, corn, coughed, kit, cat,* and *cup.* The teacher should explain how to make the "k" sound and then let the class participate in choral speaking fashion each time "K, k, k" appears in the story.

MAKING THE SPEECH SOUND

This speech sound is made like the "k" sound, except that less pressure is exerted and the vocal cords vibrate for "g."

You may call "g" the "frog" sound.

CORRECTING THE DEFICIENT SPEECH SOUND

Ask the child to place his fingers on the front of his neck to feel the movement as he says, "Go, go, go." He may make the transition from the voiceless "k" to the

299

"frog" sound by making the voice motor hum. The most common misarticulation of this sound is "d" for "g," e.g., *dum* for *gum*.

INSTRUCTIONS TO THE CHILD

"When a frog croaks, his little throat moves as he sings his glugging song. You cannot see my throat move as I say, 'g, g, g,' but you can feel the movement if you will place your hand on the front part of my throat. Now feel your own throat as you say the funny 'frog' sound with me: 'ug-ug-ug, og-og-og, ag-ag-ag, ig-ig-ig, eg-eg-eg.' Good for you! Now I will name some words that begin with the 'frog' sound. When you hear that 'frog' sound, say, 'Goody, goody, gumdrop!' Ready? *Go,* ball, *gum, goose, gate,* four, *goat.* Wasn't that fun? Did you feel the sound in your throat when you made the first sound in *go?* Did the back of your tongue rise high? We have a poem about a frog. Every time the frog sings, please help him."

I am very fond of the froggie in our pond.
Glug, glug, glug!
He sings a glugging song all the night long.
Glug, glug, glug!
With his voice so deep, he sings me to sleep.
Glug, glug, glug!

—L.B.S.

WORDS FOR PRACTICE

Initial	Medial	Final
gate	buggy	bug
garden	tiger	log
ghost	wagon	rag
gum	eagle	pig
goose	August	mug
goat	bugle	flag

300

I HEAR IT

For instructions on using this activity, refer to the "I Hear It" explanation in the "s" unit on pages 80-81.

I hear it in *gate* but not in *date.*
I hear it in *Gale* but not in *Dale.*
I hear it in *game* but not in *dame.*
I hear it in *gay* but not in *day.*
I hear it in *go* but not in *dough.*
The back of my tongue goes away up high.
I use my voice motor. Now you please try!
" 'G, g, g!' Goody, goody, gumdrop."
I hear it in *gun* but not in *done.*
I hear it in *gull* but not in *dull.*
I hear it in *group* but not in *droop.*
I hear it in *gown* but not in *down.*
I hear it in *grain* but not in *drain.*
The back of my tongue goes away up high.
I use my voice motor. Now you please try!
" 'G, g, g!' Goody, goody, gumdrop."

—L.B.S.

ARE WE LISTENING?

1. What do you see when you *go* to the zoo? Perhaps you might see a *grizzly* bear with shaggy brown hair or a small *gazelle,* which is a *graceful* antelope with beautiful eyes. You might see a *gorilla,* which is an ape and comes from Africa. You might see a Rocky Mountain *goat.* Are we listening? Let's see! What kind of bear might you see at the zoo? What kind of ape? What animal is a member of the antelope family? How would an antelope or a *gazelle* move? Which animal would come from the Rocky Mountains?

2. We have many feathered friends. The sea *gull* flies out over the ocean, but we can see it when it comes into

shore. A *goose* lays eggs. A *gander* does not. *Goose* babies are called *goslings*. Are *guppies* feathered friends? No, *guppies* are tiny fish that come from South America. A *grasshopper,* of course, is an insect and not a feathered friend. Are we listening? Let's see! What bird do we see at the seashore? What insect did I mention? Have you seen a *grasshopper?* Tell about it. What kind of fish did I name? What are *guppies?* Where do *guppies* come from? Which feathered friend lays eggs? Which one does not? What are baby *geese* called?

3. Do you know what a rodent is? It is an animal that nibbles and gnaws. Mice, squirrels, and beavers are rodents. A *guinea* pig is a rodent. Sometimes children have *guinea* pigs for pets. A *gopher* belongs to the squirrel family, and it has fur-lined pouches in its cheeks. A *greyhound* is a dog which is tall and slender, and it is a very fast runner. A *Great* Dane is a large and powerful dog with short hair. Are we listening? Let's see! Which rodent might you have for a pet? Which animal belongs to the squirrel family? Which dog is slender and is a very fast runner? Which dog is large and powerful?

—L.B.S.

WHAT DOES GLAD MEAN?

I am glad I have mittens for fingers and thumb.
I am glad when Grandmother and Grandfather come.
I am glad for a blossomy peach tree to climb;
I am glad when my Uncle Jim gives me a dime.
I am glad when I pick a sweet flower to smell;
I am glad when I have a good story to tell.
I am glad that I have some shiny new shoes;
I am glad when somebody allows me to choose.
I am glad that I have a fine family;
I am glad — very glad — I'm a person like ME!

—L.B.S.

HAPPY NOISES

Glip, glip, glip
  Goes the water in the sink,
    the water in the sink,
      the water in the sink.
        Glip, glip, glip
          Goes the water in the sink
            When I go to get a nice cool drink!

Glup, glup, glup
  Goes the milk into my cup,
    the milk into my cup,
      the milk into my cup.
        Glup, glup, glup
          Goes the milk into my cup,
            And I drink all the milk right up!

Glub, glub, glub
  Goes the froggie by the lake,
    the froggie by the lake,
      the froggie by the lake.
        Glub, glub, glub
          Goes the froggie by the lake,
          And he keeps me wide-awake!

—L.B.S.

The repetition enables the children to join in with the teacher almost at once. Words which contain the "g" speech sound are: *glip, goes, go, glup, glub,* and *froggie.*

FUNNY OLD PIG

Funny old pig,
Funny old pig,
Why do you like to dig, dig, dig?
    "I like to dig
    Because I'm a pig."
Oh! You funny old pig-ig-ig!

Funny old frog,
Funny old frog,
Why do you like to croak in a bog?
    "I croak in a bog
    Because I'm a frog."
Oh! You funny old frog-og-og!

Funny old bug,
Funny old bug,
Why do you like to creep under the rug?
    "I creep under the rug
    Because I'm a bug."
Oh! You funny old bug-ug-ug!

—L.B.S.

This nonsense rhyme provides practice on the "g" speech sound in final positon in *pig, dig, frog, bog, bug,* and *rug.* The children can join immediately in saying lines one, two, and six of each stanza.

FROGS IN A BOG

A frog family lived in a bog. And that is where they sang their garrumpy, gallumpy, glugging songs. The bog was a nice place for frogs, because the earth was dark and soft and oozy. On a warm July night the frogs sang a sere-nade — a garrumpy, gallumpy, glugging serenade. And one little frog could be heard to say:

"I am a little frog.
I live in a bog.
Just listen to my song.
I sleep all winter long.
And now I catch a fly,
And now I wink my eye,
And now and then I hop,
And now and then I stop.
Glug, glug, glug!"

If you were to listen to the frogs very long, your eyes would grow droopy and drowsy and soon the serenade would put you to sleep — that garrumpy, gallumpy, glugging serenade.

On this particular July night, Baby Frog's voice could be heard quite plainly as he said again:

> "I am a little frog.
> I live in a bog.
> Just listen to my song.
> I sleep all winter long.
> And now I catch a fly,
> And now I wink my eye,
> And now and then I hop,
> And now and then I stop.
> Glug, glug, glug!"

When you listened carefully and paid full attention to what the frog family said in their conversations, you could hear some glugging sounds in their words, and of course, if you really stop to think about it, there are glugging sounds that you can hear on the very end of such words as *fro-g*, *e-gg*, *lo-g*, and *bo-g*.

Baby Frog asked his mother, "Mummy, where did I come from?"

And his mother replied, "You came from an *e-gg*, dear. You came from an *e-gg*, and you grew into a *polliwo-g*, a sweet little *polliwo-g*."

"Oh," said Baby Frog. "Am I still a *polliwo-g*, a little *polliwo-g*?"

"No," said his mother. "You are now a *fro-g*, a delightful *fro-g*."

Baby Frog knew about himself now, so he dived into the marshy water to play leapfrog with the other little frogs. Soon Baby Frog became tired and stopped playing. He rested on a log.

"Where are you, Baby Frog?" asked his mother.

"I am resting on a *lo-g*, a *lo-g* in the *bo-g*. I'm a *fro-g* on a *lo-g*," said Baby Frog. Then he said:

> "I am a little frog.
> I live in a bog.
> Just listen to my song.
> I sleep all winter long.
> And now I catch a fly,
> And now I wink my eye,
> And now and then I hop,
> And now and then I stop.
> Glug, glug, glug!"

Suddenly, there was a BIG noise. A VERY big noise. The noise was nothing like Baby Frog had ever heard before. It went, "Bow-wow-wow!"

You and I know that it was a dog, but Baby Frog did not know this. He jumped into the water and swam away from there quickly, and the whole frog family came swimming as fast as could be right behind him. On the other side of the marshy pond, Baby Frog asked his mother, "Mummy, what WAS that noise?"

His mother replied, "It was a *do-g*, a *bi-g do-g*. The *do-g* must have heard our serenade, our garrumpy, gallumpy, glugging serenade. Maybe we awakened him from his sleep."

"Do dogs like frogs?" asked Baby Frog.

"Your father could answer that question much better if he were here. But Father Frog had swum far down the pond to seek a better and safer place for us to live," said Mother Frog.

Baby Frog said, "But I like this home, Mummy. Why do we have to leave?"

Mother Frog said, "The cranes have taken over the bog, and cranes like nothing better than plump, juicy frogs for their dinner. We no longer have any safety or privacy here. Father Frog will find another home where we can practice our garrumpy, gallumpy, glugging sounds."

"I am hungry, Mummy," said Baby Frog. His mother brought him something to eat. She said, "Here is a *bu-g*, a delicious *bu-g*."

Baby Frog thanked his mother and gobbled the bug. Then he sat down to wait for Father Frog who soon came with good news about a new home downstream, a place where the frog family would be away from the cranes and where they could have all the safety and privacy they needed to practice their garrumpy, gallumpy, glugging sounds.

Someday when you are near a bog, please listen for Baby Frog's song. It goes this way:

> "I am a little frog.
> I live in a bog.
> Just listen to my song.
> I sleep all winter long.
> And now I catch a fly,
> And now I wink my eye,
> And now and then I hop,
> And now and then I stop.
> Glug, glug, glug!"

—L.B.S.

Ask the children to feel what the back of the tongue does when they make the "frog" sound. Ask them to pronounce words in the story that end with the sound: *frog, bog, glug, egg, log, polliwog, dog,* and *big.* They will enjoy joining in with the little frog's song.

CHAPTER 13

The "P" and "B" Speech Sounds

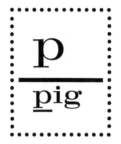

MAKING THE SPEECH SOUND

The lips are pressed together, and air is held inside the mouth. The soft palate is raised to keep the air from escaping through the nasal passages. When the lips are opened quickly, the air is released suddenly and explosively as the "p" sound. The teeth usually are slightly parted. There is no vocal-cord vibration when this sound is produced.

You may call "p" the "popcorn" or the "balloon-popping" sound.

CORRECTING THE DEFICIENT SPEECH SOUND

This is an easily imitated speech sound because it is made primarily with the lips. To demonstrate the explosive quality of the sound, ask the child to hold up a small piece of paper close to his mouth and say "p, p, p." The paper will move if the voiceless sound is made correctly. The sound should not be voiced as "puh." In cleft-palate speech or in post-polio paralytic speech, it may be necessary to close the lips more firmly than usual and exaggerate the position. If a child is prone to puff out the cheeks, ask him to hold a finger against each side of his face to see that the cheeks are not extended or puffed out. Most difficulties in producing this sound will occur in final position. The lips must be opened to let the air escape in an explosion when "p" is produced at the end of a word.

INSTRUCTIONS TO THE CHILD

"Press your lips together. Hold your finger in front of your lips and feel the little puff of air as you make the 'popping' sound: 'P, p, p.' Now let's see if you can make this paper move when you say each of these words: *pony, pig, pan*. Did you hear the 'popping' sound? Could you feel it? Make the paper move as you say these words which end with the 'popping' sound: *top, cup, lip*. Here is a poem about popcorn. When you hear the popping sound, make it with me."

The popcorn in the pan goes pop, pop, pop.
"P, p, p, p, p, p, p!"
The little yellow grains will hop, hop, hop!
"P, p, p, p, p, p, p!"
The little yellow grains will turn to white;
We'll put them in a bowl and we'll all have a bite.

—L.B.S.

WORDS FOR PRACTICE

Initial	Medial	Final
park	apple	cup
paste	shepherd	hop
peach	pepper	lip
pie	slipper	step
post	puppet	map
puff	copper	pipe

309

Consonant Blends:

*p*low	*p*rune	he*lp*	shar*p*
*p*lum	*p*ray	sca*lp*	har*p*

I HEAR IT

Refer to the unit on "s" for suggestions on using the "I Hear It" rhyme.

I hear it in *paint* but not in *faint.*
I hear it in *pan* but not in *fan.*
I hear it in *pat* but not in *fat.*
  I hear it in *pour* but not in *four.*
  I hear it in *peal* but not in *feel.*
  I press both my lips and hold the air in.
  I let it explode in *pony* and *pin.*
  "P, p, p!" *Pony* and *pin.*
I hear it in *pull* but not in *full.*
I hear it in *put* but not in *foot.*
I hear it in *pit* but not in *fit.*
  I hear it in *port* but not in *fort.*
  I hear it in *pail* but not in *fail.*
  I press both my lips and hold the air in.
  I let it explode in *pony* and *pin.*
  "P, p, p!" *Pony* and *pin.*

—L.B.S.

WHAT PETE HEARD

TEACHER: Pete heard a sound and Pete looked all around.
Was it someone opening a bottle of soda pop?

CHILDREN: "P, p, p, p!"

310

TEACHER:	Was it the slow unwinding of a spinning top?
CHILDREN:	"P, p, p, p!"
TEACHER:	Was it a puffing engine inside a boat?
CHILDREN:	"P, p, p, p!"
TEACHER:	Was it four buttons popping off a brown coat?
CHILDREN:	"P, p, p, p!"
TEACHER:	Was it someone puffing out the flame of a match?
CHILDREN:	"P, p, p, p!"
TEACHER:	Was it a pumpkin bursting in a pumpkin patch?
CHILDREN:	"P, p, p, p!"
TEACHER:	Was it grains of popcorn popping in a pan?
CHILDREN:	"P, p, p, p!"
TEACHER:	Was it pink pebbles rattling inside a can?
CHILDREN:	"P, p, p, p!"
TEACHER:	Time's up! We will have to stop this game! It was the sound at the beginning of Pete's name!
CHILDREN:	PETE!

—L.B.S.

Remind the children to press the lips together when they make the "popping" sound. For variety, ask the class to give negative complete-sentence responses instead of making the "popping" sound. Ask them to tell if their name has the "p" speech sound.

POP, POP, POP!

Pop, pop, pop, pop,
Pop, pop, pop!
Listen to the popcorn pop!

The little yellow grains
Are dancing in the heat,
And when the pan is full,
We will all have a treat!

311

Pop, pop, pop, pop,
Pop, pop, pop!
Listen to the popcorn pop!

Soon the pan is filled
With snowy grains of white.
We'll put some butter on
And we'll all have a bite!

Pop, pop, pop, pop,
Pop, pop, pop!
Listen to the popcorn pop!

—L.B.S.

Ask the children to press the lips together firmly as they make the "popcorn" sound. Part of the class may be popcorn popping as they make the voiceless "p, p, p" sound while the rest of the class says the lines.

HEAR THE LITTLE RAINDROPS

Hear the little raindrops dancing
As they patter to the ground.
Pitter-patter-pitter-patter,
With a happy raindrop sound!

Pitter-patter-pitter-patter
On the chimney tops and roofs.
Pitter-patter-pitter-patter
Like fairy pony's prancing hoofs.

Pitter-patter-pitter-patter,
Clouds will bring us warm spring
    showers.
They will find the little buds
And turn them into pretty flowers.

Pitter-patter-pitter-patter,
Pitter-patter-pitter-patter,
Pitter-patter-pitter-patter!
(*The children say the raindrop
refrain softer and softer.*)

—L.B.S.

Let the children tap their fingers lightly on the desk as they say the refrain. The "p" sound, though repeated in the words *pitter* and *patter,* is not overly emphasized, so it will not become a pedantic practice device.

PORKY PORCUPINE

Porky, porky porcupine,
With bristles on your back,
Your little neat pincushion
Is sharper than a tack!
 Porky, porky porcupine,
  Porky, porky porcupine!

Porky, porky porcupine,
How slowly you do crawl;
But when you want to go to sleep,
You curl up in a ball!
 Porky, porky porcupine,
  Porky, porky porcupine!

Porky, porky porcupine,
Your spiny quills go up
When you see a mewing cat
Or a barking pup!
 Porky, porky porcupine,
  Porky, porky porcupine!

—L.B.S.

Ask the children to press the lips together to make a good "p" speech sound in *porky* and *porcupine.*

PETS [1]

ALL: Pets, pets, pets!
Oh, pets are so much fun!
Real ones or stuffed ones,
I like them every one!

TEACHER: Would you like a fat, black piggy
That has a piggy snout?

CHILDREN: Yes, I'd like a fat, black piggy
That has a piggy snout.

TEACHER: Would you like a frisky pony
That will trot and run about?

CHILDREN: (*Respond.*)

ALL: Pets, pets, pets!
Oh, pets are SO much fun!
Real ones or stuffed ones,
I like them every one!

TEACHER: Would you like a prickly porcupine
With needles on his back?

CHILDREN: (*Respond.*)

TEACHER: Would you like a stately penguin
That is dressed in white and black?

CHILDREN: (*Respond.*)

ALL: (*Repeat refrain.*)

---

[1] Based upon "Pets," page 14, *Book B, Time for Phonics,* Louise Binder Scott, Webster Division, McGraw-Hill Book Company.

TEACHER: Would you like a hungry pelican
That eats all he can hold?

CHILDREN: (*Respond.*)

TEACHER: Would you like a gorgeous peacock,
Clad in blue and green and gold?

CHILDREN: (*Respond.*)

ALL: (*Repeat refrain.*)

TEACHER: Would you like a curious puffin
With a very curious bill?

CHILDREN: (*Respond.*)

TEACHER: Would you like a furry prairie dog
That burrows with such skill?

CHILDREN: (*Respond.*)

ALL: (*Repeat refrain.*)

—L.B.S.

Ask the children to draw pictures of their favorite pets and discuss them. Words in the poem which begin with the "p" speech sound are: *pets, piggy, pony, pretty, prickly, porcupine, penguin, pelican, peacock, puffin,* and *prairie.* Check the children's familiarity with some of the less well-known animals mentioned in the poem.

APPLE PIE

ALL: Apple pie, apple pie,
Oh, why do I like apple pie?

TEACHER: I pick a ripe apple,
And take out the core.

I cut some small slices,
One, two, three, and four.

ALL: Apple pie, apple pie,
It is my favorite kind of pie.

TEACHER: I roll out the dough
With a long rolling pin.
I smooth out the crust
In a round shiny tin.

ALL: Apple pie, apple pie,
Oh yes, I do like apple pie!

TEACHER: I put in the slices
And sprinkle with spice.
The cinnamon smell
Is oh so very nice!

ALL: Apple pie, apple pie,
That's why we all like apple pie!

—L.B.S.

The "p" speech sound is used initially in *pie* and medially in
apple. The rhyme may be acted out by the girls in the class while
the boys say the refrains. Ask the children to discuss their favorite
kinds of pie.

THE POPPING BALLOONS

Mr. Poppins, the balloon man, always stood on the
corner of Poplar Street at half-past three in the afternoon. On any afternoon he could be heard calling out,
"Balloons! Balloons! Balloons! Who will buy my pretty
balloons?"

In his hand, Mr. Poppins held balloons of every color.
You name the colors. I am sure that Mr. Poppins had at

least one balloon of every color you could think of and even some you cannot think of!

> Now balloons are round,
> And they have no sound.
> When they're filled with air,
> They fly everywhere.

Suddenly on the corner of Poplar Street at half-past three in the afternoon, and without warning, a HUGE wind came along and whisked every single balloon out of poor Mr. Poppins' hand. He reached and he grabbed and he jumped and he shouted, but the balloons sailed away.

Some children saw the balloons sailing, and they ran after them, reaching their hands up high and jumping to try to catch them.

> Pete caught a red one.
> "P!" That was that!
> The red balloon popped,
> And now it was flat! (*Children repeat.*)

> Penny caught a green one.
> "P!" That was that!
> The green balloon popped,
> And now it was flat! (*Children repeat.*)

> Patty caught a yellow one.
> "P!" That was that!
> The yellow balloon popped,
> And now it was flat! (*Children repeat.*)

> Paul caught a blue one.
> "P!" That was that!
> The blue balloon popped,
> And now it was flat! (*Children repeat.*)

Perry caught an orange one.
"P!" That was that!
The orange balloon popped,
And now it was flat! (*Children repeat.*)

Pansy caught a purple one. But — it did NOT pop!
It did not pop at all. Isn't that amazing? Pansy was very
careful with the purple balloon. She carried it back to Mr.
Poppins, who stood sadly on the corner of Poplar Street.

Mr. Poppins was sorry to lose his pretty balloons. He
said, "Keep this balloon, Pansy. It is a purple balloon.
Pansies are purple, too, so this balloon matches your name
perfectly. A purple balloon is just right for you."

Pansy caught the purple one,
But it stayed nice and round.
It never, never, never
Made a popping sound!

—L.B.S.

Remind the children that to make as good a "popping" sound
as the balloon made, we must press our lips together and hold the
air inside. Then we let the air out of our mouths in a "popping"
sound. Remind them that "p" is a quiet sound and that the voice
motor does not work. This story may be used in several ways: Read
it aloud and let the class pantomime it as they take turns being
the characters. Use it with a flannelboard, and ask the children to
cut colored construction-paper balloons to stick to the board as the
story is told or dramatized by the children themselves.

PEEPERS, THE HUNGRY·CHICK

"Peep, peep, peep!" said Peepers. "I'm hungry and
my tummy tells me that it is time to eat.

Peep, peep, peep! Peep, peep, peep!
I would like some food to eat.
Peep, peep, peep! Peep, peep, peep!"

Peepers was a little yellow chick. She was hungry and lonesome as she stood near the big red barn looking for the rest of her family. Peepers had eaten breakfast long ago in the lower garden with Mother Hen and her many brothers and sisters. Mother Hen had started back to the barnyard, with Peepers and the other chicks following along.

"Peep, peep! Peep, peep! Peep, peep!" they all said happily as they ran along the garden path. But Peepers was left behind when she chased a beautiful black-and-yellow butterfly and then stopped to watch a caterpillar crawl under a fuzzy leaf. Peepers hurried along the path to catch up with her family, but it was too late. Mother Hen and all the little brother and sister chicks had disappeared.

Peepers huddled near the big red barn. "Peep, peep, peep!" she said with her tiny voice. "Peep, peep, peep! Where is my mother and where are my brothers and sisters?

> Peep, peep, peep! Peep, peep, peep!
> I would like some food to eat.
> Peep, peep, peep! Peep, peep, peep!"

Peepers peeked inside the barn. "Peep, peep, peep!" she called. "Are you in there, Mother Hen?"

"Moo, moo!" came the answer. "Mother Hen is not here, but I am."

"It is Brown Eyes, the Cow," said Peepers. "Perhaps, she can give me something to eat." So Peepers hurried to Brown Eyes, the Cow, and said:

> "Peep, peep, peep! Peep, peep, peep!
> May I share your food with you?
> Peep, peep, peep! Peep, peep, peep!
> Just a few small bites will do."

"Moo!" replied Brown Eyes. "If you can eat hay as I do, I will be happy to share some with you!"

Peepers watched Brown Eyes munching a mouthful of hay. But she knew that her small beak was made for pecking, not for chewing. She said to Brown Eyes:

"Peep, peep, peep! Peep, peep, peep!
I thank you, Brown Eyes, but hay I cannot eat.
Peep, peep, peep! Peep, peep, peep!"

Peepers hippity-hopped right out of the barn, and there was Digger, the Dog, lying in the sun. "Perhaps Digger can give me something to eat," she said. Peepers stopped in front of the dog, who was gnawing on a large bone.

"Peep, peep, peep! Peep, peep, peep!
May I share your food with you?
Peep, peep, peep! Peep, peep, peep!
Just a few small bites will do."

"Woof!" replied Digger. "If you can eat bones as I do, I will be happy to share mine with you."

Peepers watched Digger gnawing happily on the large bone. She knew that her small beak was made for pecking, not for gnawing. So she said to Digger:

"Peep, peep, peep! Peep, peep, peep!
I thank you, Digger, but bones I cannot eat.
Peep, peep, peep! Peep, peep, peep!"

All at once, Peepers heard the sound of children's voices. "Look," said the little girl, "that baby chick is lost. Where could Mother Hen be?"

"Perhaps the baby chick is hungry," said the little boy. "Let's take it up to the house and give it some food. Then we'll look for Mother Hen."

Peepers knew right away that the children wanted to help her. She peeped loudly:

"Peep, peep, peep! Peep, peep, peep!
I would like some food to eat.
Peep, peep, peep! Peep, peep, peep!"

The children took turns cuddling Peepers gently in their hands as they walked back to the white farmhouse. Carefully they placed her inside a big cardboard box on the porch. Then they brought some tasty cracked corn to sprinkle inside the box. Peepers pecked away with her little sharp bill until her tiny tummy was full.

"Peep, peep, peep! Peep, peep, peep!
Thank you, friends. This corn I like to eat.
Peep, peep, peep! Peep, peep, peep!"

Later, the little girl and the little boy carried Peepers back to the barnyard and returned her to her family. Mother Hen clucked and scolded, but she was very happy to see her baby again. Before Peepers could even begin to explain what had happened, the children scattered several handfuls of cracked corn over the ground. Mother Hen joined the chicks, who were enjoying the treat.

Peepers was no longer hungry, for she had been fed at the farmhouse and her tummy was full. She just walked quietly beside Mother Hen and peeped:

"Peep, peep, peep! Peep, peep, peep!
Thank you, friends. This corn we like to eat.
Peep, peep, peep! Peep, peep, peep!"

—J.J.T.

The "p" sound is presented in all three positions in this story in the words *peep* and *Peepers*. Have the children repeat the refrain each time. Use the flannelboard as an aid in telling the story. The children can also act out the story in a creative dramatics activity.

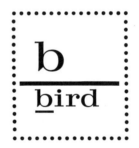

MAKING THE SPEECH SOUND

This speech sound is made like the "p" sound, except that there is slightly less force exerted and the vocal cords vibrate. Like "p," this speech sound is imitated easily because it is made primarily with the lips.

You may call "b" the "bubble" or the "babbling-baby" sound.

CORRECTING THE DEFICIENT SPEECH SOUND

Use the same techniques as for "p." It is rare that a child makes substitution for "b," since it is one of the first speech sounds he learns. However, cleft palate children may have difficulty with this sound, for labial, or lip, closure may not be possible. The palatal deficiency may permit air to escape through the nose so that insufficient pressure cannot be built up to produce a good explosive "b" sound.

INSTRUCTIONS TO THE CHILD

"Press your lips together. Be sure to use your voice motor. You hold air inside of your mouth and now you let it go: *bub*. Did you feel what your lips did when they closed firmly and then opened suddenly? Hold up your finger. As you say *bee* and *boy,* feel the puff of air that blows against your finger. Here is a rhyme which will give us practice."

> Bub, bub, bub,
> Three puppies in a tub.
> Bub, bub, bub,
> Let's give them a scrub!
>
> —L.B.S.

WORDS FOR PRACTICE

Initial	Medial	Final
butter	rabbit	tub
bark	pebble	bib
bone	marble	cab
boot	robber	web
bake	gobble	cub
beak	warble	knob

I HEAR IT

Refer to the unit on the "s" speech sound for suggestions on using the "I Hear It" rhyme.

I hear it in *bad* but not in *mad.*
I hear it in *bail* but not in *mail.*
I hear it in *bind* but not in *mind.*
 I hear it in *bare* but not in *dare.*
 I hear it in *bent* but not in *dent.*
 My lips press together; I hold the air in.
 I let it explode when I say *bin.*
 "B, b, b!" *Bin!*
I hear it in *bug* but not in *tug.*
I hear it in *boot* but not in *toot.*
I hear it in *bite* but not in *tight.*
 I hear it in *beat* but not in *neat.*
 I hear it in *bed* but not in *Ned.*
 My lips press together; I hold the air in.
 I let it explode when I say *bin.*
 "B, b, b!" *Bin!*

        —L.B.S.

BUTTONS

Buttons on a new shirt, shiny, round, and small.
Buttons on an old shirt, very few at all.

Buttons, buttons, buttons,
Yellow, green, or blue,
Red buttons, purple buttons,
Which are best for you?

Buttons in the button box for a rainy day.
Buttons that are fun when I can't go out to play.

Buttons, buttons, buttons,
Yellow, green, or blue,
Red buttons, purple buttons,
Which are best for you?

324

Painted buttons, brass buttons, every kind, I guess.
If you ask me, there must be a million, more or less!

Buttons, buttons, buttons,
Yellow, green, or blue,
Red buttons, purple buttons,
Which are best for you?

—L.B.S.

The children say the refrain each time it appears in the poem. To help teach color concepts, cut out colored construction-paper buttons for the flannelboard. Or you may wish to glue small magnets to the backs of plastic colored buttons and use these for a magnetic board. Suggest that the children take turns placing the buttons on the board as the poem is said. Ask them to describe the buttons on their own clothing.

BIG

Big is an engine that pulls a train;
Big is a storm cloud that brings the rain.
Big is a fat hippopotamus;
Big is a car and also a bus.
Big is the horse that gives me a ride;
Big is the desert, endlessly wide!
Big is a whale in the big, big sea;
Big is a stately redwood tree.
Big is a mountain, majestic and tall;
Big is the opposite of *small!*

—L.B.S.

Ask the class to tell about other things that are big. Write their responses on a wall chart. This rhyme may be used to teach the opposite concepts *big* and *small*. (See page 87 for an activity on the concept *small*.) After the rhyme has been read once or twice, ask the children to supply the last word in each couplet. Suggested bibliography: Charles and Martha Shapp, *What's Big and What's Small?* (Watts); Ethel S. Berkley, *Big and Little, Up and Down* (Young-Scott).

BUBBLES

Big, BIG bubbles I can blow!
Rainbow bubbles! Watch them go!
    Bub, bub, bub! Bub, bub, bub!

Soap makes bubbles, pink and blue,
But there are other bubbles, too.
    Bub, bub, bub! Bub, bub, bub!

I see bubbles at the top
Of my orange soda pop.
    Bub, bub, bub! Bub, bub, bub!

Water boils for Mother's tea;
Then many bubbles I can see.
    Bub, bub, bub! Bub, bub, bub!

—L.B.S.

The isolated "b" speech sound cannot be produced without adding a vowel sound. Rather than add a schwa or short *u* (which is not part of the "b" speech sound), it is best to pronounce the sound in a word or in a nonsense syllable, e.g., *bub* in the poem above. Ask the children to press the lips firmly together and use their voice motors as they make the sound. Pronounce with the class all words in the rhyme which contain the "b" sound: *big, bubbles, blow, blue,* and *boils.*

THE BABBLING BROOK

I know a little babbling brook
That sings and sings for me.
I watch it as it flows along
To join the sparkling sea.

    Babble, babble, babble
    Over stones and pebbles.
    Babble, babble, babble
    To join the sparkling sea.

It sings of thirsty animals
That stop along its way.
It sings of fish and butterflies
And frogs that leap and play.

Babble, babble, babble
Over stones and pebbles.
Babble, babble, babble
Is what it sang today.

—L.B.S.

The children say the refrain. Ask them to press their lips together and make their very best "b" speech sound as they say the word *babble*.

WHAT IS BLACK?

Black is good earth where little seeds grow;
Black is the bird that we call a crow.
Black is a berry which grows on a vine;
Black is the night, unless moon and stars shine.
Black are the shoes that you wear on your feet;
Black is the pepper on food that you eat.
Black is sweet licorice — yum, yum, yum!
Black is the spot of ink on your thumb.
Black is the skunk with stripe down his back;
Black is the engine that runs on a track.
Black is a fierce old Halloween cat;
Black is a witch's steeple hat.
Black is the marker with which you write;
Black is the opposite of *white!*

—L.B.S.

WHAT IS BLUE?

Blue is the jay that scolds you and me;
Blue is the bluebird that sings from the tree.
Blue is the sky where fluffy clouds float;
Blue is the hull on the little sailboat.

Blue is Kentucky bluegrass so sweet;
Blue is a blueberry — oh, what a treat.
Blue is the ribbon that wins the first prize;
Blue is the color of my kitten's eyes.
Blue are the bluebells that grow by the brook;
Blue is the cover on my picture book.
Blue is a color that often is seen;
Blue paint with yellow will make pretty green.

—L.B.S.

Ask individuals to name other things that are black or blue. Since both color names begin with consonant blends containing the "l" speech sound, the two poems above may be used for drill on that sound as well as on "b." After you have read each poem through, ask the children to recall and name things mentioned in the poems that were blue or black.

MY BOUNCING BALL

Tractors, trucks, and trains make noise;
So do girls, and so do boys.
But the noise that I like the best of all
Is the noise that is made by a bouncing ball!

ALL: Bumpety, bumpety, bumpety, bump,
Bumpety, bumpety, bump!

Whistles on top of factories blow;
Sirens are shrill, and foghorns, low.
But I like the noise of my bouncing ball
As it bumps against the side of the wall.

ALL: Bumpety, bumpety, bumpety, bump,
Bumpety, bumpety, bump!

—L.B.S.

The children say the refrain. Read the rhyme slowly enough so that the children can duplicate the rhythm of the lines by bouncing a real or an imaginary ball.

Baby Bass was a fish that lived in a cool stream of fresh, clear water. Baby Bass liked to blow bubbles out of his mouth: "B, b, b, b!" (*Children imitate.*)

If you have ever seen bubbles coming from a fish's mouth, you will know what I mean. When you press your lips together firmly and let the air come out in a big "b" sound, you can make the sound Baby Bass made.

One evening, there was to be a bubble-blowing contest in the big blue lake at the end of the little stream where Baby Bass lived. All of the fishes gathered for the event. Mrs. Guppy was to be the judge. She was so small she couldn't blow bubbles that would be big enough to judge in the contest. But everyone agreed that Mrs. Guppy would make a fine judge.

Mr. Bullfrog was to be second judge. He could puff out his chest and say, "Glug, glug," but no matter how hard he tried he just could not blow bubbles.

Little Miss Firefly was to be the third judge. She carried a pale-green lantern that made a lovely glow, but of course she could not blow bubbles, either.

So there were three judges, Mrs. Guppy, Mr. Bullfrog, and Miss Firefly, and everyone agreed that they would make splendid judges for the bubble contest.

Just as the sun was going down behind the big hill in the west, all of the water creatures gathered. And when Mrs. Cricket gave the signal by playing a crickly-crackly note on her cricket flute, a big fish began to blow the first bubbles of the contest.

It was Mr. Carp. He took a big breath and out came bubbles: "B, b, b, b!" (*Children imitate.*)

"Four bubbles," called Miss Firefly.

"Four bubbles," repeated Mrs. Guppy.

"Four bubbles," glugged Mr. Bullfrog.

It was now Mrs. Halibut's turn. She took a big breath and out came some bubbles: "B, b, b, b, b!"

"Five bubbles," sang Miss Firefly.

"Five bubbles," called Mrs. Guppy.

"Five bubbles," croaked Mr. Bullfrog.

Baby Bass was waiting his turn in line. When the judges called out, "Next," Baby Bass took a big breath and out came bubbles, bubbles, and more bubbles: "B, b, b, b, b, b, b, b, b, b!" (*Children imitate.*)

"Ten bubbles," called Miss Firefly.

"Ten bubbles," cried Mrs. Guppy.

"Ten bubbles," glugged Mr. Bullfrog.

Of course, every fish wanted a turn and all had a chance to try out for first prize. All of the fish tried their very best, but none of them could make as many bubbles as Baby Bass. And do you know why? Baby Bass practiced! And you can make a good bubbly-bubbling sound, too, if you will practice and say these words that end with the "bubble" sound: *tu-b, cri-b, bi-b, we-b, cu-b.* And you can make the "bubble" sound at the beginning of each of these words: *ball, bug, bag, bit, boy.* And you can make three "bubble" sounds when you say Baby Bass's name, because it has three *b*'s: *Baby Bass.* See how easy it is?

Since bubbles have every color of the rainbow, perhaps you can show me that you know your colors.

> Bubbles, bubbles,
> Bubbles so round!
> Six bubbles will be seen:
> Blue and yellow,
> Red and purple,
> Orange and green!

> —L.B.S.

Cut colored construction-paper circles to represent bubbles and place them on the flannelboard as the "color" rhyme is said.

THE BABY BOYS

Once there was a remarkable Baby Boy:

> He had blue eyes
> Like sunny skies.
> He had brown hair,
> And his skin was fair.

He was an English baby. When he talked to his mother and father, he made many sounds. Sometimes he went like this: "Bah, bah, bah, pa-pa, ma-ma, buh, buh, buh! GUH!" (*Children imitate*.) Oh, he was a MOST remarkable Baby Boy.

There was another remarkable Baby Boy:

> He was a cute little fellow,
> And his skin was yellow.
> His name was Yo-San,
> And he lived in Japan.

He was a Japanese baby. He talked to his mother and father and they were SO proud of him. The Japanese baby said all sorts of nonsense things like: "Bah, bah, bah, pa-pa, ma-ma, buh, buh, buh! GUH!"

There was another remarkable Baby Boy:

> This baby was carried
> On his mother's back.
> His hair was curly,
> And his skin was black.

He was an African baby. And he made all sorts of nonsense noises, which his mother and his father listened to with great joy: "Bah, bah, bah, pa-pa, ma-ma, buh, buh, buh! GUH!"

There was another remarkable Baby Boy.

He lived across the border
In a Mexican town.
He had a big smile,
And his skin was lovely brown.

He was a Mexican baby. He said nonsense things to his mother and father, too. And they loved him very much. "Bah, bah, bah, pa-pa, ma-ma, buh, buh, buh! GUH!"

And all of the Baby Boys — the English Baby Boy, the Japanese Baby Boy, the African Baby Boy, and the Mexican Baby Boy — all babbled exactly the same way. They all talked *baby language* because they were only a few months old, and the baby language helped them to learn grown-up language!

—L.B.S.

Note: Authorities agree that babies babble in the same way in every language. Syllables may appear around the sixth or seventh month and this vocal play continues even through the stage of imitation.

CHAPTER 14

The "Wh" and "W" Speech Sounds

MAKING THE SPEECH SOUND

The lips are rounded as for long "oo" in *moon*. The back of the tongue is elevated toward the soft palate. As the breath stream is blown out steadily, the tongue, teeth, and lips move quickly and smoothly from the "oo" position to the position for the succeeding vowel sound. The soft palate is raised and the vocal cords do not vibrate.

You may call "wh" the "blowing," the "pinwheel," or the "whistling" sound.

CORRECTING THE DEFICIENT SPEECH SOUND

Blowing out the breath precedes the production of the vowel sound which follows the "wh" sound. After the lips are rounded, and the breath stream is blown out for "wh," the jaw moves down for the vowel sound which follows, e.g., short "e" in *when* and long "i" in *why*. The sound should be demonstrated by holding up a slip of paper and making it move as words are said: *where, wheat, what, which*. The child may construct a pinwheel, attach it to a pencil eraser with a pin, and use it for practice. A large proportion of people in the United States do not differentiate between the voiced "w" and the voiceless "wh," e.g., *wen* for *when*.

INSTRUCTIONS TO THE CHILD

"When we name question words like *what, where, when,* and *why,* our lips are rounded in a very small circle. Do this with me. Now blow softly like this. (*Demonstrate.*) Name these words after me and watch the paper blow." (*Repeat word list above.*)

> My lips form a circle
> Just like small *o.*
> I can make this paper move
> When I blow:
> "Wh! Wh! Wh! Whoa!"
>
> —L.B.S.

WORDS FOR PRACTICE

Initial	Medial	Final
what	pinwheel	——
wheat	anywhere	
whiskers	nowhere	
whistle	snow-white	
whirl	bullwhip	
why	meanwhile	

I HEAR IT

Refer to the unit on "s" for suggestions on using this "I Hear It" rhyme.

I hear it in *whale* but not in *wail.*
I hear it in *what* but not in *watt.*
I hear it in *where* but not in *wear.*

I hear it in *which* but not in *witch.*
I hear it in *whether* but not in *weather.*
Whenever I make this blowing sound,
I make my lips very small and round.
"Wh, wh, wh!" *Where* and *what.*

I hear it in *whine* but not in *wine.*
I hear it in *why* but not in *Y.*
I hear it in *whit* but not in *wit.*

I hear it in *whir* but not in *were.*
I hear it in *whee* but not in *wee.*
Whenever I make this blowing sound,
I make my lips very small and round.
"Wh, wh, wh!" *Why* and *whirl.*

—L.B.S.

WHISTLING FOR GOBLINS

There are two goblins sitting in a tree.
Whistle, and I will let you see! (*Children whistle.*)
Along comes another, now there are three.
Whistle, and I will let you see! (*Children whistle.*)
Along comes another, now there are four.
Oh, please don't whistle anymore!
   (*Children whistle.*)
White-whiskered goblins I simply adore,
But I get scared of more than four!

—L.B.S.

Each time the children whistle, add a green construction-paper goblin to the flannelboard. Use white pipe cleaners for whiskers.

BLOWING OUT CANDLES

Do you have a birthday?
How old are you today?
Shall we have a party?
And what games shall we play?
Let's have a big white birthday cake
With candles burning bright,
And when we blow the candles out,
We'll have a nice big bite!
          "Wh— wh— wh— wh— wh— wh!"
Blow with all your might,
          "Wh— wh— wh— wh— wh!"
Until there's not one light!

—L.B.S.

Ask the children to pretend their fingers are candles on a cake. As they blow out the "candles," they bend their fingers down one at a time.

BIRTHDAY CANDLES

SOLO: Today, I have a birthday.
        I'm six years old, you see;
        And here I have a birthday cake
        Which you may share with me.

ALL: First, we'll count the candles;
        Count them every one.
        One, two, three, four, five, six;
        The counting now is done.

SOLO: Let's blow out the candles;
        Out each flame will go,
        "Wh! Wh! Wh! Wh! Wh! Wh!"
        As one by one we blow.

—J.J.T.

A cardboard cake with removable candles and paper flames will add to the fun as the children blow out their candles with a "wh" sound.

MAKING A BLOWING SOUND

I want to say *when, wheat,* and *what,*
So my lips must be round.
I take a breath, and then I blow
To make this quiet sound:
      "Wh, wh, wh!
      Wh, wh, wh!"

I practice saying *why* and *where*
And *which* and *whoa* and *white.*
I practice until I can make
That blowing sound just right!
      "Wh, wh, wh!
      Wh, wh, wh!"

                                       —L.B.S.

Ask each child to hold a slip of paper in front of his lips and make the paper move as he practices saying the words in the poem that begin with the "blowing" sound.

SWEET SUSIE

Where, O where does our sweet Susie go?
She goes to the meadow where blue flowers grow.
WHERE?
      To the meadow where soft breezes blow.
WHERE?
      To the meadow where brook waters flow.

When, O when does our sweet Susie return?
She comes when the butter is ready to churn.
WHEN?
      When the twilight falls soft on the fern.
WHEN?
      When our fire for the night starts to burn.

Why, O why does our sweet Susie cry?
She cries for the rainbow that arches the sky.
WHY?
For the sunlight beginning to die.
WHY?
For the swallow that darts swiftly by.

—J.J.T.

This poem imitates the style of a mountain ballad and can be set to music easily. The "wh" sound is emphasized in the words *where, when,* and *why.*

THE "PINWHEEL" SOUND

Blow the pinwheel! Make it go
As you say, "Whoa, whoa, whoa!"

Blow the pinwheel! Blow again
As you say, "When, when, when!"

Blow the pinwheel! Give it air
As you say, "Where, where, where!"

Blow the pinwheel! Make it fly
As you say, "Why, why, why!"

Blow the pinwheel! Do it right
When you say, "White, white, white!"

—L.B.S.

This exercise emphasizes the "wh" speech sound in initial position in *whoa, when, where, why,* and *white,* and in medial position in *pinwheel.* A commercial pinwheel can be used to demonstrate the blowing quality of the "wh" sound as it causes the pinwheel to turn.

WHITE HORSE, WHITE HORSE

White horse, white horse, on a high hill,
White horse, white horse, standing so still.

338

What would you do if I stood by your side?
Where would we go if I wanted to ride?
We could gallop to work,
We could gallop to play,
We could gallop
and gallop
and gallop away!
When can I come to stand by your side?
Why can't we go for a galloping ride?
White horse, white horse, don't go away.
White horse, white horse, why can't we play?

—J.J.T.

The "wh" sound in *white, what, where, when,* and *why* is contrasted with the "w" sound in *we* and *would*. Point out the difference between the two sounds and ask the children to listen for and feel the difference as the poem is said.

LOST PUPPY

O where is my puppy?
Where, where, where?
Is he hiding underneath
Daddy's big chair?
CHILDREN: Where are you, puppy?
             Where, where, where?

Is he hiding under
The crib or the stair?
I can't find my puppy
At all — anywhere!
CHILDREN: Where are you, puppy?
             Where, where, where?

Have you seen my puppy?
He has a pug nose
And very sad eyes
And some white on his toes.

CHILDREN: Where are you, puppy?
Where, where, where?

His name? It is Blackie,
Because he is black.
He has a name tag,
And a short tail in back.
CHILDREN: O where is my puppy?
O where, O where, O where?

—L.B.S.

The children are afforded practice on the "wh" sound in *where*.
Ask them to make up a stanza telling where the puppy was finally
found.

WHISKERS

Dogs have whiskers,
So do rats,
Rabbits have whiskers,
So do cats.
Tigers and lions
In the zoo,
Both have whiskers;
Mice do, too.
Santa has whiskers
Snowy white.
I wear whiskers
Halloween night.
Daddy has whiskers;
He shaves each day.
What else has whiskers?
Can you say?

—L.B.S.

Motivate this rhyme by asking the children to tell what has
whiskers. Provide a sentence pattern so the children will use the
word *whiskers* in a complete sentence.

WHIPPOORWILL

Whippoorwill, whippoorwill,
  with little specks of white,
    I have heard you singing
      in the still of the night.
        Whippoorwill, whippoorwill,
        Whippoorwill, whippoorwill!
        (High and quick, in imita-
        tion of the bird's call.)
Whippoorwill, whippoorwill,
  with feathers brown and gray,
    I see you sitting on a log,
      sleeping there by day.
        Whippoorwill, whippoorwill,
        Whippoorwill, whippoorwill!
Whippoorwill, whippoorwill,
  I can see why you
    rest so still upon that log,
      because it looks like you!
        Whippoorwill, whippoorwill,
        Whippoorwill, whippoorwill!
Whippoorwill, whippoorwill,
  in the night you fly
    to catch your supper on the wing,
      as little bugs go by!
        Whippoorwill, whippoorwill,
        Whippoorwill, whippoorwill!
Whippoorwill, whippoorwill,
  the night is dark and long;
    But how I like to listen to
      your sad and lovely song:
        Whippoorwill, whippoorwill,
        Whippoorwill, whippoorwill!

                        —L.B.S.

Thorough practice on the "wh" speech sound is provided by the frequent repetition of the word *whippoorwill.*

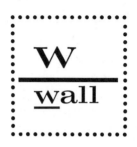

MAKING THE SPEECH SOUND

This sound is made like the voiceless "wh," except that less pressure is exerted and the vocal cords vibrate.

Suggest that the children round the lips for "oo" as in *moon,* and follow the sound with "uh" as "oo-uh, oo-uh." Then, ask the class to blend both sounds quickly if the sound is made in isolation. Like "wh," the "w" speech sound is used initially and medially, but not in final position. The child should use the "w" sound in such words as *way, we, wood, went, one, walk, weed,* and *wide* to gain experience in combining "w" with a variety of vowel sounds. Call "w" the "watch-dog" sound.

CORRECTING THE DEFICIENT SPEECH SOUND

The explanations given under *Making the Speech Sound* offer suggestions that can be used to help a child make the sound correctly. Since this sound is one of the very first speech sounds a child masters in his speech, it is misarticulated only infrequently.

INSTRUCTIONS TO THE CHILD

"To make a barking sound, the lips must first be rounded in a small ring. Look into a mirror to see if your lips are doing so. We can pretend we are big dogs and bark, 'Wow, wow, wow!' Try it. We can be medium-sized dogs and bark, 'Woo, woo, woo!' Try it with me. Then we can be little dogs and bark, 'Wuff, wuff, wuff!' Do it with me now. When we use our lips carefully, people can understand us better when we talk."

WORDS FOR PRACTICE

Initial	Medial	Final
wagon	wigwag	——
water	sidewalk	
web	hardware	
wife	beeswax	
wing	inkwell	
woman	forward	

I HEAR IT

Refer to the section on "s" for information on using this "I Hear It" rhyme.

I hear it in *wake* but not in *rake*.
I hear it in *wag* but not in *rag*.
I hear it in *weed* but not in *read*.
I hear it in *witch* but not in *rich*.
I hear it in *west* but not in *rest*.
I make my lips very small and round.
I use my voice and I make an "oo" sound.
"Oo— oo— oo!" *Witch* and *watch*.
I hear it in *wait* but not in *late*.
I hear it in *wet* but not in *let*.
I hear it in *week* but not in *leak*.
I hear it in *weep* but not in *leap*.
I hear it in *way* but not in *lay*.
I make my lips very small and round.
I use my voice and I make the "oo" sound.
"Oo— oo— oo!" *Witch* and *watch*.

—L.B.S.

WOLFIE, THE WATCH DOG

Wolfie says, "I'm master
When I guard the farm.

I'll bark at anything I think
Might do the animals harm.
       "Wuh, wuh, wuh! Wuff, wuff, wuff!
       Wuh, wuh, wuh! Wuff, wuff, wuff!"

Wolfie barks so crossly,
But there is not a trace
Of fierceness when he comes to me
And licks me on the face.
       "Wuh, wuh, wuh! Wuff, wuff, wuff!
       Wuh, wuh, wuh! Wuff, wuff, wuff!
       Lap, lap, lap!"

—L.B.S.

This rhyme gives practice not only on the "w" speech sound in *Wolfie, wuh,* and *wuff,* but also on the "l" sound in *licks* and *lap.*

ONCE THERE WAS A DUCKLING

Once there was a duckling
With a lovely yellow bill.
She walked down the road, and
She came to a hill.

    With a waddle, waddle, waddle
    And a quack, quack, quack,
    She waddled up the hill and
    She waddled right back!

This fuzzy-wuzzy duckling
With a lovely yellow bill
Tripped on a pebble and
She almost took a spill.

    With a waddle, waddle, waddle
    And a quack, quack, quack,
    She waddled up the hill and
    She waddled right back!

—L.B.S.

The children may take small waddling "duck" steps as the refrain is said.

THE WINTER WIND

The winter wind howls so loudly today.
It rattles the chimney and blows things away.
    "Woo— woo— woo!
    Woo— woo— woo!"
It pounds on the windows and bangs the doors;
It jiggles the shutters and soars and roars.
    "Woo— woo— woo!
    Woo— woo— woo!"
My! It's exciting to hear the wind blow
And see swirling and fluttering flakes of snow!
    "Woo— woo— woo!
    Woo— woo— woo!"

—L.B.S.

Ask the children to round the lips as they make the "wind" sound. Ask them to "paint pictures" with their voices by using good vocal interpretation as they imitate the sound of the wind.

WIGGLE WORM

For his house in this wide, wide wonderful world, Wiggle Worm chose the warm, wonderful earth, which to him was softer and sweeter smelling than anything else ever could be. Wiggle Worm was an earthworm.

One June day the earth tasted especially good to Wiggle Worm, for there had been a shower which had lasted only a few minutes. The shower had lasted just long enough to give the earth — the warm, wonderful earth — that very special fragrance of freshly grown grass and little seeds beginning to sprout.

Wiggle Worm's food was the earth — the moist earth that was his home and that was full of tiny morsels of food that were so good to eat. Wiggle Worm took a mouthful of the delicious earth, and he pushed some aside to make his little tunnel-house through the earth. Of course, every time Wiggle Worm took a bite of food, he made his house just a little bigger.

Wonderful, wonderful Wiggle Worm
In a wide, wide wonderful world —
Exploring all by himself — his wonderful self!

Wiggle Worm pushed himself through the soft earth to the top of the ground, and he knew he was in a wonderful world.

Every nerve fiber told him that it was a wonderful world.

Every cell and muscle in his wiggly body told him so.

As he crawled along, the bristles on his little sleek body, that was made of parts all knitted together in a most marvelous way, helped him move over the ground.

Wonderful, wonderful Wiggle Worm
In a wide, wide wonderful world —
Exploring all by himself — his wonderful self!

Wiggle Worm was one year old, and he had learned many things — oh, very many things — in that one year.

Though he had neither head nor arms nor legs, and though he had no eyes with which to see, he did have a brain — a most wonderful brain for an earthworm — for he knew how to get the best tastes out of the earth. He also knew that it was best not to go outside by day, because the sun made his skin too dry. So he explored at night when the air was cool and the ground was fresh and moist with the fresh fallen dew.

Wonderful, wonderful Wiggle Worm
In a wide, wide wonderful world —
Exploring all by himself — his wonderful self!

Wiggle Worm had many, many friends in the wonderful world above his earth house. There was gentle ladybug with spots of black scattered all over her red shiny back. And of course there was grasshopper, who could flex the strong-as-steel muscles in his hind legs and leap far and wide just as easy as you please. Gay old grasshopper could spread his wings, too, and sail through the air like a magic flying chariot.

But Wiggle Worm knew that it was not safe to go near the barnyard, because harm could come to him there. Wiggle Worm knew that Mrs. Duck would gobble him up, or Mother Hen just might catch him to feed to her baby chicks.

One time, Wiggle Worm did a FABULOUS thing! He covered a cold seed with warm, moist earth, and the seed grew and grew and finally became a plant. Imagine!

> Wonderful, wonderful Wiggle Worm
> In a wide, wide wonderful world —
> Exploring all by himself — his wonderful self!

And Wiggle Worm, when night had passed, crawled back into the earth — his very own earth — the delicious earth that fed him and cared for him and protected him and gave him his own little tunnel-house to live in.

—L.B.S.

The children say the refrain each time it occurs. Through the functional use of vocabulary in the refrain, emphasis and drill on the "w" speech sound is provided in a natural, unpedantic setting.

CHAPTER 15

The Nasal Speech Sounds, "M," "N," and "NG"

MAKING THE SPEECH SOUND

This nasal speech sound is made by pressing the lips together lightly to prevent air from escaping through the mouth. The soft palate is lowered to permit air to pass through the nose in a resonant humming sound. The vocal cords vibrate. The tongue is relaxed and is in a flat position in the mouth. The teeth are parted slightly.

You may call "m" the "mosquito," the "humming," or the "mewing" sound.

CORRECTING THE DEFICIENT SPEECH SOUND

Often, voices lack proper resonance because the breath stream is not being properly directed. In such cases, humming exercises will help improve the quality of the voice. Humming a familiar tune with the "m" sound is one of the easiest and most adaptable of such exercises. The child should be able to feel vocal vibrations by placing his fingers beside his nose, or by placing his hand on the front part of his neck or against his cheek or forehead as he hums the continuant "mmmm."

INSTRUCTIONS TO THE CHILD

"Say 'mmm' with me. Place your fingers beside your nose and say 'mmm' again. Did you feel your voice motor work? Now say 'mmm' again and pinch your nostrils together. The sound was shut off, wasn't it? So now you know that your nose is the doorway for this 'humming' sound you hear at the beginning of *mother, me,* and *my.* Name these words with me and listen to the 'humming' sound: *may, mouse, mew, moo.* Here is a poem about a kitten. Say the kitten's *mew* with me each time we hear it in the poem."

"Mmmmmew, mmmmmew," said the baby kitten small.
"I am not a very big kitten at all,
So I will make a little *mmmmew* for you.
Mmmmew, mmmmew, mmmmew!"

—L.B.S.

WORDS FOR PRACTICE

Initial	*Medial*	*Final*
mule	hamster	lamb
mouse	lemon	comb
moth	primer	drum
monkey	Tommy	Jim
match	number	bomb
men	playmate	broom

349

I HEAR IT

Nasal blockage, resulting from colds, allergies, enlarged tonsils and adenoids, or other conditions which cause nasal passages to inflame and swell, causes denasalization of three nasal speech sounds, "m," "n," and "ng." Substitution for the "m" sound is "b," e.g., *be* for *me*.

The "I Hear It" exercise affords practice on both the defective and correct speech sound. Even if the child's nasal obstruction prevents him from producing the nasal sound, the aural experience in hearing the difference between these sounds is valuable. It is rare, otherwise, that a child would substitute for "m," since this is one of the first speech sounds he learns and uses prolifically. However, children with a repaired lip may have difficulty in effecting closure.

I hear it in *me* but not in *be*.
I hear it in *mad* but not in *bad*.
I hear it in *make* but not in *bake*.
> I hear it in *man* but not in *Nan*.
> I hear it in *map* but not in *nap*.
> My lips are pressed together just so,
> And then I can hear the humming go:
> "Mmmmm— mmmmm— mmmmm!"
I hear it in *melt* but not in *belt*.
I hear it in *mend* but not in *bend*.
I hear it in *mill* but not in *bill*.
> I hear it in *mine* but not in *nine*.
> I hear it in *moon* but not in *noon*.
> My lips are pressed together just so,
> And then I can hear the humming go:
> "Mmmmm— mmmmm— mmmmm!"

—L.B.S.

THE HUMMING SOUND

I like to make the "humming" sound.
"Mmmm— mmmm— mmmm!"
(Prolong the sound.)
I press my lips together so;

Then my voice motor starts to go.
My pinky tongue tip does not show.
"Mmmm— mmmm— mmmm!"

I like to make the "humming" sound.
"Mmmm— mmmm— mmmm!"
I feel the humming in my face
And up here in my breathing space
And on my neck and every place!
"Mmmm— mmmm— mmmm!"

I like to make the "humming" sound.
"Mmmm— mmmm— mmmm!"
Mosquitos hum and I can, too.
It sounds so pretty when I do;
I want to teach that sound to you.
"Mmmm— mmmm— mmmm!"

—L.B.S.

The children make the prolonged "m" sound. The second time
the poem is read it may be pantomimed by touching parts of the
face and neck with the finger tips.

MY BLACK CAT

My sleek black cat is a witch's cat.
And she stays with me all day.
She has her meals — I am glad of that —
She usually sleeps upon her mat;
But at night she runs away!
　　　Mee-ow! Mee-ow! Mee-ow! Mee-ow!
　　　But at night she runs away!

She meets a witch in a haunted glade
Deep in the gloomy wood.
They sit by the fire the witch has made
And whisper mysterious tricks they've played.
I'm afraid they never should!

Mee-ow! Mee-ow! Mee-ow! Mee-ow!
I'm afraid they never should!

Then they begin to ride the skies,
Holding the broomstick tight.
No wonder my cat has sleepy eyes!
"It comes," says Daddy, who's very wise,
"Of broom-stick riding at night!"
Mee-ow! Mee-ow! Mee-ow! Mee-ow!
Of broom-stick riding at night.

—ADAPTED BY L.B.S. FROM AN ANONYMOUS POEM.

The children say the refrain. Added practice for the "frightened-kitten" sound (see the unit on the "f" speech sound) may be introduced at the end of each stanza by having the children say, "F, f, f!"

THE BOBTAIL CAT

Mark Alan has a bobtail cat.
Me-ew, me-ew, me-ew!
Mark Alan's cat is thin, not fat —
So small he fits in Daddy's hat.
His furry paws
Have sharp, sharp claws.
Me-ew, me-ew, me-ew!

Mark Alan's cat stays home all day.
Me-ow, me-ow, me-ow!
When Mark returns from school to play,
His bobtail cat has lots to say;
And in a ring
He'll chase a string.
Me-ow, me-ow, me-ow!

Mark Alan's cat likes milk to drink.
Me-yum, me-yum, me-yum.

Mark Alan's cat is black as ink,
Except his little tongue — that's pink!
Just stroke his fur
And hear him purr.
Mee-yum, me-yum, me-yum!
  (*Prolong the final "m" sound.*)

—J.J.T.

The children participate by saying the cat sounds in each stanza. Remind them that the lips are pressed together when they make the "m" sound. Substitute three-syllable names of children in the class for the name of the boy in the poem. For programming purposes, assign the narrative lines in the poem to various children.

THE MONKEY GAME

Ten little monkeys play this game.
Each one has a number name.
Monkey One, sit on the floor.
Monkey Two, shut the door.
Monkey Three, sit on a chair.
Monkey Four, comb your hair.
Monkey Five, bend your knees.
Monkey Six, give a sneeze.
Monkey Seven, stand up tall.
Monkey Eight, touch the wall.
Monkey Nine, bend way down.
Monkey Ten, be a clown.

—J.J.T.

The rhyme presents the "m" sound in initial position in the word *monkey*. Note that *n* spells the medial "ng" sound in *monkey*. Use the poem for a finger play by having the children raise a finger as each monkey is introduced. Use the poem as a pantomime activity by selecting ten children to act it out.

MOTHER, MOTHER!

Mother, Mother, have you heard?
Mary gave me a mockingbird.

My — oh — my!
A mockingbird!

Mother, Mother, did you know?
My mockingbird sings like a crow.
My — oh — my!
Sings like a crow!

Mother, Mother, did you see?
My mockingbird flew away from me.
My — oh — my!
Away from me!

—J.J.T.

This poem presents the "m" sound in initial position in *Mother, Mary, mockingbird,* and *my.* The sound occurs in final position in *from.* After they are familiar with the poem, have the children prolong the "m" sound in "My — oh — my!" This will improve their awareness of the humming quality of the sound.

THE HUMMINGBIRD'S SOUND

It was spring on the farm. The orchard trees were bursting with lovely blossoms and the garden was a picture of color. The lawn in front of the white farmhouse was green after a fine warm shower.

Penelope heard the sound as she walked through the orchard. "Mmmmmmmmmmm— mmmmmmmmmmm!" It was a humming sound. "Mmmmmmmmmmm!" Was it a bumblebee? It could have been, but it wasn't. It was a lovely hummmmmmmmmmm.

And there it was! Penelope saw! It was a tiny hummingbird. He was flying around the plum tree, and he wasn't much bigger than the bumblebee Penelope thought she had heard. But the hummingbird could fly ever so much faster than a bumblebee.

354

Penelope watched the hummingbird closely, shading her eyes from the sun. Suddenly, he left the plum tree and flew into the garden where he flitted from flower to flower as he continued to hum: "Mmmmmmmmmmm!"

The brilliant red patch on his throat glowed like a red coal of fire. The little hummingbird sparkled like a jewel, especially when the sunlight caught the flashing green colors of the feathers on his tiny head and back.

"Mmmmmmmmmmmmmmmmm!"

Penelope said, "He is MY hummingbird and I am going to name him Sparkle."

Now Sparkle was less than four inches long from the tip of his beak to the tip of his tail, so of course you know that he must have been one of the smallest birds in the world.

Penelope said, "I will help Sparkle hum." And she did. "Mmmmmmmmmmm!" She sat by the hour watching Sparkle do stunts. He could fly straight up like a helicopter and dart straight down in a flash. He could even fly backward. Imagine that! And all the time Sparkle hummed: "Mmmmmmmmmmm." (*Children imitate.*)

The most interesting thing about his flying was that he could stay suspended right in mid-air. When he hovered in one spot, he was absolutely still except for his wings, which whirred and hummed as fast as the blades on an electric fan.

Penelope told her classmates at school about her new friend. On *Monday* she said, "Sparkle poised over a morning glory yesterday. He was almost standing still in the air. His wings moved so fast they looked like a blur."

On *Tuesday,* Penelope said to the class, "This morning, I saw Sparkle sipping nectar from a morning glory with his long tongue." The class was surprised to find out that hummingbirds have tongues. But everyone knew that hummingbirds could hummmmmmmmmmm with their wings. (*Children imitate sound.*)

355

On *Wednesday,* Penelope again told her friends about Sparkle. "Sparkle flew in a kind of half circle right in front of me. He just barely missed my head. And then, with a hum, he was out of sight in a second. 'Mmmmmmmmm-mm.' " (*Children imitate.*)

On *Thursday,* Penelope told more about Sparkle. "I asked our librarian about Sparkle, and she told me that he has a long tongue that forms a kind of tube. Through his tongue tube, Sparkle can sip nectar and insects. He can sip through his tongue just like you can sip through a drinking straw. I can hear Sparkle humming in our or- chard now. 'Mmmmmmmmmm.' " (*Children imitate.*)

On *Friday,* Penelope said, "I found a little bottle and put some sugar water in it. I wrapped the bottle with red tissue paper because Sparkle likes red. Then I went to the orchard and fastened the bottle to the branch of the plum tree. And soon Sparkle was having a drink of sugar water."

"What makes Sparkle hum?" asked one of Penelope's friends.

Penelope answered, "His wings do it. He can flap his wings as fast as fifty or more times a second."

So every day after that, Penelope had something new to say about Sparkle. There were scarcely enough days to tell everything she knew about Sparkle. The class not only learned a lot about hummingbirds, but they also learned a new speech sound that we use when we talk: "Mmmmm-mmmmm." (*Children imitate.*)

—L.B.S.

MARY MELISSA MAKES POEMS

"Mmmm," went Mother Mosquito as she flew over a peaceful little pond near a large swamp. Mother Mos- quito's hum was very soft and quiet. Sometimes she hummed up the scale, and sometimes she hummed down. Try it with me. "Mmmmmmmm! Mmmmmmmm!" (*Hum up the scale and then down. Children imitate.*)

Mary Melissa was six years old. She sat on a log near the pond and listened to the humming sound. It made Mary Melissa want to hum, too, and she did. Her little nose tickled with the humming.

"Mmmm," hummed Mary Melissa. "I feel a poem coming," she said.

"A crumb on my thumb. 'Mmmm!'
A *plummm* on my thumb. 'Mmmm!'
Some *gummm* on my thumb. 'Mmmm!'"
(*Children imitate.*)

It was really quite an amusing poem. It didn't make a bit of sense, but no matter, Mary Melissa was having fun.

Mother Mosquito kept on humming! "Mmmmmmmm!" (*Children imitate.*)

Mary Melissa said, "I like that humming sound. My name begins with the mosquito sound: *Mmmmary Mmmmelissa.*"

Mary Melissa felt the humming in her nose when she said her name.

"I feel another poem coming," said Mary Melissa. She cleared her throat and said, "I sweep my *roommm* with a *broommm.*" Mary Melissa said, "I made a *poemmmm.*" (But of course she said *po-em* and not *pome*.)

Then Mary Melissa rhymed words with other words: And that was glorious fun, too: *be - me; by - my; bud - mud; bill - mill; bad - mad.* (*Children repeat each pair of words after you.*)

Mother Mosquito hummed and hummed and hummed, and Mary Melissa made up more and more rhymes. Mother Mosquito and Mary Melissa just never seemed to get tired at all.

And I'll bet you can think of many words that begin with that beautiful humming sound. You might even make a poem!

—L.B.S.

n
nose

MAKING THE SPEECH SOUND

This nasal speech sound is produced very much like "t" or "d." However, with "n" the tongue tip is held lightly against the upper gum ridge behind the teeth so that the sound is continued instead of being exploded. As in the "m" sound, the soft palate is lowered and the air passes through the nose to produce the nasal sound. The vocal cords vibrate, and the lips and the teeth are parted.

You may call "n" the "sewing-machine" sound.

CORRECTING THE DEFICIENT SPEECH SOUND

The child should open his mouth, hold his chin with his hand, and "reach" with the tip of his tongue to touch the gum ridge behind the upper teeth. He should hum: "Nnnnnn." It is important that a mirror be used so that the child can view the position of his tongue tip. The tongue tip is narrowed and sometimes pointed, depending upon the vowel which follows the "n" sound. If the child can produce "t" or "d," have him work from these known tip-of-tongue speech sounds. If "n" is denasalized as "d," e.g., *do* for *new,* this may be a temporary defect caused by the common cold, or it may indicate sinus infection, hay fever, an adenoidal condition, or some other more serious and permanent nasal blockage.

INSTRUCTIONS TO THE CHILD

"Watch me make a new sound: 'nnn— nnn— nnn.' Did you see my tongue tip go up high and touch the shelf behind my upper teeth? Try it with me. Look into this mirror. Make your tongue tip fly high and say 'nnn.' Did you hear the hum? Make it again and pinch your nostrils together. What happened to the hum? You have discovered that your nose is a very special speech helper, haven't you? It helps to make your speech sounds pleasant to listen to. Name some words after me and listen for the 'nnn' sound: *name, new, no,* and *none.*"

WORDS FOR PRACTICE

Initial	*Medial*	*Final*
number	rainbow	pan
nation	candy	tin
needle	window	gun
nickel	banana	moon
noise	penny	green
nut	hundred	bone

I HEAR IT

The "d" speech sound as a denasalized substitute for "n" is emphasized in this drill. See the unit on "s" for added information on the use of the "I Hear It" rhyme.

I hear it in *nail* but not in *Dale.*
I hear it in *name* but not in *dame.*
I hear it in *Nan* but not in *Dan.*
 I here it in *near* but not in *dear.*
 I hear it in *neat* but not in *meat.*
 My tongue tip goes up and a hum I hear,
 And the sound I make comes right back to my ear.
 "Nnnn— nnnn— nnnn."

I hear it in *neck* but not in *deck*.
I hear it in *new* but not in *do*.
I hear it in *need* but not in *deed*.
I hear it in *net* but not in *met*.
I hear it in *nice* but not in *mice*.
My tongue tip goes up and a hum I hear,
And the sound I make comes right back to my ear.
"Nnnn— nnnn— nnnn."

—L.B.S.

LITTLE BUG'S SONG

Little Bug liked to sing
Up the scale and down,
"Nnnnn, nnnnn,"
As jolly as a clown.

It made Bug Mother worry
To hear him sing so gay,
"Nnnnn, nnnnn,"
In such a careless way.

She said, "Beware, my darling,
If you sing your song
'Nnnnn, nnnnn,'
You won't last very long."

Little Bug grew more careful,
And as he flew along,
"Nnn, nnn, nnn,"
Went his humming song.

—J.J.T.

Have the children make their voices go up and down the scale,
except in the last stanza, as they hum Little Bug's song.

WHAT SHALL WE SEE?

What shall we see when we go to the zoo,
With a nay-nee-nie-noo,
When we go to the zoo?
We shall go see the penguin, with a nay-nee-nie-nay,
The penguin who walks in the funniest way.

What shall we see when we go to the zoo,
With a nay-nee-nie-noo,
When we go to the zoo?
We shall go see the lion, with a nay-nee-nie-no,
The lion that paces his cage to and fro.

What shall we see when we go to the zoo,
With a nay-nee-nie-noo,
When we go to the zoo?
We shall go see the monkey, with a nay-nee-nie-nee,
The monkey who swings by his tail from a tree.

What else shall we see when we go to the zoo,
With a nay-nee-nie-noo,
When we go to the zoo?
There are camels, bears, tigers, and elephants, too.
There is so much to see when we go to the zoo.

—J.J.T.

Have the children repeat the nonsense phrase, *nay-nee-nie-noo*
and variations, each time it occurs. Instruct them to make the "n"
sound precisely, in order to get the proper nasal resonance. Children may wish to add other verses of their own to the rhyme.

A BABY IS NEW

TEACHER: A baby is new,
And very young, too.
What is a baby cow?
Can you tell me now?

CHILDREN:	A baby cow is a calf.
	A baby calf is new,
	And very young, too.
TEACHER:	What is a new baby horse?
	You must know, of course.
CHILDREN:	A baby horse is a colt.
	A baby colt is new,
	And very young, too.
TEACHER:	What is a new baby cat?
	Can you tell me that?
CHILDREN:	A baby cat is a kitten.
	A kitten is new,
	And very young, too.

—L.B.S.

The children gain practice on the "n" speech sound in the word *new*. Other baby animals may be added: *goat-kid, dog-puppy, duck-duckling, goose-gosling,* and *swan-cygnet.*

THE SONG OF THE SEWING MACHINE

Hear the gay song of the sewing machine
As it stitches and sews a new dress for Marlene.
    "Nnnnnnnnnn! Nnnnnnnnnn!"
It sings in a hurry sometimes as it goes
When mother is sewing our new school clothes.
    "Nnnnnnnnnn! Nnnnnnnnnn!"
It sings very slow when it sews up a tear
Or stitches a ribbon to go in Jill's hair.
    "Nnnnnnnnnn! Nnnnnnnnnn!"
But whether it sings very fast or quite slow,
The song that it sings is a song you now know.
    "Nnnnnnnnnn! Nnnnnnnnnn!"

—J.J.T.

Children hum to imitate the song of the sewing machine. The "n" sound is prolonged to give the effect of a motor running. By varying the pitch level of the humming, the sewing machine can be made to sound as though working rapidly or slowly.

362

THE MAGIC SEWING MACHINE

Once there was a maiden named Nora, and she was lovely to behold. Her eyes sparkled like clear water in sunlight, her hair was like black, silky floss, and her hands were small and delicate.

You may think that one so beautiful would possess rich jewels and wear silken garments and lovely brocades, but Nora had none of these. Her dress was all patched and worn and threadbare, but her shoes were polished. It was true that Nora had no fine clothes and sometimes scarcely enough to eat, but she was happy. Many times during the day, people who passed by the cottage where Nora lived were enchanted with her singing:

> "I do not need fine jewels
> Or a fancy silken dress.
> I do not need a golden crown
> To bring me happiness."

But in her heart, Nora dreamed, as most maidens do, of a fine king who would come by one day and make her his queen.

Now Nora had one possession which she prized above all others among her lowly treasures. It was a sewing machine. In days when things were better, Nora had fine cloth with which to sew garments for the villagers. But she charged so little for her work that the demands for the garments were too great, and at last Nora could no longer afford to buy cloth.

In happier days, the sewing machine sang its own song:

> " 'Nnnnn— nnnnn!' (*Children repeat.*)
> Hear my humming song.
> 'Nnnnn— nnnnn!'
> To Nora I belong."

And Nora would add her own song to the humming song of the sewing machine:

> "I do not need fine jewels (*Children repeat.*)
> Or a fancy silken dress.
> I do not need a golden crown
> To bring me happiness."

But now the sewing machine had stopped singing because there was nothing to sew. The days seemed longer than long without a song. But of course Nora still dreamed of a king who would some day come and make her his queen.

Once when Nora went to the cupboard and found only a small crust of bread, she began to cry. Suddenly, there was a low rumble and a great burst of noise, and there appeared a funny little old gnome with a long nose. On his head he wore a small cap with a tassel, and his wizened face and twisted body resembled a brown autumn leaf.

"Do not fear," said the little old gnome. "I heard you crying and I thought that you might want my help. May I do something for you?" Nora dried her tears, but before she could reply, the little old gnome went on. "I will help you by turning your sewing machine into a *magic* sewing machine. A-one and a-two and a-three and a-four and NO MORE!"

The sewing machine itself didn't look a bit different, but it was astonishing to see bolts and bolts of bright-colored cloth of every hue stacked neatly at one side of the room. And at the very minute the cloth *appeared,* the little old gnome *disappeared* just as suddenly as he had come.

As Nora excitedly laid patterns upon the cloth and cut them out, the sewing machine began to sew magically all by itself. As it sewed, it sang:

" 'Nnnnn— nnnnn!' (*Children repeat.*)
I am a magic sewing machine.
'Nnnnn— nnnn!'
Soon Nora will be a lovely queen!"

Nora wondered about the meaning of the magic sewing machine's words, but of course it could tell her nothing more. It just kept right on stitching and stitching and turning out more and more garments until every room in the house was filled. Nora prospered now, for the villagers came once more to buy.

The song Nora sang was still the same:

> "I do not need fine jewels (*Children repeat.*)
> Or a fancy silken dress.
> I do not need a golden crown
> To bring me happiness."

Then one day there was a low rumble and a great burst of noise, and once again there appeared the little old gnome with the long nose.

"Good day, Nora," he said. "And have you been prosperous?"

"Yes," replied Nora, "I am indeed prosperous. I have all the riches of happiness, because there are so many around me who are happy with their beautiful new clothes. I am grateful to you for bringing this about, and I thank you from the bottom of my heart for making such wonderful magic possible. Is there something I might do to repay you for your kindness?"

The little old gnome said, "Yes, lovely Nora. You can repay me by being my wife."

Nora looked at the funny little gnome, with his wizened face and twisted body, and she thought, "If I marry the gnome, my dream of the king will never come true. I cannot be queen of a realm, but it matters not. The little gnome is kind, and he will make a fine husband."

The moment Nora said, "Yes," the funny little old gnome disappeared just as suddenly as he had come. Then the magic sewing machine began to sing:

> " 'Nnnnn— nnnnn!' (*Children repeat.*)
> I am a magic sewing machine.
> 'Nnnnn— nnnnn!'
> Soon Nora will be a lovely queen."

"I will never be a queen," said Nora, "but it matters not." As she said these words, there was a low rumble and a great burst of noise and there appeared a handsome king, dressed in purple velvet adorned with rich trim.

The handsome king turned to Nora and said, "I was the gnome that you promised to wed. A wicked witch turned me into a gnome. But because you have promised to marry me, the spell has been broken and I am now a king again."

So Nora and the king were wed and lived happily ever after. The magic sewing machine became just a plain sewing machine once more, but it still was Nora's favorite possession. Nora took the sewing machine with her when she went to live in the castle, and from time to time she would sing the old song:

> "I do not need fine jewels (*Children repeat.*)
> Or a fancy silken dress.
> I do not need a golden crown
> To bring me happiness."

Now and then, when Nora asked the sewing machine to make a dress or a cloak, which it could no longer do by itself, it would sing:

> " 'Nnnnn— nnnnn!' (*Children repeat.*)
> I am just a plain sewing machine.
> 'Nnnnn— nnnnn!'
> Now Nora is a lovely queen."

—L.B.S.

366

ng

so̲ng

MAKING THE SPEECH SOUND

This sound is similar to the "k" and "g" sounds in that the rear portion of the tongue is raised to contact the soft palate. In making the "ng" sound the soft palate is lowered to allow the air to pass through the nasal passages. A continuous nasal sound is then produced. The vocal cords vibrate. The lips and the teeth are parted slightly, and the tip of the tongue usually is on the floor of the mouth. The "ng" sound is one of the most frequently mispronounced sounds in the English language. The usual substitution for "ng" is "n," e.g., *goin'* for *going*. Another misarticulation is the addition of a hard "g" to the "ng" sound, e.g., *sing-guh* for *sing*.

You may call "ng" the "bell" or the "foghorn" sound.

CORRECTING THE DEFICIENT SPEECH SOUND

The use of a mirror will help the child to note the difference between "ng," "m," and "n." A wide-open mouth will allow the child to check the back-of-tongue position. Emphasis on pointing the tip of the tongue down and touching the lower front teeth should also be given. If the child notes that his tongue tip is down, he can better visualize back-of-tongue movement. Ask him to say "ah," then direct him to raise the back of the tongue *lightly* for "ng." Pressing the back of the tongue too rigidly against the soft palate may result in a hard "g" sound.

367

INSTRUCTIONS TO THE CHILD

"Let your tongue lie asleep with the tip pointing toward your lower teeth. Now say 'ah' with me. Let the back of your tongue go up and hum with me: 'ng-ng-ng.' Say *ding-dong* with me now. Did you feel the humming in your nose?"

WORDS FOR PRACTICE

Initial	Medial	Final
——	songbird	string
	lengthy	young
	singer	hang
	thank	king
	bringing	strong
	ink	among

The medial "ng" sound usually is followed by the hard *g* sound. *N* sometimes has the *ng* sound, e.g., *think, honk,* and *bank.*

I HEAR IT

The substitution of hard "g" for the "ng" sound is included in this drill. Refer to the unit on "s" for suggestions on the use of the "I Hear It" rhyme.

I hear it in *bing* but not in *big.*
I hear it in *ping* but not in *pig.*
I hear it in *long* but not in *log.*
    I hear it in *bang* but not in *bag.*
    I hear it in *rang* but not in *rag.*
    I hum when I raise the back of my tongue.
    I heard it just then:
    Tongue———! (*Prolong the "ng" sound.*)
I hear it in *ring* but not in *rig.*
I hear it in *wing* but not in *wig.*
I hear it in *sang* but not in *sag.*

I hear it in *hung* but not in *hug.*
I hear it in *rung* but not in *rug.*
I hum when I raise the back of my tongue.
I heard it just then:
Tongue——!

—L.B.S.

BELLS

The doorbell rings out in the hall
To say a friend has come to call.
    Ring-ing-ing!
    The doorbell rings.

The telephone rings in the den.
It rings nine times, and sometimes ten.
    Ring-ing-ing!
    The telephone rings.

The big bells in the old church tower
Ring day and night to tell the hour.
    Ring-ing-ing!
    The church bells ring.

Puppy's bell has a tinkling sound
To tell us where he can be found.
    Ring-ing-ing!
    The puppy's bell rings.

The little song bells ring and ring,
And happy little children sing.
    Ring-ing-ing!
    The song bells ring.

—L.B.S.

Ask the children to prolong the "ng" sound in *ring* each time it occurs. Words that contain the "ng" sound are: *rings, ring, sing, tinkling,* and *song.*

EACH FOGGY DAY

Out in the harbor, out in the bay,
Calls the big horn on a foggy day:
"Ng-ah, ng-ah, ng-ah!"

Big ships and small ships follow its sound.
They know it means safety when danger's around.
"Ng-ah, ng-ah, ng-ah!"

—J.J.T.

IF I WERE A CLOCK

If I were a clock
And I should strike one,
I would make a loud bong,
And *that* would be fun! BONG! (*Loudly.*)

If I were a clock
And I should strike two,
I would make my sounds softly
As I struck for you. *Bong, bong!* (*Softly.*)

If I were a clock
And I should strike three,
I would make every bong
As fast as could be! Bong-bong-bong! (*Quickly.*)

If I were a clock
And I should strike four,
I would take a whole minute,
Or maybe two more. Bong— bong— bong— bong! (*Slowly.*)

If I were a clock
And I should strike five,
I would make my sounds cheerful
And glad and alive. Bong, bong, bong, bong, bong!
  (*Briskly and cheerfully.*)

If I were a clock
And I should strike six,
I would make my sounds pretty,
And also my ticks! Bong, bong, bong, bong, bong, bong!
   (*Melodiously.*)
Ticka-ticka-ticka-ticka-tick!

—L.B.S.

Use this selection not only for the "ng" speech sound, but also to emphasize voice variety: loudness, softness, fastness, slowness, cheerfulness, and melodiousness.

CHRISTMAS TIME

Snow is falling, falling, falling,
   (*Raise arms above head. Move fingers as arms are lowered.*)
Coming down in cold white flakes.
Snow is falling, falling, falling,
Covering the roads and lakes.

Sleet is rushing, rushing, rushing,
   (*Rub palms together.*)
Wrap your scarf around your throat.
Sleet is rushing, rushing, rushing,
Button up your overcoat!

Winter winds are blowing, blowing!
   (*Wave arms.*)
Drifts are piling higher, higher.
Winter winds are blowing, blowing,
We are warm beside the fire. (*Hug body.*)

Hear the reindeer prancing, prancing,
   (*Tap fingers on desk.*)
On the rooftops overhead.
Hear the reindeer prancing, prancing,
I am snug inside my bed. (*Hug body.*)

Santa Claus comes creeping, creeping,
   (*Finger at side of lips.*)
Down the chimney to our tree.
Santa Claus comes creeping, creeping,
Leaving gifts for you and me.

Let us all sing, "Merry Christmas!"
On this happy Christmas morn.
Let us all sing, "Merry Christmas,"
For a little Child is born.

—L.B.S.

Follow the pantomiming suggestions included with the poem. Children may get practice on the "ng" sound in these words: *falling, coming, covering, rushing, blowing, piling, prancing, creeping, leaving,* and *sing.*

THE FOGHORN PRINCE

Lena lived in a house near the ocean. Her father was a fisherman who spent most of his days far out at sea. Lena liked to sit by her bedroom window late in the afternoon and watch for her father's boat to chug-chug into the harbor. When the boat came closer, she would wave a white scarf from the window. Her father and her brother, Max, who was learning to be a fisherman, would wave back when they saw her. Sometimes Lena was sorry that she was a little girl and couldn't go out into the big ocean and help catch fish.

One summer day while her father and Max were out with their nets, Lena was happy to hear the sound of the big foghorn outside the harbor. She had heard that sound many times, so many times that she knew exactly what the big foghorn was saying when it called out across the rolling waves:

" 'Ng-ah! Ng-ah! Ng-ah!' (*Children repeat.*)
That's the sound I say.
'Ng-ah! Ng-ah! Ng-ah!'
I guide ships on their way."

Lena had read the fairy tale about *The Frog Prince,* and often at night she would pretend that the foghorn was a fairy prince who had been turned into a large frog by a wicked witch. She imagined that if she could stay awake just long enough to count the "ng-ah" sound of the foghorn frog one hundred and one times, the magic spell of the witch would be broken and the fairy prince would be free.

"Ng-ah! Ng-ah! Ng-ah!" the bewitched prince seemed to call, but Lena never could seem to stay awake long enough to count to one hundred and one. This she must do to set the prince free.

Lena knew that the foghorn was a real friend. When an unexpected thunderstorm had come rumbling and grumbling across the water that day, the foghorn had guided her father's boat safely back to the harbor with its welcome call:

" 'Ng-ah! Ng-ah! Ng-ah!' (*Children repeat.*)
That's the sound I say.
'Ng-ah! Ng-ah! Ng-ah!'
I guide ships on their way."

One night when Lena had gone to bed, she listened as she always did to the comforting sound of the big friendly foghorn. "It is the fairy prince," she said to herself, "and tonight I shall set him free. I will break the spell of the wicked witch who turned him into a foghorn frog. I'll count the sounds he makes until I reach one hundred and one!"

So she began her game of "pretend" as the voice of the foghorn came through the thick white blanket of fog:

" 'Ng-ah! Ng-ah! Ng-ah!' (*Children repeat.*)
That's the sound I say.
'Ng-ah! Ng-ah! Ng-ah!'
I guide ships on their way."

Lena kept counting. She reached fifty. "Fifty-one — 'Ng-ah!' Fifty-two — 'Ng-ah!' Fifty-three!" Her eyelids grew heavy. Oh, if she could stay awake long enough to free her prince!

"Ng-ah! Ng-ah! Ng-ah!" called the bewitched prince, but his voice faded farther and farther away. Lena kept counting.

"Ng-ah! Ng-ah! Ng-ah!" The voice became softer. "Ng-ah! Ng-ah! Ng-ah!"

Lena did not know when the sound of the foghorn disappeared. But her eyes opened to see a huge frog with a head shaped like a big foghorn on the beach below her house, and suddenly the frog turned into a handsome prince! Then the handsome prince rode up to Lena's house on a beautiful white stallion and called to her, "Le-na! Le-na!" She ran out to meet the prince, and he lifted her up onto the horse behind him. Then off into the night the white horse galloped, its hoofs beating faintly against the white, fog-covered sand along the ocean's edge.

In her dream, Lena's game of "pretend" had freed the prince after all. Perhaps when the fog hangs over the harbor, you, too, can pretend to free the prince if you will count the sounds of the foghorn frog one hundred and one times — that is, if you can stay awake long enough to do it!

—J.J.T.

The back of the tongue presses against the soft palate to produce the humming sound of "ng" and then drops down for "-ah."

CHAPTER 16

The "Y" and "H" Speech Sounds

MAKING THE SPEECH SOUND

The tongue is pressed lightly against the sides of the teeth in the same position as for the sound of long *e*. The lips are parted and drawn back slightly. The soft palate is raised and the vocal cords vibrate. The lips and tongue glide immediately into position for the vowel sound which follows.

You may call "y" the "yip-yip," the "yes-yes," or the "yum-yum" sound.

CORRECTING THE DEFICIENT SPEECH SOUND

Children may be aided in making this speech sound correctly by asking them to produce the sound of "ee" and follow it with the sound of "uh" or another of the vowel sounds, e.g., "ee-um" (*yum*), "ee-ess" (*yes*), and "ee-am" (*yam*).

Common mispronunciations of this sound are "w" or "l" for "y," e.g., *lellow* or *wewwow* for *yellow*. Actually, the consonant *y* is a semi-vowel which cannot be pronounced in isolation except by adding a vowel sound. It is not recommended that such speech sounds as plosives or *y* be produced in isolation, unless they are given a personality and dramatized for purposes of introducing the sound to the children. The final *y* in words like *my* (long *i*) or *happy* (short *i*) is not discussed in this book.

INSTRUCTIONS TO THE CHILD

"Do you hear the sound 'ee'? Make your tongue rise and press against your upper teeth: 'ee,' 'ee.' Did you hear it? Now very quickly say with me: 'ee-um,' 'ee-um' (*yum*). Now put the sounds together rapidly: Yum, yum, yum! Clap with me as we say a little poem."

> Yum, yum, yum!
> Come, come, come
> To have some ice cream.
> Yum, yum, yum!
>
> —L.B.S.

"Let's try to name some words that begin like *yum: yes, yellow, you, your, yip.*"

WORDS FOR PRACTICE

Initial	Medial	Final
yarn	yo-yo	——
your	barnyard	
yesterday	yum-yum	
you	stallion	
yet	union	
yellow	New York	

I HEAR IT

Refer to the section on "s" for instructions for using the following "I Hear It" activity.

I hear it in *yam* but not in *lamb*.
I hear it in *yard* but not in *lard*.
I hear it in *young* but not in *lung*.
    I hear it in *yoke* but not in *woke*.
    I hear it in *yell* but not in *well*.
    My tongue is flat as it can be,
    Just like the way I make an "ee."
    "Ee-ee-ee." "Ee-es (*yes*)." "Ee-ellow (*yellow*)."
I hear it in *yale* but not in *wail*.
I hear it in *yet* but not in *wet*.
I hear it in *you* but not in *woo*.
    I hear it in *yip* but not in *lip*.
    I hear it in *Yak* but not in *lack*.
    My tongue is flat as it can be,
    Just like the way I make an "ee."
    "Ee-ee-ee." "Ee-es (*yes*)." "Ee-ellow (*yellow*)."

—L.B.S.

IS THE SKY YELLOW?

Is the sky yellow, yellow as can be?
No, the sky is blue as you can plainly see.

Is the grass yellow, yellow as can be?
No, the grass is green as you can plainly see.

Is a fire engine yellow, yellow as can be?
No, a fire engine's red as you can plainly see.

Is the snow yellow, yellow as can be?
No, the snow is white as you can plainly see.

Then tell me what is yellow, yellow as can be.
The shining sun is yellow as you can plainly see.

A baby duck is yellow, yellow as can be.
A daffodil is yellow as you can plainly see.

—J.J.T.

This question-answer rhyme can be used to teach color concepts as well as the pronunciation of "y" in *yellow*. The teacher may extend the activity by adding other things that are yellow: banana, grapefruit, and sunflower.

YES, YES, YES

TEACHER:	Mister Spider, what are you spinning?
FIRST CHILD:	Can't you guess?
TEACHER:	Are you spinning webs of silver?
FIRST CHILD:	Yes, yes, yes!
TEACHER:	Little Bear, why are you crying?
SECOND CHILD:	Can't you guess?
TEACHER:	Did someone eat your breakfast porridge?
SECOND CHILD:	Yes, yes, yes!
TEACHER:	Mother Hubbard, where are you going?
THIRD CHILD:	Can't you guess?
TEACHER:	To get a bone for your poor doggie?
THIRD CHILD:	Yes, yes, yes!
TEACHER:	Tommy Tucker, why are you singing?
FOURTH CHILD:	Can't you guess?
TEACHER:	Are you singing for your supper?
FOURTH CHILD:	Yes, yes, yes!

—J.J.T.

Other nursery rhymes may be put into the same pattern as the activity above, to provide additional question-and-answer dialogues between the teacher and the children. The repetitive use of *yes* provides practice on the "y" sound in initial position.

ALL KINDS OF YO-YOS

Yo-yos are purple and yo-yos are green.
Yo-yos are black, red, or blue.
Yo-yos have speckles and yo-yos have stripes.
Yo-yos have polka dots, too.
You choose a yo-yo, a yo-yo you like.
Let it spin fast on a string.
I'll choose a yo-yo, a yo-yo I like.
Together our yo-yos will sing.
Yo-yos are purple and yo-yos are green.
Yo-yos are black, red, or blue.
Yo-yos have speckles and yo-yos have stripes.
Yo-yos have polka dots, too.

—J.J.T.

The "y" speech sound is presented in both initial and medial position in *yo-yo*. Pictures of appropriately colored and patterned yo-yos can be used to stimulate descriptive responses from the children.

YELLOW

A squash may be yellow; and lemonade, too.
The big yellow sun shines down upon you.
A crayon is yellow for coloring things
Like fishes and new baby ducklings and rings.
Some flowers are yellow; they smell, oh, so sweet.
A banana, when yellow, is yummy to eat!
Some leaves are bright yellow; they dance in the
    breeze.
A big puff of wind — and they fall from the trees.
Yellow is cheerful and pretty to see.
Yellow is what I want all things to be.

—L.B.S.

Ask the children to name other things that are yellow. Ask them to draw and color the objects described in the poem and use them with the flannelboard as the poem is said.

YELLOW STALLION

Yellow Stallion was sleek and especially handsome, with his bright yellow body, his sparkling eyes, his wide nostrils, and his flowing mane and tail. He looked like a stallion, except that he was much too yellow. But instead of furry hide, Yellow Stallion had a thick coat of yellow paint. Have you guessed yet? Yellow Stallion was a rocking horse!

Now Yellow Stallion belonged to twin brothers named Jacques and Joseph. Jacques and Joseph lived in a big city, high up on the sixth floor in a house called a tenement, which had many stairs, many floors, and many fire escapes. Though there was only one Yellow Stallion for two children, there was really no problem at all. Jacques and Joseph simply took turns riding Yellow Stallion.

There was an exciting song which Yellow Stallion loved. Whenever he heard that song, his eye flashed and he rocked and rocked so hard that often his rider almost took a spill. It was a song which the twins had heard on a Western TV show — a most exciting cowboy song that went this way:

"Yippi-yi-yi! (*Children participate.*)
Yippi-yi-yi!
Over the prairie we will fly!
Yippi-yi-yi!
Yippi-yi-yi!
My fine yellow stallion and I!"

Jacques and Joseph had never seen real cowboys except on television. But that was almost as good as visiting Wyoming, Montana, Texas, or any big western state that had cowboys who rode the range and herded cattle as they sang, "Yippi-yi-yi!"

So Jacques and Joseph pretended they were cowboys on the wide plains as they took turns riding Yellow Stallion and singing:

> "Yippi-yi-yi! (*Children participate.*)
> Yippi-yi-yi!
> Over the prairie we will fly!
> Yippi-yi-yi!
> Yippi-yi-yi!
> My fine yellow stallion and I!"

One day, Yellow Stallion was listening to this happy song. Carrying Jacques on his back, he was rocking, rocking, rocking, faster and faster and faster, when all at once — Crack! Crash! Splinter! Yellow Stallion's rocker broke and Jacques took a spill. It was not a serious spill, but it did frighten Jacques and he began to cry.

"Are you awfully much hurt?" asked Joseph as he helped Jacques to his feet.

"No — I guess not," said Jacques, rubbing a sore place on his knee. "But Yellow Stallion is hurt! Look at his rocker! It is broken!"

While Jacques and Joseph were wondering what to do about Yellow Stallion, maman came into the room. Because they were French children, Jacques and Joseph called her maman (*mah-máw[n]*) and of course *maman* is French for Mother.

She said, "Never mind, mes chéris (*may shayree:* my darlings). See? Part of Yellow Stallion's mane and tail are gone. He is a very old horse. Look how his yellow paint is chipped. He belonged to your papa when he was a little boy. This horse must be at least twenty-five years old. It is time Yellow Stallion retired."

"But we *love* Yellow Stallion," sobbed the twins. "We sing an exciting song only for him, maman. What shall we do about our song? But more important, what shall we do about our dear Yellow Stallion?"

"We will put Yellow Stallion in the storeroom where the tenants store their trunks," said maman. "He will be perfectly safe there and papa will buy you a new rocking horse."

So they all helped carry the pieces of Yellow Stallion to the storeroom, and a new rocking horse came to live with Jacques and Joseph. Once more they could sing:

"Yippi-yi-yi!
Yippi-yi-yi!
Over the prairie we will fly!
Yippi-yi-yi!
Yippi-yi-yi!
My fine yellow stallion and I!"

But there was no heart in the song, and somehow it was all wrong singing Yellow Stallion's song to a new rocking horse. So Jacques and Joseph stopped singing, and the new rocking horse stood neglected in a corner of the room.

One day, maman said, "Mes chéris, you are sad. What is troubling you?"

And Jacques and Joseph replied, "We miss our dear Yellow Stallion, and we know how lonely he must feel in the storeroom."

"Ah," said maman softly. "Papa and I will fix things. We will send the new rocking horse away and you may bring Yellow Stallion back to the living room."

"Merci, maman," cried the twins. "Merci, merci!"

A van came that afternoon and took the new rocking horse to the children's hospital, and Yellow Stallion was brought back downstairs, right where he belonged.

What a busy household it was!

Papa, maman, Jacques, and Joseph hammered and mended and painted until Yellow Stallion looked fine enough for a display window. Once again, Jacques and Joseph could sing with all their heart:

"Yippi-yi-yi!
Yippi-yi-yi!
Over the prairie we will fly!
Yippi-yi-yi!
Yippi-yi-yi!
My fine yellow stallion and I!"

Now when Yellow Stallion rocked too fast and too hard, nobody worried about it. Certainly Yellow Stallion never worried, for he knew he belonged forever and ever to two little boys who lived on the sixth floor of a big tenement in the city.

—L.B.S.

As the refrains are said by the children, practice is gained on the "y" speech sound in *yippi-yi-yi*. The "y" sound also occurs initially in *yellow* and medially in *stallion*.

THE RED YO-YO

Enoch was very busy. A big yo-yo contest was going to be held at his school and he wanted to win. He had been practicing and practicing with his favorite red yo-yo, so that he could make it do all kinds of tricks. He could make it whirl around his head and over his shoulder. He could make it spin in the air without climbing its string and then, suddenly, as if by silent command, slowly climb back to his hand.

How Enoch practiced with his red yo-yo! Finally, on the night before the contest, he was so excited that he could hardly finish dinner. Before he went to bed, he practiced once more every yo-yo trick he knew. Then, he polished his yo-yo carefully and placed it on the bed table. Enoch tossed and turned with excitement until he finally fell asleep.

Then a bright light began to glow. It became so brilliant that Enoch had to close his eyes. He heard the door of his bedroom open slowly, and he quickly opened his eyes to see who it was. An enormous RED yo-yo was rolling into his bedroom. It was so tall and wide that it could scarcely get through the doorway. The red yo-yo rolled right up to the bed and spoke to Enoch.

"I am Der, the Yo-yo King.
Help me do tricks upon a string."

Enoch looked in amazement at the red Yo-yo King. "You are much too big and heavy for me. Why I would have to climb to the top of a tall building and then ask my friends to help me hold you up. All of us working together could never make you roll fast enough even to climb your string."

"Then," said Der, the Yo-yo King, "I will turn you into a giant, so that you can hold me and teach me to do tricks upon a string."

"Please don't," Enoch urged. "I must be ready for the yo-yo contest tomorrow. I know that giants cannot enter the contest, so please let me stay just as I am."

The Yo-yo King answered:

"Oh, no, no, no!
You must grow, Enoch, grow.
You must help your king
Do tricks on a string."

Enoch heard the bedroom door open again and as he watched, he saw an enormous BLUE yo-yo roll in and stop beside his bed. The blue yo-yo spoke to him.

"I am a son of the Yo-yo King.
(*Children repeat.*)
Help me do tricks upon a string."

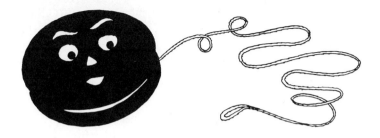

"Well," said Enoch, "as I was just telling the king—"
He was interrupted as the bedroom door opened a third
time, and an enormous BLACK yo-yo rolled into the room,
right up to his bed, and spoke to him.

"I am a son of the Yo-yo King.
   (*Children repeat.*)
Help me do tricks upon a string."

Enoch wondered how he could satisfy these huge yo-yos
that were filling his room. But even as he wondered to
himself, the bedroom door opened wide again and in
rolled an enormous YELLOW yo-yo. The new arrival
spoke to him.

"I am a son of the Yo-yo King.
   (*Children repeat.*)
Help me do tricks upon a string."

Enoch tried to think of something to say. But how
could a boy his size make these huge yo-yos do tricks? His
thoughts were quickly interrupted when his bedroom door
opened again. This time an enormous WHITE yo-yo
rolled in and spoke:

"I am a son of the Yo-yo King.
   (*Children repeat.*)
Help me do tricks upon a string."

The yo-yos immediately formed themselves into a large ring and rolled rapidly around and around, singing as they rolled:

"We're yo-yos of yellow and yo-yos of blue,
  (*Children repeat.*)
Yo-yos of white and of black and red, too.
We've come to ask you for one simple thing —
Help us to whirl, twirl, and spin on a string."

Faster and faster they rolled — around and around and around. Enoch felt himself beginning to grow as he watched the yo-yos rolling around in their ring. His feet stretched out over the foot of his bed and his head bumped against the wall. The yo-yos rolled faster and faster as they sang:

"We're yo-yos of yellow and yo-yos of blue,
  (*Children repeat.*)
Yo-yos of white and of black and red, too.
We've come to ask you for one simple thing —
Help us to whirl, twirl, and spin on a string."

Thump-bump! The bed broke. Enoch kept growing and growing until his feet smashed against the walls, which cracked and ripped apart. His head pushed right through the ceiling — *cr-r-rash!*

Then, it was very quiet. Enoch slowly opened his eyes. His room was empty and the morning sunlight streamed brightly through the window.

"Wow!" he said to himself. "What a dream! I must have been thinking too much about that yo-yo contest." He sat up and looked at the yo-yo, his favorite red yo-yo, on the table right beside his bed.

"Hmmm!" he thought. "It is as red as the Yo-yo King in my dream. Maybe it will be king of the yo-yos when the contest is over today." He jumped out of bed, dressed quickly, put his favorite red yo-yo into his pocket, and said happily:

"Here is *one* red Yo-yo King
That CAN do tricks upon a string."

—J.J.T.

The "y" sound is emphasized in the repetition of the word *yo-yo.* The sound also occurs in *yellow, you,* and *your.*

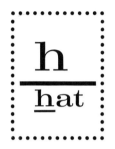

MAKING THE SPEECH SOUND

The vocal cords are partially closed, but not enough so that they vibrate. The lips, tongue, and teeth are in position for producing the vowel which immediately follows the voiceless "h." The soft palate is raised. The breath makes a slight noise as it is pushed through the throat. The sound is a continuant; that is, it can be produced continuously without interruption, unlike the explosive sounds, "p," "b," "t," "d," "k," and "g."

You may call "h" the "tired-puppy," the "huffing," or the "ho-ho" sound.

CORRECTING THE DEFICIENT SPEECH SOUND

The most common deviation in the production of this sound is the complete omission of the sound, e.g., *at* for *hat.* Ask the child to hold up a slip of paper, name some words that begin with the "h" sound, and watch the paper move: *hat, house, hen.* Ask him to listen for the "h" sound and clap when he hears it in words: *horse,* ball, *hide, heel, heart, hand.*

INSTRUCTIONS TO THE CHILD

"Hold up your hand so that your palm is in front of your mouth. Say *at* with me. Now say *hat.* Did you feel the difference? Did you feel a little puff of breath blow against your hand when you said *hat? (Use the words listed above for further practice.)* Puppy makes that sound when he is tired. Here is a poem about my puppy. When you hear the panting sound, make it with me."

> My puppy likes to chase his tail
> Around, around, around;
> And when he stops to rest awhile,
> He makes this panting sound:
> "H, h, h, h, h, h!"

—L.B.S.

WORDS FOR PRACTICE

Initial	*Medial*	*Final*
honey	birdhouse	——
hen	uphill	
hundred	groundhog	
hall	bellhop	
hatchet	sweetheart	
helicopter	childhood	

I HEAR IT

See the section on "s" for instructions on how to use the "I Hear It" selection.

I hear it in *hair* but not in *air.*
I hear it in *harm* but not in *arm.*
I hear it in *hat* but not in *at.*

I hear it in *heel* but not in *eel*.
I hear it in *hem* but not in *M*.
I let out my breath;
My lips come apart
When I say *hand* and *head* and *heart*.
"H, h, h!" *Hand! Head! Heart!*
I hear it in *hate* but not in *ate*.
I hear it in *hark* but not in *ark*.
I hear it in *hoe* but not in *Oh*.
I hear it in *hold* but not in *old*.
I hear it in *heart* but not in *art*.
I let out my breath;
My lips come apart
When I say *hand* and *head* and *heart*.
"H, h, h!" *Hand! Head! Heart!*

—L.B.S.

"HOO— HOO— HOO!"

The barn owl flies in the dark of the night!
Still as a shadow he makes his flight.
"Hoo— hoo— hoo!
Hoo— hoo— hoo!"

He *can* see in the daytime, but *best* at dark,
When the crickets chirp and the fireflies spark.
"Hoo— hoo— hoo!
Hoo— hoo— hoo!"

His round eyes glow as he searches and prowls,
Looking for food for his baby owls.
"Hoo— hoo— hoo!
Hoo— hoo— hoo!"

—L.B.S.

The refrain should be said slowly and mysteriously by the whole class, with the long "oo" prolonged. Individual children may take turns saying the narrative lines.

THE PANTING SOUND

Big dogs, little dogs,
Happy-snappy middle dogs,
Long dogs, short dogs,
Rolley-polley jolly dogs,
Funny dogs, sad dogs,
Even sort-of-bad dogs!
When dogs are resting from their play,
They make a panting sound this way:
"H, h, h, h, h, h!"

—L.B.S.

Ask the children to make the panting sound of dogs at rest. Ask them to describe dogs they have seen or those which are pets.

MY PUPPY

TEACHER: My puppy is little — about this size,
(*Indicate with hands.*)
With ENORMOUS ears and the saddest brown eyes.

CHILDREN: "Woof, woof, woof! 'H, h, h, h!' "

TEACHER: Puppy's tail is a stub, with some white at the tip.
Sometimes puppy barks with a sharp little yip!

CHILDREN: "Yip, yip, yip! 'H, h, h, h!' "

TEACHER: He makes that old tiger-cat run up a tree,
But when he gets tired, he runs back to me.

CHILDREN: "H, h, h, h, h, h, h, h!" (*Very quickly.*)

TEACHER: But dogs make a *soft* panting sound, don't you see?
I know *you* can make it, so do it with me.

CHILDREN: "H, h, h, h, h, h, h, h!" (*Softly and slowly.*)

TEACHER: Now hold up your hand. Feel your breath as
you say
Hand, head, heart, and *health* — yes, that is
the way! (*The children repeat each word
after you.*)

—L.B.S.

I AM SANTA CLAUS

ALL: I am Santa Claus! Ho, ho, ho!
Over the housetops I will go!
Ho, ho, ho! Ho, ho, ho!
Ho, ho, ho, ho, ho, ho, ho!

SOLO 1: Here is a dolly in my pack.
SOLO 2: Here is a wiggly jumping jack.
SOLO 3: Here is a spaceman in his ship.
SOLO 4: Here is a jump rope you can skip.

ALL: I am Santa Claus! Ho, ho, ho!
Over the housetops I will go!
Ho, ho, ho! Ho, ho, ho!
Ho, ho, ho, ho, ho, ho, ho!

SOLO 5: Here is a panda black and white.
SOLO 6: Here is a silver Japanese kite.
SOLO 7: Here is a licorice lollipop.
SOLO 8: Here is a bunny, hop, hop, hop!

ALL: I am Santa Claus! Ho, ho, ho!
Over the housetops I will go!
Ho, ho, ho! Ho, ho, ho!
Ho, ho, ho, ho, ho, ho, ho!

—L.B.S.

Half the class may hum the song "Up on the Housetops" while
the other half says the lines. Ask the children to say "Ho, ho, ho!"
in one breath as practice for establishing better breath control.

391

HAPPY HALLOWEEN

ALL: Happy Halloween! Happy Halloween!
Funny sights are seen
On happy Halloween!

CHILD 1: I'll bring a pumpkin,
CHILD 2: I'll bring a pumpkin,
CHILD 3: I'll bring a pumpkin,

ALL: For Happy Halloween.
Happy Halloween! Happy Halloween!
Funny sights are seen
On happy Halloween!

CHILD 4: I'll scrape the insides,
CHILD 5: I'll scrape the insides,
CHILD 6: I'll scrape the insides,

ALL: For Happy Halloween.
(*Repeat the first three lines of the poem.*)

—L.B.S.

These solo lines may be added to the poem: "I'll cut a crooked mouth," "I'll cut the eyes and nose," "I'll put the candle in," and "I'll light the candle." Suggest that the class make a tune for this rhyme, which provides simple practice for more ambitious choric and dramatization activities. Repetitive words beginning with the "h" speech sound are *happy* and *Halloween*.

WHAT IS FINE

September is fine for skipping time. Hooray! Hurrah!
October is fine for harvest time. Hooray! Hurrah!
November is fine for turkey time. Hooray! Hurrah!
December is fine for Santa time. Hooray! Hurrah!
January is fine for snowman time. Hooray! Hurrah!
February is fine for valentine time. Hooray! Hurrah!

March is fine for windy kite time. Hooray! Hurrah!
April is fine for umbrella time. Hooray! Hurrah!
May is fine for May-basket time. Hooray! Hurrah!
June is fine for vacation time. Hooray! Hurrah!

—L.B.S.

This rhyme affords practice on the "h" sound in *hooray* and *hurrah,* which should be said with feeling. Months of the year are reviewed. Ask members of the class to tell which months they like best and why.

WHAT IS HIGH?

High is the kite that sails in the sky;
High goes the plane when it takes off to fly.

High is the back of a Halloween cat;
High is an Abraham Lincoln top hat.

High is my baby brother's high chair;
High is my head when I swing through the air.

High is the branch way up on a tree;
High is the mast on a ship out at sea.

High are the clouds all puffy and white;
High is the sun overhead, shining bright.

High are the ragweeds if we let them grow;
High is the opposite of *low*.

—L.B.S.

Ask the children to name other things that are high. Use this rhyme to teach the opposite concepts *high* and *low*. After the class has listened to the rhyme once or twice, the children will be able to supply the last word in each couplet.

HAVE YOU EVER SEEN?

TEACHER:	Have you ever seen
	A hippo in a hat?
CHILDREN:	A hippo in a *hat?*
TEACHER:	Just imagine that!
ALL:	I have not seen a hippo in a hat.
TEACHER:	Have you ever seen
	A house full of hay?
CHILDREN:	A house full of *hay?*
TEACHER:	No, not any day!
ALL:	I have never seen a house full of hay.
TEACHER:	Have you ever seen a horse asleep in the hall?
CHILDREN:	A horse asleep in the *hall?*
TEACHER:	A horse sleeps in a STALL!
ALL:	I have never seen a horse asleep in the hall.
TEACHER:	Have you ever seen
	A hen in a hive?
CHILDREN:	A hen in a *hive?*
TEACHER:	Oh, my sakes alive!
ALL:	I have never seen a hen in a hive.
TEACHER:	Have you ever seen
	A hog blow a horn?
CHILDREN:	A hog blow a *horn?*
TEACHER:	As sure as I'm born!
ALL:	I have never seen a hog blow a horn.

—L.B.S.

Words beginning with the "tired-puppy" sound are *have, hippo, hat, house, hay, horse, hall, hen, hive, hog,* and *horn.*

THE KING'S POCKET

Once upon a time, his Majesty the Jovial King of Laughland sent a proclamation to everyone in his kingdom:

"To the one who, in three guesses, can tell what is in my pocket, I will give my beautiful daughter in marriage."

Now, the challenge which this proclamation set forth seemed quite simple to the young men of the kingdom, and since the Princess Holly was very lovely, it was certain that many swains would come from north, south, east, and west to try their skill at guessing what was in the king's pocket.

"Oh, Father," Princess Holly pleaded when she heard what the king had done, "I want to choose my own husband. It is not right that I marry one who has done nothing more than make a lucky guess about what is in your pocket."

The Jovial King laughed, "Ho, ho, ho! And you *shall,* you know. You *shall* marry one of your own choice, for nobody will *ever* guess what is in my pocket. Ho, ho, ho!"

The princess did not understand, so she asked, "How is this possible, Father? Surely someone will be lucky enough to guess right!"

"Never!" roared the Jovial King. "Ho, ho, ho!"

The princess asked, "Can you give me a hint, Father? What IS in your pocket that would make it so difficult to guess?"

The Jovial King laughed again, and then he cleared his throat. "Ahem!

> It is something to have,
> But nothing to hold.
> It is something to hide,
> But not silver or gold."

The Princess Holly still wondered. If it was nothing to hold, then how could it possibly be kept in one's pocket? If it was something that should be hidden, then why would anybody want it? But the Princess Holly trusted her father and knew that what he said must be true.

The first suitor who came was from the East and his ears were the size of an elephant's. He rode a black, high-spirited horse.

395

"I am here," announced the suitor with ears the size of an elephant's. "I am here, your Majesty, to make three guesses. Could you, by any chance, give me one hint as to what is in your pocket?"

The Jovial King laughed. "Ho, ho, ho! Why not?

It is something to have,
But nothing to hold.
It is something to hide,
But not silver or gold.
And it begins with *H*."

"Well," said the suitor with ears the size of an elephant's, "if it is nothing to hold, then

It cannot be heard
Like a hummingbird,
Nor a horn you can blow,
Nor a big hello!
Hummingbird? Horn? Hello?
NO! I give up!"

And the suitor rode away on his black, high-spirited horse.

The second suitor was a prince with a nose three-feet long. "I am here, your Majesty," said the prince with a nose three-feet long, "to make three guesses. Can you, by any chance, give me a hint as to what is in your pocket?"

The Jovial King laughed. "Ho, ho, ho! Why not?

It is something to have,
But nothing to hold.
It is something to hide,
But not silver or gold.
And it begins with *H*."

The prince with a nose three-feet long thought about this. "Hmmmmm," he said to himself.

"It cannot be a hen,
Nor a ball-point pen,
Nor a harmonica to play,
Nor a wisp of hay.
Hen? Harmonica? Hay?
  NO. I give up."

And the prince with a nose three-feet long went away.

Next came a prince with shoulders three arm-lengths wide. Like the others, he asked the king, "Can you by any chance give me a hint as to what is in your pocket?"

The king laughed. "Ho, ho, ho! Why not?

It is something to have,
But nothing to hold.
It is something to hide,
But not silver or gold.
And it begins with *H*."

The prince made three guesses.

"Would it be a hairbrush to brush your hair,
Or a pair of hose that you can wear?
Or a handkerchief to use when you sneeze?
Hairbrush? Hose? Handkerchief? NO. None of these!"

So the prince with shoulders three arm-lengths wide gave up and went away.

Word got around that nobody had guessed what was in the Jovial King's pocket. Everybody thought, "What's the use?" and gave up trying. No more suitors came to try their luck and the Princess Holly was free to choose her own husband, which is exactly what she did.

A long time after that, the Princess Holly was thinking about all of these things that had happened, and she decided to ask the Jovial King what was in his pocket.

She said, "Father, I cannot contain my curiosity any longer. Please tell me what is in your pocket."

The Jovial King replied:

> "It is something to have,
> But nothing to hold.
> It is something to hide,
> But not silver or gold."

And then the Jovial King did something very amusing. He turned his pocket wrong side out. And really and truly there was nothing in his pocket. Nothing at all.

> There was something to have,
> But nothing to hold.
> There was something to hide,
> But not silver or gold.
> It was a HOLE —
> A HOLE in the king's pocket!

—L.B.S.

Words in the story that contain "h" are *his, Holly, heard, husband, Ho, have, hold, hide, hidden, her, he, who, horse, here, hint, hummingbird, horn, hoe, hen, harmonica, hay, hairbrush, hair, hose, handkerchief,* and *hole.* The children may say the refrain each time it occurs in the story. This story lends itself easily to creative dramatics and to use with puppets or a flannelboard.

INDEX OF ACTIVITIES BY UNITS

This index is useful for organizing activities with a common theme into integrated study units or into programs of material for observing holidays and other special events. As the authors pointed out in Chapter One, the selections serve many purposes beyond speech correction and improvement. A complete discussion of ways to enrich the presentation and use of materials may be found on pages 12 through 21. The following index will help the teacher take advantage of the many learning values offered by these selections.

400

BIBLIOGRAPHIES

The following basic bibliographies provide the classroom teacher with five convenient lists of handbooks and activity books which are approved and recommended by speech specialists and clinicians. The teacher will find these books helpful in understanding the child with a speech problem and will discover additional techniques and activities for helping the child to improve or correct his speech.

BOOKS OF GENERAL INFORMATION

Ogilvie, Mardel: *Speech in the Elementary School,* McGraw-Hill, Inc., New York, New York, 1954.

Pronovost, Wilbert: *The Teaching of Listening and Speaking in the Elementary School,* McKay, New York, New York, 1959.

Rasmussen, Carrie: *Speech Methods in the Elementary School,* Ronald Press, New York, New York, 1962.

Scott, Louise Binder, and Thompson, J. J.: *Speech Ways,* McGraw-Hill, Inc., New York, New York, 1955.

SPEECH CORRECTION

Anderson, Virgil: *Improving the Child's Speech,* Oxford University Press, New York, New York, 1953.

Backus, Ollie, and Beasley, Jane: *Speech Therapy with Children,* Houghton-Mifflin, Boston, Massachusetts, 1951.

Byrne, Margaret C.: *A Child Speaks,* Harper and Row, New York, New York, 1964.

Eisenson, Jon, and Ogilvie, Mardel: *Speech Correction in the Schools,* Macmillan, New York, New York, 1963.

Hahn, Elise, and others: *Basic Voice Training for Speech,* McGraw-Hill, Inc., New York, New York, 1957.

Johnson, Wendell: *Speech Handicapped School Children,* Harper and Row, New York, New York, 1956.

Lewis, M. M.: *How Children Learn to Speak,* Basic Books, New York, New York, 1959.

Mellencamp, Virginia Lynn: *Play It and Say It,* Expression Co., Magnolia, Massachusetts, 1962.

Nemoy, Elizabeth, and Davis, Serena: *The Correction of Defective Consonant Sounds,* Expression Co., Magnolia, Massachusetts.

Schoolfield, Lucille D.: *Better Spelling and Better Reading,* Expression Co., Magnolia, Massachusetts.

Schreiber, Flora Rheta: *Your Child's Speech,* G. P. Putnam, New York, New York, 1956.

Van Riper, Charles: *Speech Correction: Principles and Methods,* Prentice-Hall, Englewood Cliffs, New Jersey, 1963.

Williams, Rona M.: *Speech Difficulties in Children,* George G. Harrup Co., Ltd., London, 1962.

STORYTELLING AND CHILDREN'S LITERATURE

Hollowell, Lillian: *A Book of Children's Literature,* Holt, Rinehart and Winston, New York, New York, 1950.

Huck, Charlotte, and Young, Doris A.: *Children's Literature in the Elementary School,* Holt, Rinehart and Winston, New York, New York, 1961.

Martignoni, Margaret (ed.): *Illustrated Treasury of Children's Literature,* Holt, Rinehart and Winston, New York, New York, 1955.

Siks, Geraldine: *Children's Literature for Dramatization,* Harper and Row, New York, New York, 1964.

Wagner, Joseph, and Smith, R. W.: *Teacher's Guide to Storytelling,* Wm. C. Brown Co., Dubuque, Iowa, 1958.

CHORIC SPEAKING

Austin, Mary C., and Mills, Queenie B.: *The Sound of Poetry,* Allyn and Bacon, Rockleigh, New Jersey, 1963.

Huber, Miriam Blanton (ed.): *Story and Verse for Children,* Macmillan, New York, New York, 1955.

Hughes, Rosalind (ed.): *Let's Enjoy Poetry,* Houghton-Mifflin, Boston, Massachusetts, 1958.

Keppie, Elizabeth, Wedberg, Conrad, and Kesslar, Miriam: *Speech Improvement Through Choral Speaking,* Expression Co., Magnolia, Massachusetts.

Scott, Louise Binder: *Fairy Tale Plays in Rhyme,* F. A. Owen Publishing Co., Dansville, New York, 1961.

CREATIVE DRAMATICS

Burger, Isabel: *Creative Play Acting,* A. S. Barnes and Co., New York, New York, 1950.

Durland, Frances C.: *Creative Dramatics for Children,* Antioch Press, Yellow Springs, Ohio, 1952.

Hoaga, Agnes, and Ronales, Patricia: *Supplementary Materials for Use in Creative Dramatics with Children,* University of Washington Press, Seattle, Washington, 1952.

Scott, Louise Binder: *Stories That Stick,* F. A. Owen Publishing Co., Dansville, New York, 1959.

Scott, Louise Binder, and others: *Puppets for All Grades,* F. A. Owen Publishing Co., Dansville, New York, 1960.

Scott, Louise Binder, and Thompson, J. J.: *Rhymes for Fingers and Flannelboards,* McGraw-Hill, Inc., New York, New York, 1960.

Siks, Geraldine: *Creative Dramatics,* Harper and Row, New York, New York, 1958.

Slade, Peter: *Child Drama,* University of London Press, London, 1954.

Torrance, Ellis P.: *Guiding Creative Talent,* Prentice-Hall, Englewood Cliffs, New Jersey, 1962.

Ward, Winifred: *Playmaking with Children,* Appleton-Century-Crofts, New York, New York, 1957.